Women in the Medieval Common Law c.1200–1500

This book examines the view of women held by medieval common lawyers and legislators, and considers medieval women's treatment by and participation in the processes of the common law. Surveying a wide range of points of contact between women and the common law, from their appearance (or not) in statutes, through their participation (or not) as witnesses, to their treatment as complainants or defendants, it argues for closer consideration of women within the standard narratives of classical legal history, and for re-examination of some previous conclusions on the relationship between women and the common law. It will appeal to scholars and students of medieval history, as well as those interested in legal history, gender studies and the history of women.

Gwen Seabourne is Professor of Legal History in the School of Law, University of Bristol, UK. She specialises in medieval legal history, and has written on medieval crime, economic regulation and medieval women.

Studies in Medieval History and Culture

Recent titles include

From Justinian to Branimir
The Making of the Middle Ages in Dalmatia
Danijel Džino

The Triumph of an Accursed Lineage
Kingship in Castile from Alfonso X to Alfonso XI (1252–1350)
Fernando Arias Guillén

Franks and Lombards in Italian Carolingian Texts
Memories of the Vanquished
Luigi Andrea Berto

The Bible and Jews in Medieval Spain
Norman Roth

The Cursed Carolers in Context
Edited by Lynneth Miller Renberg and Bradley Phillis

Women in the Medieval Common Law c.1200–1500
Gwen Seabourne

Jews and Converts in Late Medieval Castile
Breaking with the Past
Cecil D. Reid

Mobile Saints
Relic Circulation, Devotion, and Conflict in the Central Middle Ages
Kate M. Craig

For more information about this series, please visit: https://www.routledge.com/Studies-in-Medieval-History-and-Culture/book-series/SMHC

Women in the Medieval Common Law c.1200–1500

Gwen Seabourne

Routledge
Taylor & Francis Group
LONDON AND NEW YORK

First published 2021
by Routledge
2 Park Square, Milton Park, Abingdon, Oxon OX14 4RN

and by Routledge
52 Vanderbilt Avenue, New York, NY 10017

Routledge is an imprint of the Taylor & Francis Group, an informa business

British Library Cataloguing-in-Publication Data
A catalogue record for this book is available from the British Library

Library of Congress Cataloging-in-Publication Data
A catalog record has been requested for this book

ISBN: 978-1-4724-3980-2 (hbk)
ISBN: 978-0-3677-4522-6 (pbk)
ISBN: 978-1-315-54672-8 (ebk)

Typeset in Times New Roman
by codeMantra

To my mother, Margot Seabourne,
who, in my own deep past,
took me to countless castles and cathedrals,
shared her gloves on cold days
and always had a spare sweet for the sermon;
with love and thanks for a lifetime of care, conversation, inspiration
and general magnificence.

Contents

Figures

Preface

Argument in an early twentieth-century Court of Appeal case, *Bebb v. Law Society*,[1] made reference to a few words of law-French from the anonymous late thirteenth-century treatise known as *The Mirror of Justices: 'Fems ne poient mie estre attorneyes'*.[2] Thus a medieval statement of the impossibility of women being *attorneyes* was brought into discussion in an important case in the much more recent dispute as to whether or not the Law Society was entitled to exclude women from qualification as solicitors in England and Wales. Different views of the meaning of the *Mirror*'s statement were put forward in the case, with disagreement as to whether it asserted the exclusion of all women from the role of attorney or only married women, and as to what was an 'attorney' for these purposes. This medieval statement was cited by the early modern lawyer Sir Edward Coke (1552–1634), and this citation by a figure regarded as particularly authoritative, coupled with Coke's own elaboration, damaged Miss Bebb's case.[3] The fact that the *Mirror* statement was discussed in the twentieth century is a reminder that sources from the deep past of the common law may be used in much later periods. In legal practice, and some legal scholarship, sources from the medieval period are mediated, and may be distorted, by legal commentators of intervening periods, giving an over-simplified view of medieval legal thought and practice. In *Bebb*, for example, seeing the *Mirror* statement through the lens of Coke's *Institutes* tended to smooth over the changes in the meaning of 'attorney' which had occurred between the thirteenth and seventeenth centuries, giving an inaccurate sense of a venerable and monolithic ban on women acting in a way which could be assimilated to the early twentieth-century role of solicitor, and used to exclude Miss Bebb from legal practice. The particular fight in *Bebb* has long since been won, but there is a need to throw off the weight

1 [1914] Ch 286.

2 *Mirror*, Book II, c. 31. This is not a text which is well regarded for its accuracy. Pollock, editor of the Law Reports, criticised Coke's use of it: [1914] Ch 286 295, notes 28 and 29.

3 Lord Cozens-Hardy at 294: 'the opinion of Lord Coke on the question of what is or what is not the common law is one which requires no sanction from anybody else'.

of the over-simplified past from discussion of many areas of law relating to women, from ideas about sex and gender to specific legal doctrines.[4]

The importance of studying medieval women and the common law, however, is not merely instrumental, a way of ensuring accuracy in current legal discourses and disputes; it is also essential to understanding the lives and worlds of those medieval women, and contemporary ideas and practice relating to them. The women recorded in medieval plea rolls, reduced to a name and a few bare facts or allegations, and the now-nameless many subject to statements as to what women could not do, were as human as we are and deserve as full consideration as the nature of the records will allow. I hope that this book will contribute to the huge task of doing them some sort of justice.

4 On history in legal discourse, see, in particular, F.W. Maitland, 'A Survey of the Century' (1901) in *Collected Papers of Frederic William Maitland*, ed. by H.A.L. Fisher (Cambridge, 1912), Vol 3, 432 at 439; Enid Campbell, 'Lawyers' Uses of History', *University of Queensland Law Journal* 6 (1968), 1–23, 21; Mark Leeming, 'Lawyers' uses of history, from *Entick v Carrington* to *Smethurst v Commissioner of Police*' (2020); Russell Sandberg, 'The Time for Legal History: Some Reflections on Maitland and Milson Fifty Years on', *Law & Justice*, 180 (2018), p. 21–37, 25; C.H.S. Fifoot, *Frederic William Maitland* (Cambridge, MA, 1971) 143.

Abbreviations and citation conventions

National archives manuscript classes

CP 40	Plea Rolls of the Common Bench/Court of Common Pleas
KB 9	Indictment Files, Court of King's Bench
KB 26 and 27	Plea Rolls, King's Bench
SC8	Ancient Petitions
JUST 1	Justices in Eyre, of Assize, of Oyer and Terminer, and of the Peace: Rolls and Files
JUST 2	Coroners' Rolls and Files
JUST 3	Gaol Delivery Rolls and Files

Electronic databases

Where manuscripts are included in the Anglo-American Legal Tradition digitisation project, http://aalt.law.uh.edu/AALT.html, they are cited by manuscript membrane and AALT image number, e.g. JUST 1/564 m. 11 (IMG 7332).

For reasons of space, I have opted to cite Year Book cases by reference to their number in 'Seipp's Abridgement' of Year Book reports, http://www.bu.edu/law/faculty-scholarship/legal-history-the-year-books/. These appear in the form 'Seipp 1489.008'. Traditional legal citations such as Y.B. Hil. 4 Hen. VII, fo. 5, pl. 8 may be found in 'Seipp's Abridgement'.

Other abbreviations

AHR	*American Historical Review*
AJLH	*American Journal of Legal History*
Baker, *Introduction*	J.H. Baker, *Introduction to English Legal History*, 5th edn (Oxford: Oxford University Press, 2019).
Bl. Comm.	William Blackstone, *Commentaries on the Laws of England* (4 vols, Oxford: Clarendon Press, 1765–9).

Bracton	Woodbine, George and Samuel Thorne (eds), *Bracton on the Laws and Customs of England* (4 vols, Cambridge MA: Harvard University Press, 1968–77).
Britton	*Britton*, ed. F. Nichols (2 vols, Oxford: Clarendon Press, 1865).
BMOC	Selden Society Supplementary Series vol. 18 (2 vols) *The Men of Court 1440–1550: A Prosopography of the Inns of Court and Chancery and the Courts of Law* ed. by J.H. Baker (London: Selden Society, 2012).
BNB	Maitland, Frederic (ed.), *Bracton's Note Book: a Collection of Cases Decided in the King's Courts During the Reign of Henry III* (3 vols, London: C.J. Clay, 1887).
c.	chapter
CCR	*Calendar of Close Rolls* (London: HMSO, 1892–1963).
CPR	*Calendar of Patent Rolls* (London, HMSO, 1891–).
CRR	*Curia Regis Rolls preserved in the Public Record Office* (London: HMSO, 1922–).
CLJ	*Cambridge Law Journa*l
Co. Inst.	Edward Coke, *Institutes of the Laws of England* (1628–44) 4 vols. Vols II-IV. Vol. I is referred to as *Co. Litt.*
Co. Litt.	*Institutes of the Laws of England* (1628–44) 4 vols, vol. I.
*D.*1.5.9	Citations in this form are from the *Digest of Justinian*, following conventional practice. See *The Digest of Justinian*, ed. and tr. by Theodor Mommsen, Paul Krueger and Alan Watson (Philadelphia: University of Pennsylvania Press, 1985).
Dialogus de Scacc.	*The Course of the Exchequer and Constitutio Domus Regis*, ed. by Charles Johnson, F. E. L. Carter and D. E. Greenway (Oxford: Clarendon Press, 1983).
Fortescue, *DLNL*	John Fortescue, *De Natura Legis Naturae* tr. by Chichester Foitescue in *Works* ed. by T. Fortescue (London, 1869).
Fleta Fleta vols 2–4,	ed. by H.G. Richardson and G.O. Sayles (3 vols, London: Selden Society, 1955–84).
Glanvill	*The Treatise on the Laws and Customs of the Realm of England commonly called Glanvill*, ed. by G.D.G. Hall (London: Nelson, 1965).
H	husband (in notes).

Hale *HPC*	Matthew Hale, *Historia Placitorum Coronae* (London: Nutt and Gosling, 1736).
HR	*Historical Research*
JBS	*Journal of British Studies*
JLH	*Journal of Legal History*
JMH	*Journal of Medieval History*
LHR	*Law and History Review*
LQR	*Law Quarterly Review*
LHP	*Leges Henrici Primi*, ed. Leslie John Downer (Oxford: Clarendon Press, 1972).
Lincs RS 22	The Earliest Lincolnshire Assize Rolls AD 1202–1209, ed. by Doris M. Stenton (Lincoln: Lincoln Record Society, 1924).
Litt.	Thomas Littleton, *Tenures*, ed. by Eugene Wambaugh (Washington, DC: John Byrne and Co., 1903).
MLR	*Modern Law Review*
Mirror	*The Mirror of Justices*, ed. W. Whittaker, *Selden Society* vol. 7 (Oxford: Professional Books, 1893).
Northumb. AR	*Three Early Assize Rolls for the county of Northumberland, saec XIII* ed. by W. Page, (Durham: Surtees Society, 1891).
OHLE	*Oxford History of the Laws of England*
P & M	Pollock, Frederick and Maitland, Frederic, *The History of English Law Before the Time of Edward I*, (Cambridge: Cambridge University Press, 1895).
P & P	*Past and Present*
Palmer, *ELABD*	Robert C. Palmer, *English Law in the Age of the Black Death 1348–81* (Chapel Hill: University of North Carolina Press, 1993).
Plac. Abbrev.	*Placitorum Abbreviatio* (London: Record Commissioners, 1811).
PROME	*The Parliament Rolls of Medieval England*, ed. by Chris Given-Wilson and others (16 vols, Woodbridge: Boydell Press, 2005).
PCCG	*Pleas of the Crown for the County of Gloucestershire*, ed. by F.W. Maitland (London: Macmillan and Co., 1884).
Placita Corone	*Placita Corone or La Corone Pledee Devant Justices* (London: Selden Society, 1986).
RP	*Rotuli Parliamentorum; ut et Petitiones, et Placita in Parliamento*, (London: Record Commission, 1783).
SR	*Statutes of the Realm*, ed. by A. Luders, T.E. Tomlins, J. France, W.E. Taunton and J. Raithby (London: Record Commission, 1810–27).

SS	Selden Society volumes. These are generally cited by volume number, with the exception of those which are discrete, original medieval treatises, such as the *Mirror of Justices*. Full titles of those volumes cited are in the Bibliography.
st.	Statute (in notes).
Seabourne, *IMW*	Gwen Seabourne, *Imprisoning Medieval Women: The Non-Judicial Confinement and Abduction of Women in England, c.1170–1509* (Farnham: Ashgate, 2011).
Somersetshire Pleas	*Somersetshire Pleas, Civil and Criminal from the Rolls of the Itinerant Justices c. 1200–56* (1897) ed. by C.E.H. Chadwyck-Healey (London: Harlison and Sons, 1897).
TNA	The National Archives, Kew.
W	wife (in notes).
WHR	Women's History Review
Wilts GD and T	Wiltshire Gaol Delivery and Trailbaston Trials 1275–1306 ed. by R.B. Pugh (Devizes: Wiltshire Record Society, 1978).

Introduction

Women, the common law and the legal historians

A recent work devoted to landmark moments in the relationship between women and the law declared that '[L]egal history scholarship in the UK and Ireland largely ignores women'.[1] Such a claim may raise the hackles of the many excellent scholars whose work does in fact deal with women and law in the various jurisdictions which might be considered to be covered by 'the U.K. and Ireland', but at least as far as the tradition of teaching and researching legal history, in law schools, in England, is concerned, there has been some truth in it. At times, women are quite spectacularly absent.

Some of the best-known visual representations of the medieval English common law at work are to be found in the four images, now held by the Inner Temple, of the central courts at Westminster, in the mid-fifteenth century. They show an entirely masculine world: men are judges, lawyers, officials, litigants, defendants and spectators, and no women appear to be present.[2] Though women were subject to the common law, and did take part in litigation, they were not thought worthy of depiction. One of these images, that of the King's Bench, was reproduced on the front cover of the Legal History textbook I used as an undergraduate law student in the 1990s.[3] Women are sometimes equally hard to find in the sort of legal

1 'Introduction', in *Women's Legal Landmarks: Celebrating the History of Women and Law in the UK and Ireland*, ed. by Erika Rackley and Rosemary Auchmuty (Oxford, 2018), p. 8; Maria Drakopoulou, 'Feminist Historiography of Law', in *The Oxford Handbook of Legal History*, ed. by Markus D. Dubber and Christopher Tomlins (Oxford, 2018), c. 32, p. 605. For recent attention on (mostly modern) women's legal history, see *New Perspectives on European Women's Legal History*, ed. by Sara L. Kimble and Marion Röwekamp (New York, 2016); Rosemary Auchmuty 'Legal History', in *Great Debates in Gender and Law*, ed. by Rosemary Auchmuty (London, 2018), pp. 173–84.

2 https://www.innertemplelibrary.org.uk/collections/manuscript-collection/four-illuminated-manuscripts/, anon., 1460s. The plea rolls of the central courts contain a few illustrations of women, e.g., JUST 1/564 m. 11 (IMG 7332); CP 40/51 m. 13d (1283); CP 40/840 m. 226 (IMG 451); m. 411 (IMG 791). See Elizabeth A. Danbury and Kathleen L. Scott, 'The Plea Rolls of the Court of Common Pleas: an Unused Source for the Art and History of Later Medieval England. 1422–1509', *Antiquaries Journal*, 95 (2015), 157–210, 184.

3 J.H. Baker, *Introduction to English Legal History*, 3rd edn (London, 1990). See p. 2.

Figure 0.1 Court of Kings Bench. ©Inner Temple Library. Used with permission of The Masters of the Bench of the Inner Temple.

history which has traditionally been taught in English law schools. Such was my own acceptance of the assumptions of the discipline being revealed to me that it did not strike me to ask where the women were, either in the image or in the material I was studying.

Such 'law school legal history' in England has been dominated by the 'classical' tradition and framework established by F.W. Maitland (1850–1906).[4] In the hugely influential two-volume work on medieval law usually known as 'Pollock and Maitland',[5] women are not absent, but the fact that they appear in the list of 'the sorts and conditions of men', only in eleventh place, after, for example, 'lepers, lunatics and idiots' excommunicates Jews, aliens and long after earls, barons and knights, does suggest a certain lack of enthusiasm.[6] Maitland was at times content with summaries of the area of women and the law which were elegant in style but which did not measure up to the levels of insight he displayed on other matters.[7] Despite the fact that he lived in an era of intense debate about women and law, and took some part in the disputes as to how educational institutions should treat women, this intellectual and political turmoil did not leave a serious imprint on his ideas about the priorities of legal history. Rather than inspiring an interest in women's treatment by the common law, Maitland saw his participation in debates around whether his university should award degrees to women as a distraction from his legal historical work, memorably writing in a letter to a (male) colleague, 'Meanwhile there are these women - drat them'.[8]

4 For classification of legal historians' 'schools', see, e.g., Jonathan Rose, 'Studying the Past: The Nature and Development of Legal History as an Academic Discipline,' *JLH* 31 (2010), 101–28; Michael Lobban, 'The Varieties of Legal History', *Clio Themis* 5 (2012), 1–29; David Ibbetson, 'What is Legal History a History of?', in *Law and History* (Current Legal Issues 6), ed. by Andrew Lewis and Michael Lobban (Oxford, 2004), pp. 33–40; Alan Hunt, 'The New Legal History: Prospects and Perspectives', *Crime, Law and Social Change* 10 (1986), 201–8; Sandberg, 'The Time for Legal History', pp. 24, 30. Classical legal history, in England and Wales in particular, has been very male-dominated; see, e.g., *The History of English Law, Centenary Essays on 'Pollock and Maitland'*, ed. by John Hudson (Oxford, 1996) (all male authors and ending with a cricket anecdote); and the editors' introductory comments in *Crossing Borders: Boundaries and Margins in Medieval and Early Modern Britain. Essays in Honour of Cynthia J. Neville*, ed. by Sara M. Butler and Krista J. Kesselring (Leiden and Boston, MA, 2018), p. 1.

5 Frederick Pollock and Frederic William Maitland, *The History of English Law before the Time of Edward I* (2 vols, Cambridge, 1895) (hereafter, *P & M*).

6 *P & M* II, c. 2, pp. 465–8. For the brevity of Maitland's treatment of women in some contexts, see, e.g., P.R. Hyams, 'Maitland and the Rest of Us', in *History of English Law*, ed. by Hudson (Oxford, 1996), pp. 213–41, 231; Margaret H. Kerr, 'Husband and Wife in Criminal Procedure in Medieval England', in *Women, Marriage and Family in Medieval Christendom: Essays in Memory of Michael M. Sheehan CSB*, ed. by Constance M. Rousseau and Joel T. Rosenthal (Kalamazoo, 1998), p. 211.

7 Hyams, 'Maitland', p. 224; F.W. Maitland, 'The Law of Real Property', in *Collected Papers* vol. I (Cambridge, 1911), p. 176.

8 *SS* Supplementary Series 1, *Letters of F.W. Maitland*, vol. 1, (London, 1965), p. 188, letter 188 (to H.A.L. Fisher, 1897). Late nineteenth-century 'founding fathers' of English legal

Maitland's lack of interest has been influential. S.F.C. Milsom, introducing a reissue of 'Pollock and Maitland' in the totemic year 1968, had nothing further to add on women.[9] The Selden Society has published two volumes on public works in medieval law, but none focusing on women.[10] Women are not a major focus of the volumes of the weighty *Oxford History of the Laws of England* series which have so far appeared.[11] The major current student text on English legal history still devotes only short sections to legal thought on women and the effect on women of legal developments.[12] To the great surprise of my undergraduate legal history students, the latest edition of this book, which runs to almost 600 pages, deals with rape, an offence of unarguable significance to women,[13] and a major area of enquiry for modern scholars of law, women and gender, within a section on personal injuries in general, in four sentences and two footnotes, ending its account in 1285. It should be borne in mind that considerably less space is given to 'criminal law' than to rights in land, or to 'obligations', but, even so, this is a considerably shorter account in words and chronological duration than those relating to other offences such as burglary, robbery and larceny, and it shows little change over the editions of this text since 1971.[14] As long ago as 1986, Janet Loengard asked serious questions about the reasons for the lack of sustained treatment of medieval women and the law,[15] and, since that time, the fact that women have not been brought closer to the core of the mission of classical legal history has begun to look odder still, set against the increasing focus in law schools over the last few decades on sex, gender

history were not above including misogynist comments; see C.S. Kenny, *The History of the Law of England as to the Effects of Marriage on Property and on the Wife's Legal Capacity* (London, 1879), p. 12. For attention to women's treatment by the common law, see the less lauded Arthur Rackham Cleveland, *Woman under the English Law: from the Landing of the Saxons to the Present Time* (London, 1896), pp. vii, 71, 299, 300.

9 S.F.C. Milsom, introduction to *P & M* 2nd edn. reissue (Cambridge, 1968).

10 Vols. 32 and 40.

11 John Hudson, *OHLE vol. II, 871–1216* (Oxford, 2012), deals with women mainly in sections concerning 'family and marriage'. J.H. Baker, *OHLE vol. VI 1483–1558* (Oxford, 2003), considers the law's attitude to women as a separate issue, but devotes only five pages to it out of 880, rather less than the space given to aliens or corporations.

12 Baker, *Introduction*, 5th edn (Oxford, 2019). David Ibbetson, *A Historical Introduction to the Law of Obligations*' (Oxford, 1999), pp. 208, 211, gives more attention to a case about a lost owl than to the contractual (in)capacity of married women. I note that my 2003 book, hardly in this league, but a good example nonetheless, did not even have 'women' in its index: Gwen Seabourne, *Royal Regulation. of Loans and Sales in Medieval England: Monkish Superstition and Civil Tyranny* (Woodbridge, 2003).

13 Traditionally, rape was an offence which could only be committed by a male principal against a woman.

14 Baker, *Introduction*, p. 573; Baker, *Introduction*, 1st edn (1971), p. 288; 2nd edn (1979), p. 430; 3rd edn (1990), p. 603; 4th edn (2002), p. 531.

15 Janet S. Loengard, 'Legal History and the Medieval Englishwoman: a Fragmented View', *LHR* 4 (1986), 161–78, 172.

and law, as well as the considerable interest in medieval women, gender and law outside the confines of classical legal history.[16]

A partial justification for a lack of general discussion of women and the law in classical legal history has been the idea that, during the formative medieval period and for centuries thereafter, there was no coherent common law treatment of the position of women. As Maitland put it, 'No text-writer, no statute, ever makes any general statement as to the position of women. This is treated as obvious...'.[17] It is not entirely true to say that there is no such statement in medieval common law sources, for the thirteenth-century treatise *Bracton* includes the statement *[D]ifferunt feminæ a masculis in multis, quia earum deterior est condicio quam masculorum* ('Women differ from men in many respects, for their position is inferior to that of men'), though it is not far from the truth.[18] It is clearly correct to note that '[t]he law relating to women in general ... was not a discrete legal topic in the common law'.[19] The fact that there is no comprehensive or clear statement of the position of women is hardly surprising, given that legal sources from medieval England often do not treat as discrete, substantive, topics matters which modern lawyers or historians would regard in this way,[20] and the fact that there is a lack of 'general statements' about a particular area or the fact that arguably connected matters were not formerly seen as 'discrete legal topic[s]' would not usually stop legal historians from exploring them. Is it any more anachronistic to discuss women and the common law than to discuss, for example, the 'law of obligations' in medieval England, by tracking down dispersed comments and deducing principles from terse case records and reports, to impose upon a medieval legal world concepts of property which it did not use, or to use the conventional modern categories 'crime' and 'tort' or 'criminal' and 'civil' cases, when discussing a system which made no such clear distinctions?[21] The scattered statements about women in common law sources, and the telling silences, can also be brought together, if one wishes to do so.

16 For examples of the large body of scholarship on gender and law and on medieval women, see Joanne Conaghan, *Law and Gender* (Oxford, 2013); Shulamith Shahar tr. by Chaya Galai, *The Fourth Estate: A History of Women in the Middle Ages* (London, 1983), *Women and Power in the Middle Ages*, ed. by Mary Erler and Maryanne Kowaleski (Athens, GA, 1988); *A History of Women in the West II: Silences of the Middle Ages*, ed. by Christiane Klapisch-Zuber and others (Cambridge, MA, 1992).

17 *P & M* I, p. 482.

18 *Bracton*, II, 31. This is borrowing from civilian sources: *P & M* II, p. 465; 8 *SS* 8, pp. 57, 60, 63.

19 132 *SS*, lxix.

20 *P & M* I, p. 482. Contrast the unified Welsh treatment: *The Welsh Law of Women*, ed. by Dafydd Jenkins and Morfydd E. Owen (Cardiff, 2017), p. 2; Sara Elin Roberts, 'The Welsh Legal Triads: Selden Society Lecture 16th July 2008', *Welsh Legal History Society* 12 (2012), 1–22, 16.

21 Ibbetson, *Historical Introduction*; David J. Seipp, 'The Concept of Property in the Early Common Law', *LHR* 12 (1994), 29–91, 30; Susan Reynolds, 'Tenure and Property in Medieval England', *HR* 88 (2015), 563–75. Use of 'criminal' and 'civil' is conventional

This may require a certain amount of speculation, tentatively filling in some of the gaps in the record, but speculation has been admitted in some other areas of legal historical scholarship.[22] Such an endeavour is unlikely to produce a neat theory, immune from criticism by those not in sympathy with the attempt. It will certainly not be possible to make confident statements about clear chronological changes in some aggregated overall legal 'position of women'. Nevertheless, it appears to me to be incumbent upon legal historians to try to reveal what they can of the conceptions and constructions of women explicit or implicit in the sources and literature of the common law. Legal historians should engage with and contribute to the historically sensitive study of law within law schools, and they also have something of worth to offer to the historical study of women, in terms of a perspective which spans a wide range of legal activities and doctrines, as well as seeing the ways in which aspects of law have been received, understood and used over the intervening period.

Some further explanation of the choice of subject matter for this monograph, and the nature of the enquiry, is in order. First of all, it is necessary to say something about 'the common law', what it is, or was, and why it is my focus. The common law of England is understood to be that system which proceeded from royal law-making and from the central royal courts, as they developed from the later twelfth century onwards, in a process described and debated by many distinguished scholars, and involving central royal or 'governmental' action, the contributions of nascent legal professions through the building up of practice and discussion of legal principle, and the participation of some lay people (overwhelmingly men).[23] It was certainly not the only system of law relevant to women in medieval England: aspects of their lives might also be governed by the law of the church, and local laws and customs, as common lawyers accepted.[24] These other jurisdictions

---

in legal history, but while these words do occur in Glanvill 1, 1, they were not usual in medieval legal sources, and the two categories are not distinct.

22 Thomas Green, *Verdict According to Conscience: Perspectives on the English Criminal Jury 1200–1800* (Chicago, IL, 1985), p. 64.

23 See, e.g., Paul Brand, *The Making of the Common Law* (London, 1992); Thomas J. McSweeney, *Priests of the Law: Roman Law and the Making of the Common Law's First Legal Professionals* (Oxford, 2019), p. 97; Anthony Musson and W. Mark Ormrod, *The Evolution of English Justice: Law, Politics and Society in the Fourteenth Century* (London, 1999); Edward Powell, *Kingship, Law and Society: Criminal Justice in the Reign of Henry V* (Oxford, 1989), pp. 1, 9.

24 *P & M* II, pp. 363, 373; Paul Brand, 'Local Custom in Early Common Law', in *Law, Laity and Soidarities: Essays in Honour of Susan Reynolds*, ed. by Pauline Stafford, Janet L. Nelson and Jane Martindale (Manchester, 2001), pp. 150–9; R.M. Smith, 'Women's Property Rights under Customary Law: Some Developments in the Thirteenth and Fourteenth Centuries', *TRHS* 36 (1986), 165–94; R.H. Helmholz, 'Harboring Sexual Offenders: Ecclesiastical Courts and Controlling Misbehavior', *JBS* 37 (1998), 258–68; Shannon McSheffrey, 'Jurors, Respectable Masculinity and Christian Morality: A Comment on Marjorie McIntosh's *Controlling Misbehavior*', *JBS* 37 (1998), 269–78; Hanawalt, *Wealth*, c. 8.

might have subtly or significantly different balances between men and women in terms of substance and procedure. A number of recent works on medieval women focus on systems other than the common law.[25] This is enormously enriching and interesting. There remains a need, however, to revisit the sources of the common law, which are far from having given up all they have to offer with regard to women. The mass of such material which is accessible to researchers continues to swell through the publication of scholarly editions of legal texts, but commentary does not always keep up with this. Without keeping under review what can be gleaned about women from available common law material, both studies of common law and studies of medieval women will be more incomplete than they have to be.

There is an additional and different stratum to the question of what amounts to 'the common law', and should thus fall within the remit of a book like this: it concerns the possibility of different understandings of 'law' itself.[26] Although one prominent legal historian describes the 'extensive literature on the proper definition of "law" and the "legal" as "a slough to be avoided"',[27] it is necessary for anyone looking at legal history at least to be aware of the existence of the different ways in which these words might be interpreted.[28] 'Common law' could, in theory, be restricted to definitive and authoritative statements of rules emanating from the king or his justices. This, however, is not always a practical possibility. Identifying 'the rules' may not be straightforward, as, in many cases, it is difficult to be sure that one has the 'official' text of a statute, or the correct, contemporary interpretation of its words or its perceived legitimacy or temporal scope, and sources emanating from medieval common lawyers do not always give answers to the substantive legal questions modern scholars wish to ask of them. It is often necessary to deduce the rules from the existing evidence of what people did in practice. This necessity encourages a 'realistic' view of law,

25 E.g., *Women in England c 1275–1525*, ed. by P.J.P. Goldberg (Manchester, 1995). The *JBS* special edition, *Women Negotiating the Boundaries of Justice in Britain, 1300–1700* (vol. 58, 2019), contains no chapter concentrating on common law. See also *Legalism: Property and Ownership*, ed. by Georgy Kantor, Tom Lambert and Hannah Skoda (Oxford, 2017), Introduction, p. 27.

26 See Hall's introduction to *Glanvill*, xi, Ibbetson, 'What is Legal History a History Of?', p. 34; Catherine L. Fisk, '&: Law Society in Historical Legal Research', in *Oxford Handbook of Legal History* (Oxford, 2018), c. 26, p. 486.

27 William Ian Miller, 'Choosing the Avenger: Some Aspects of the Bloodfeud in Medieval Iceland and England', *LHR* 1 (1983), 159–204, 161.

28 See, e.g., Michael Freeman, *Lloyd's Introduction to Jurisprudence*, 9th edn (London, 2014), cc. 3, 9; Naomi Creutzfeldt, 'Traditions of Studying the Social and the Legal', in *Routledge Handbook of Socio-Legal Theory and Methods*, ed. by Naomi Creutzfeldt, Marc Mason and Kirsten McConnachie (Abingdon, 2020), pp. 9–34, 97–109. Note that questioning the nature of law is nothing new; see Edward M. Peters, 'Introduction: The Reordering of Law and the Illicit in Eleventh- and Twelfth-Century Europe', in *Law and the Illicit in Medieval Europe*, ed. by Ruth Mazo Karras, Joel Kaye and E. Ann Matter (Philadelphia, 2008); *Glanvill*, Prologue, 2–3; *Bracton* II, p. 22.

as including not only the available statements as to what people should do, but also what actually happened.[29] This book will take a relatively broad view of '[common] law', accepting that contemporaries did not see it as only immutable rules backed by inevitable consequence or sanction. Complicating and tempering factors such as mercy, settlement and arbitration should not necessarily be treated as external to the common law, but as practices accepted and assumed by it. This being so, it is necessary to keep a critical eye on the extent to which it is appropriate to draw sharp contrasts between 'law' and 'practice', or 'law' and 'communal values' or 'law, theory and practice' in relation to women and the medieval common law.[30]

It is, nevertheless, not desirable fully to renounce the idea of law as a category apart from social practice or prevailing thought. There has been a long-standing tendency to treat law as something separate from the actions and preferences of the individuals involved in making it. The idea of a body of common rules, and common learning, was growing over the later medieval period amongst practitioners of the common law,[31] and lawyers, now and in the past, have had a tendency to speak of law as if it were a force independent of themselves or even as if it were a person.[32] In the formative period of 'classical legal history', too, such ways of thinking can be seen. Frederick Pollock, for example, portrayed the common law as a woman ('our lady of the common law') and scholars or practitioners of the common law as 'her men of life and limb':

> We are here to do homage to our lady of the common law, we are her men of life and limb and earthly worship.[33]

Although we might not follow such an overblown metaphorical model, there is some historical justification for seeing the medieval common law as

29 See, e.g., Roscoe Pound, 'Law in Books and Law in Action', *American Law Review* 44 (1910), 12–36; Leeming, 'Lawyers' Uses', and, for a different dichotomy, between 'the law as found in books of authority and the law as it operates in real situations (whether in or out of court)', or between case law/statutes and 'common learning', see J.H. Baker, *The Law's Two Bodies* (Oxford, 2001), p. 1.

30 Drawing such contrasts, and questioning them: Eileen Power, 'The Position of Women', in *The Legacy of the Middle Ages*, ed. by C.G. Crump and E.F. Jacob (Oxford, 1926), p. 401; Sandy Bardsley, *Women's Roles in the Middle Ages* (Westport, CT and London, 2007), pp. 129, 145; Green, *Verdict according to Conscience*, c. 2; Elizabeth Papp Kamali and Thomas A. Green, 'A Crossroads in Criminal Procedure: the Assumptions Underlying England's Adoption of Trial by Jury', in *Law and Society in Later Medieval England and Ireland: Essays in Honour of Paul Brand*, ed. by Travis R. Baker (London and New York, 2018), pp. 51–82, 52, 68–70; Elizabeth Papp Kamali, *Felony and the Guilty Mind in Medieval England* (Cambridge, 2019), p. 50; Janet S. Loengard, 'Rationabilis Dos: Magna Carta and the Widow's "Fair Share" in the Earlier Thirteenth Century', in *Wife and Widow in Medieval England*, ed. by Sue Sheridan Walker (Ann Arbor, 1993), pp. 59–80, 62–8.

31 J.H. Baker, *The Law's Two Bodies* (Oxford, 2001).

32 See, e.g., Gunther Teubner, *Law as an Autopoietic System* (Oxford, 1993).

33 Frederick Pollock, *The Genius of the Common Law* (New York, 1912), p. 2.

possessing a certain autonomy. In any case, a book like this must at times refer to the common law as 'having a view', for example, if it is not to become hopelessly unwieldy, though this is done in the understanding that there is some artificiality in such expressions, and that the law was in fact shaped by numerous deliberate decisions by individuals, even if, in many cases, we do not know their names.

In seeking to explore the treatment of women in and by the medieval common law, it is to the traditional sources that this book will refer: statutes and other legislative acts, records of the courts of common law, law reports and legal writings.[34] There is a vast corpus of potentially relevant material. Much work has been done, particularly since the time of Maitland and under the auspices of the Selden Society and regional historical record societies, to edit and publish important sources of common law history, and digital scanning and other online projects have made some of this more easily accessible,[35] but much remains in manuscript. To make a start with a short monograph-length study of women in the common law is to admit that one cannot possibly see and comment on every relevant document (particularly not during the restrictions consequent upon a pandemic), nor engage with many of the debates and disputes as to documents' provenance and accuracy as representation of legal practice. It is to accept the known pitfalls of using such documents, and their limitations when subjected to our questions. One must avoid the assumption that medieval statutes, case records and reports and treatises are to be understood as essentially similar to modern statutes, law reports and textbooks.[36] Medieval legal documents do not offer a straightforward, factually accurate picture of litigation or the circumstances behind it, and are influenced by the ideas of those making them and the purposes for which they were made. They may exaggerate or use acceptable stereotypes to make a more effective case. The 'voices' of women apparent on the face of the records are seldom if ever unmediated, and all of the records to be examined were man-made in predominantly

34 On this material, see, e.g., Baker, *Introduction*, cc. 11 and 12; Kamali, *Felony*, pp. 15–19; Paul Brand, 'The Age of *Bracton*', in *History of English Law*, ed. by John Hudson (Oxford, 1996), pp. 65–89; Paul Brand, introduction to 111 *SS*; F.W. Maitland, 'Of the Year Books in General', in 17 SS, pp. ix–xx; David J. Seipp, 'The Law's Many Bodies and the Manuscript Tradition in English Legal History', *JLH* 25 (2004), 74–83; Paul Brand, 'Inside the Courtroom: Lawyers, Litigants and Justices in England in the Later Middle Ages', in *The Moral World of the Law*, ed. by Peter Coss (Cambridge, 2000), pp. 91–112, 92–3.

35 See, in particular, the Anglo-American Legal Tradition, http://aalt.law.uh.edu/AALT.html, and 'Seipp's Abridgement' of Year Book reports, http://www.bu.edu/law/faculty-scholarship/legal-history-the-year-books/.

36 33 *SS*, p. xviii; Christine Carpenter, 'Law, Justice and Landowners in Late Medieval England', *LHR* 1 (1983), 205–37; Edward Powell, 'Arbitration and the Law in England in the Late Middle Ages', *TRHS* 33 (1983), 49–67.

or wholly male environments.[37] An additional layer of difficulty of the extant and available records is that they may not record definitive views and may not conclude on points of law.[38] Though the texts of statutes may be imperfect, however, a perusal of the standard sources such as the *Statutes of the Realm* and *Rolls of Parliament* suffices to give at least a general picture of legislative intervention.[39] Legal records at least show us what was plausible or acceptable, even if not strictly true, and that plausibility is a clue to reality. All records might be man-made, but the attitudes of elite males and common lawyers, forming the legal world in which they lived, necessarily had an impact on women's lives. In sum, despite its flaws, as this book aims to demonstrate, there is still much to be learned about women and law from this, the evidence which we have. An exploration in this area must also acknowledge and use the achievements of the classical school of legal history, even as it argues for the need to expand upon its view of worthy subjects for comment and investigation, and must build upon the work of many historians of women and gender, while, again, at times differing in approach or perspective.

Taking a thematic approach, it is the aim of this book to survey the field of women's interactions with the common law, and ideas about women to be found in the sources of the common law, to note areas of (contemporary and current) certainty and uncertainty, presence and absence, to suggest alterations to some orthodoxies in the histories of medieval women and the medieval common law, and directions for further exploration. I hope to do all of this with, as an early modern pioneer of the investigation of women and the law put it, 'as little tediousnesse as I can'.[40]

37 See, e.g., 24 *SS* 103; S.F.C. Milsom, 'Trespass from Henry III to Edward III', *LQR* (1958), 195–224, 222–3; 30 *SS*, xlix; 50 *SS* xxxiii ff; Noël J. Menuge, 'Reading Constructed Narratives: An Orphaned Medieval Heiress and the Legal Case as Literature', in *Medieval Women: Texts and Contexts in Late Medieval Britain*, ed. by Noël J. Menuge (Leiden, 2000), pp, 115–29, 117; Paul Strohm, *Hochon's Arrow: The Social Imagination of Fourteenth-Century Texts* (Princeton, NJ, 1992), pp. 122, 133; Jeremy Goldberg, 'Echoes, Whispers, Ventriloquisms: On Recovering Women's Voices from the Court of York in the Later Middle Ages', in *Women, Agency and the Law 1300–1700*, ed. by Bronach Kane and Fiona Williamson (London, 2015), pp. 31–41, 31; Cordelia Beattie, 'Your Oratrice: Women's Petitions to the Late Medieval Court of Chancery', in the same volume, pp, 17–30, 18.

38 See Ibbetson, 'What is Legal History a History Of?', p. 34.

39 On legislation, see Paul Brand, *Kings, Barons and Justices: the Making and Enforcement of Legislation in Thirteenth Century England* (Cambridge, 2003); T.F.T. Plucknett, *Legislation of Edward I* (Oxford, 1949).

40 *The Lawe's Resolutions of Women's Rights, A. D., 1632*, cited in J.J.S. Wharton, *An Exposition of the Laws Relating to the Women of England* (London, 1853), p. i.

Part I

Unions and divisions

Women and the common law

A rather unlauded work on women and law, Arthur Rackham Cleveland's *Woman under the English Law* of 1896 pronounced that 'every nation which has attained to such a degree of civilization as to have reduced its system of jurisprudence to writing' made distinctions in its laws between women and 'the general body of the people owing obedience to these laws'. There was, Cleveland opined, no exception to this rule, and nor was it possible to imagine 'any state of society composed of men and women, whose system of jurisprudence could be such, that the same laws would apply equally to the two sexes'. In setting out separate laws for men and women, 'lawgivers in all past ages' were not making a choice, but recognising an eternal fact: 'the legal status of woman was of necessity different from that of man'.[1]

This passage might emphasise division of laws applicable to men and women as clear and fundamental throughout history, but the works of contemporaries more influential on the nascent classical legal history tradition had a different perspective, emphasising divisions between women, generally on the basis of marital status, and pre-eminently in the context of rights over land rather than presenting women as a coherent, separate, legal category. In modern historical study too, questions are asked about treating the women of past periods as a unified category, with frequent emphasis on divisions amongst them, in terms of 'life-cycle-stage' or social position, and on the complexity of historical (and contemporary) ideas of sex and gender categorisation, in line with ideas of identity and intersectionality with which modern scholarship has been enriched.[2] The category 'women' is also the subject of considerable current legal and political controversy.[3]

1 Cleveland, *Woman under the English Law*, pp. iii, vi. On its reception, see *Times*, Friday, 4th September, 1896, p. 6.

2 See, e.g., Patricia Skinner, *Studying Gender in Medieval Europe: Historical Approaches* (London, 2018); Joan W. Scott, 'Gender: a Useful Category of Historical Analysis', *AHR* 91 (1986), 1053–75; Elisabeth van Houts, 'Introduction', in *Medieval Memories: Men, Women and the Past, 700–1300*, ed. by Elisabeth van Houts (London and New York, 2013), p. 2; Seabourne, *IMW*, pp. 10–12; Pauline Stafford, 'Women and the Norman Conquest', *TRHS* 6 ser. IV (1994), 221–49, 230; Kimberlé Williams Crenshaw, 'Mapping the Margins: Intersectionality, Identity Politics, and Violence against Women of Color', *Stanford Law Review* 43 (1991), 1241–99; S.H. Rigby, *English Society in the Later Middle Ages: Class, Status and Gender* (London, 1995).

3 See, e.g., *R. on the application of Harry Miller v. The College of Policing and the Chief Constable of Humberside* [2020] EWHC 225 (Admin); Alex Sharpe, 'Will Gender

As far as a consideration of the medieval common law is concerned, however, while we must certainly take account of separate provision for different groups of women and the possibility of fluidity of ideas around gender, it should be noted that differentiation between men and women was treated as fundamental in the common law system. It is also clear that the existence of rules for one group of women could have an impact on the lives and legal treatment of other groups, so that it is important to question statements which treat the legal situation of the married woman as something entirely separable from the situation of women as such.[4] An insistence on considering married and unmarried women separately allows for an unbalanced description of the legal picture, for example positing a 'rule' of women's full rights in private law, with the considerable disabilities of the married woman diminished as an 'exception', however extensive the impact of those 'exceptional' disabilities might have been,[5] or presenting the unlimited and limited positions of women at different stages or in different situations as being in some sort of balance, as can be seen in a comment by C.T. Flower in a Selden Society volume from the 1940s:

> All that need be said in general about the status of women is that the widow or spinster was an unfettered litigant, while the married woman was unable to appear without her husband, whom she was bound to obey...

While it is true that there were separate legal rules for women with differing marital status, including variation in relation to the ability to litigate alone, the presentation of groups of women as somehow insulated one from another, with rules affecting only one particular group, and having no more general impact, is not one which stands up to scrutiny. Not all women would marry, but it is inconceivable that rules for married women had no impact upon unmarried women, given the importance of marriage as a present reality or a future expectation in the lives of such a large proportion of women,

---

Self-Declaration Undermine Women's Rights and Lead to an Increase in Harms?', *MLR* 83 (2020), 539–57; Alessandra Asterti and Rebecca Bull, 'Gender Self-Declaration and Women's Rights: How Self-Identification Undermines Women's Rights and Will Lead to an Increase in Harms: A Reply to Alex Sharpe', *MLR* comment: https://www.modernlawreview.co.uk/asteriti-bull-sharpe/ Accessed 25th July, 2020. On sex/gender in legal scholarship, at a more theoretical level, see, e.g., Joanne Conaghan, *Law and Gender* (Oxford, 2013).

4 62 *SS*, 235.

5 See, e.g., the statement in *P & M* II, p. 465, that women had equal private law rights to men, 'with few exceptions'; J. Everard, 'Public Authority and Private Rights: Women in the English Royal Courts of Justice 1196–1250', in *Sexuality and Gender in History*, ed. by Penelope Hetherington and Philippa Maddern (Western Australia, 1993), pp. 123–44, 137.

as the same author, on the same page, recognises.[6] Differentiation is important, but it should not be 'all that need be said'.

This part of the book will consider both 'unified' and 'separated' aspects of common law thinking and practice in relation to women, noting common law's attention both to 'women' and to subsets of women and the interplay between the two perspectives. It will highlight the difficulties which might be found in differentiating subsets of women and some of the silences and ambiguities about women in medieval common law sources which can and should be interrogated.

6 62 *SS*, 235: 'Wedlock was very much the normal state ...'. See also the remarks of Phillimore LJ in *Bebb* [1914] 1 Ch., 299.

1 'Their position is inferior to that of men'[7]

Differentiation, inclusion, omission

The work of modern historians has emphasised the presence in medieval thought of different ideas of sex categorisation, and the presence in medieval life of some degree of fluidity as to gender roles and expectations.[8] It has been shown that there was some contemporary support for different models of sex categorisation: the three sex model (men, 'hermaphrodites' and women), the two sex model (men and women) and the one sex model (with women as defective men).[9] The one sex model was taken up by Thomas Laqueur in the late twentieth century, and presented as having been prevalent through the medieval period and until the eighteenth century.[10] This has proved a very popular encapsulation. Its accuracy has, however, been challenged, and it seems clear that a one sex model was not dominant in medieval medical theory, nor in other areas of medieval thought.[11] As this chapter will show, medieval common law materials generally present and rely upon a model of humanity divided into two sexes. For the most part, this division was treated as unproblematic and fundamental, both intellectually and practically, and it is important to give due weight to this view in wider discussions of sex and

7 *Bracton* II, p. 31.

8 See, e.g., Leah DeVun, 'Erecting Sex: Hermaphrodites and the Medieval Science of Surgery', *Osiris*, 30, *Scientific Masculinities* (2015), 17–37.

9 See Aristotle, *Generation of Animals*, tr. by A.L. Peck (Cambridge, MA: Harvard University Press, 1943), p. 175; Claude Thomasset, 'The Nature of Women', in *A History of Women in the West* II, ed. by Klapisch-Zuber (Cambridge, MA: Belknap Press of Harvard University Press), pp. 43–69.

10 Thomas Laqueur, *Making Sex: Body and Gender from the Greeks to Freud* (Cambridge, MA, 1990), adopted, e.g., in Veronica Sanz, 'No Way out of the Binary: A Critical History of the Scientific Production of Sex', *Signs* 43 (2017), 1–27, 3–4.

11 See, e.g., Katharine Park and Robert A. Nye, 'Destiny is Anatomy', *New Republic* (18 February, 1991), 53–7; Joan Cadden, *Meanings of Sex Difference in the Middle Ages* (Cambridge, 1993), pp. 198–202; V.A. Rosario, 'Fustigating the 'One-Sex Body' Thesis', *Studies in History and Philosophy of Biology & Biomedical Science* 48 (2014), 112–14; Monica H. Green, 'Bodies, Gender, Health, Disease: Recent Work on Medieval Women's Medicine', *Studies in Medieval and Renaissance History,* 3rd series 2 (2005), 1–46, 6–12; Helen King, *The One Sex Body on Trial: the Classical and Early Modern Evidence* (Farnham, 2013); DeVun, 'Erecting Sex', pp. 18–19.

gender in medieval studies, as well as noting the clear recognition by common law of differences between sub-groups of women.[12]

To some extent, the emphasis in legal documents on men and women as a clear binary is to be expected: as Elliot has noted, [13] broadly legal procedural documents were less susceptible to 'prestidigital feats of gender-bending' than was the case with literary and theological texts. Her examples of less creative documents are 'the manorial roll, the episcopal visitation record, the census [and] the will', but this greater simplicity is equally true of common law plea rolls: the more practical records of the common law had significantly less room for flights of intellectual curiosity than could be included in other species of text. Nevertheless, some common law sources do also include material which indicates a degree of fluidity of thinking with regard to gender. Some of the instances of fluidity or uncertainty are reminiscent of ideas and statements in other discourses, while others are linked to issues of language and interpretation specific to, and especially important to, legal discussion.

'Women', sex and gender

In statements on medieval common law and the arguments of common lawyers, 'women' is generally assumed to be a relevant and self-explanatory category and the language of differentiation of women and men is that of sex. In relation to succession, for example, *Bracton* states that 'Sex ...makes one a nearer heir', and also notes that it is 'because of [their] sex' that women are unable to do some of the things which men can do.[14]

Both the statement from *Bracton* that 'Women differ from men in many respects, for their position is inferior to that of men' and c. 54 of Magna Carta 1215 (c. 34 of the 1225 version which lawyers generally cite), limiting women's ability to bring appeals, for example, treat 'women' as a relevant category, coherent, clearly separate from 'men' and subject to common law attention and intervention.[15] It is 'women' who are barred or exempted from attending certain legal sessions, who cannot be outlawed, but must instead be 'waived', about whom there is controversy as to whether they could be regarded as 'on royal service' so as to allow a delay of court proceedings, who are to be punished differently to men and treated differently in legal procedure, whose different treatment to men is pointed out, or who are, at times explicitly to be treated in the same way as men.[16] It is women who are

12 *P & M* I, p. 468.

13 Dyan Elliot, 'The Three Ages of Joan Scott', *AHR* 113 (2008), 1390–403, 1390.

14 *Bracton* II, pp. 190, 403; III, p. 285. See also *Bracton* II, p. 342; III, pp. 26, 84; IV, p. 361.

15 *Bracton*, II, p. 31; *Magna Carta* 1215, c. 54, *SR* I, p. 12; Peter Goodrich, 'Gynaetopia: Feminine Genealogies of Common Law', *Journal of Law and Society* 20 (1993), 276–308, 278.

16 See, e.g., *Bracton* II, pp. 353–4; *Mirror* book 4 c. 4, p. 126; *Britton*, book 1, c. 13 no. 3; 24 *SS*, p. 106. *Litt.*, book II, c. 11 no. 186 (outlawry/waiving); 102 *SS*, p. 121; *SR* I, p. 56; *Mirror*,

'weak', 'simple' and vulnerable to predation by adventurers, whose moral, physical and intellectual inferiority is noted, including their lack of wisdom compared to men, the inconstancy of their minds and their vanity.[17] It is women's blood which is less worthy than that of men, and the seisin of women which is not as 'high' as that of men.[18] It is women upon whom the role of staying at home and keeping quiet is imposed,[19] and whose lack of capacity to perform military roles such as defending a castle is stated as truth or as 'common presumption'.[20] All of this appears to treat as unproblematic, a distinction based on and anchored to a two sex model.

References to a one sex idea (with women as deformed men) are extremely uncommon.[21] *Bracton* and *Fleta* do mention 'hermaphrodites', a group sometimes regarded as constituting a third sex.[22] The treatises' accounts are, however, brief and simplified forms of classical ideas, and are inflected with a strong 'two sex' sensibility. It does not seem that their authors accepted that 'hermaphrodites' were genuinely neither male nor female: although they might not look like a typical male or female, they were 'really' one or the other.[23] Simple observation of the 'preponderance' of the sexual organs would make it possible to categorise a 'hermaphrodite' as either male or female, and doing so was necessary and appropriate.[24] Even this passing

---

preface. *SR* I, p. 217 (femina). The Assize of Bread and Ale used feminine word-endings rather than specifying *woman*, but later legislation on the topic used *femme*: *SR* I, pp. 200, 201; 13 Ric II st. 1 c. 8, *SR* II, p. 63; st. 5 Hen. IV c. 2, *SR* II, p. 144.

17 st. 31 Hen. VI c. 9, *SR* II, p. 367; 132 *SS*, pp. 227, 370; *Seipp* 1457.017; 1313.305ss; 1376.012.

18 98 *SS*, p. 542, JUST 1/633 m.71; *P & M* II, pp. 295, 258, 266, 299; *Seipp* 1306.136rs; 1312.003ss; 1382.051am; 1310.219ss; 1311.041ss; 1294.001rs.

19 Fortescue, *DNLN*, p. 257.

20 132 *SS*, pp. 31, 43, 49.

21 Fortescue, *DNLN*, p. 257 Part 2 c. 8.

22 On 'hermaphroditism' and modern categories, see De Vun, 'Erecting', pp. 18–19; Frederik Pedersen, 'Privates on Parade: Impotence Cases as Evidence for Medieval Gender', in *Law and Private Life in the Middle Ages*, ed. by Per Andersen, Mia Műnster-Swensen and Helle Vogt (Copenhagen, 2011), pp. 81–104, 90. Maitland noted mention of 'hermaphrodites' in *Bracton* and Matthew Paris, but this did not strike him as worthy of discussion: *Collected Papers* I, p. 401; 8 *SS*, pp. 8, 57, 62, 63; *Fleta*, book 1 c. 5. *Bracton* II, p. 24.

23 For medical and theological thought as to whether the 'perfect' hermaphrodite existed, see De Vun, 'Erecting', p. 22; Christof Rolker, '"The Two Laws" and the Three Sexes: Ambiguous Bodies in Canon Law and Roman Law (12th to 16th centuries)', *Zeitschrift der Savigny-Stiftung für Rechtsgeschichte: Kanonistische Abteilung* 100 (2014), 178–222, 192.

24 *Bracton* II, p. 32; 8 *SS*, pp. 57, 62; *D*.1.5.9; *Fleta* book 1, c. 5. European surgical sources described 'hermaphroditism' in adults and its 'correction', but are uninformative on assessment of babies: DeVun, 'Erecting', p. 37. For the idea of the 'prevailing sex', see Rolker, 'The Two Laws', p. 203. The hermaphrodite was a familiar enough idea that it had a metaphorical usage: Rolker, 'The Two Laws', p. 191; Ernst H. Kantorowicz, *The King's Two Bodies: A Study in Mediaeval Political Theology* (Princeton, NJ, 1997), pp. 10–11. See also Cary J. Nederman and Jacqui True, 'The Third Sex: The Idea of the Hermaphrodite in Twelfth-Century Europe', *Journal of the History of Sexuality* 6 (1996), 497–517; L. DeVun, 'The Jesus Hermaphrodite: Science and Sex Difference in Premodern Europe', *Journal of the History of Ideas* 69 (2008), 193–218, 212.

interest in questioning the distinction seems to have faded over the medieval period. Later discussions of entitlements and succession to land proceeded without expressing any difficulty in making the distinctions between males and females upon which the system was founded. The late fifteenth-century treatise, Littleton's *Tenures*, for example, rested its discussions of fees simple and tail on a two sex model without exploring the question of 'hermaphrodites'. It would be Coke's seventeenth-century commentary on this passage which would take up, once more, the possibility of uncertainty on this issue.[25]

No evidence of common law cases in which a court was confronted with an individual challenging apparent biological sex has, thus far, emerged, though there are a number of areas in which one might have imagined possible disputes as to whether an individual was male or female: above all in relation to succession to land. The common law's system of succession made distinction between male and female crucial. The importance of this clear and stark division can be seen, for example, in one fifteenth-century common lawyer's reported statement that 'it is against the law of England that a daughter shall inherit, when there is a son alive'.[26] Since there is always likely to have been a percentage of the population with some ambiguity in genital appearance, one might have expected some disputes as to whether X was in fact a son, and thus qualified to inherit, and displace a daughter, or not. Doubt or subterfuge in this area was not outside contemporary literary imagination: an attempt to evade an English rule of succession which bars female inheritance, by bringing up as a boy a child apparently biologically female, according to contemporary standards, lies at the heart of the *Romance of Silence*.[27] If such cases came before common law courts, however, no traces of them have yet been discovered in the records. Nor is there anything in common law records which appears to dispute sexual identity in the manner of the much-commented-upon London jurisdiction criminal case of John/Eleanor Rykener, which has been described variously as one of cross-dressing or transgender.[28] Common law records include

25 *Litt.*, book 1 cc. 1, 2; *Co. Litt.* 8a, 29b.

26 51 *SS*, p. 26 case 9, *R. v Reginald Cobham* (1418): Martyn sjt.

27 Caitlin G. Watt, '"Car vallés sui et nient mescine": Trans Heroism and Literary Masculinity in Le Roman de Silence', *Medieval Feminist Forum* 5 (2019), 135–73; Heldris de Cornuaille, *Le Roman de Silence*, ed. by Lewis Thorpe (Cambridge, 1972).

28 See, e.g., Ruth Mazo Karras and David Lorenzo Boyd, '"Ut cum muliere": A Male Transvestite Prostitute in Fourteenth-Century London', in *Premodern Sexualities*, ed. by Louise Fradenburg and Carla Freccero (London, 1996), pp. 99–116. Ruth Mazo Karras and Tom Linkinen, 'John/Eleanor Ryekener Revisited', in *Founding Feminisms: Essays in Honor of E. Jane Burns*, ed. by Laine E. Dogget and Daniel E. O'Sullivan (Woodbridge, 2016); Kadin Henningsen, '"Calling [herself Eleanor": Gender Labor and Becoming a Woman in the Rykener Case', *Medieval Feminist Forum* 55 (2019), 249–66; Judith M. Bennett, 'England: Women and Gender', in *A Companion to Britain in the Later Middle Ages*, ed. by S.H. Rigby (Malden, MA, 2003), pp. 87–106; Carolyn Dinshaw, 'Good

occasional references to men dressing as women, or women dressing as men, for the purposes of disguising their identities whilst engaging in offences. Thus, in Warwickshire in 1306, the sister of an alleged killer who had fled to a church is said to have exchanged clothes with him, so that he could escape in disguise as a woman.[29] Such cross-dressing is, however, understood to be a temporary ruse rather than assertion of a different identity.[30] Similarly, the occasional description of a woman as a *virago* is a criticism of her conduct as inappropriate for a woman rather than evidence of a belief that she is, or regards herself as, a man.[31]

The discussion amongst common lawyers at Westminster, as reported in the Year Books, does, however, show some fascinating, if fleeting, signs of a certain fluidity of ideas in relation to gender. On occasion, in reported courtroom dialogue, we see male pleaders and judges taking on the persona of a female client or hypothetical woman. Thus, for example, in a case of 1312, Chief Justice William Bereford was reported to have cast himself as a woman, in a metaphorical passage in which he was instructing a lawyer who was attempting to formulate his pleading to best effect,[32] and a prominent justice of the fifteenth century, Sir John Fortescue, used a metaphor of pregnancy with regard to his production of an argument in a treatise, effectively casting himself as a pregnant woman.[33] As will be discussed in Chapter 4, pleaders in common law courts seem to have felt no inhibition in identifying themselves with female clients, speaking as the client herself.

This apparent mental flexibility must, however, be seen alongside the more rigid gender stereotyping and misogyny encountered in records emanating

---

Vibrations: John/Eleanor, Dame Alys, the Pardoner, and Foucault', in *Getting Medieval: Sexualities and Communities, Pre- and Postmodern* (Durham, NC, 1999), pp. 102–42; Judith M. Bennett and Shannon McSheffrey, 'Early, Erotic and Alien: Women Dressed as Men in Late Medieval London', *History Workshop Journal* 77 (2014), 1–25. For recent developments in this area, see Roisin Cossar, Ruth Mazo Karras, and Shannon McSheffrey, "The Case of Rolandina Ronchaia, a 14th - century transwoman?," *Middle Ages for Educators*, July 22, 2020. Accessed [17th December, 2020]. https://middleagesforeducators.princeton.edu/node/886/

29 JUST 1/966 m. 8 (IMG 8919).

30 See also, e.g., SC 8 295/14747: allegation that men dressed as women to carry out an ambush.

31 *CRR* III, p. 323; 62 *SS*, p. 8. On usages of 'virago', see Mitchell, *Portraits*, p. 133; Coral Lumbley, 'Imperatrix, Domina, Rex: Conceptualizing the Female King in Twelfth-Century England', *Medieval Feminist Forum* 55 (2019), 64–99. For concern at cross-dressing, see, e.g., Valerie Hotchkiss, *Clothes Make the Man: Female Cross-Dressing in Medieval Europe* (New York, 2012); Ralph V. Turner, *Eleanor of Aquitaine* (New Haven, CT and London, 2009), pp. 227, 271; *Deuteronomy* 21:5; *Knighton's Chronicle 1337–1396*, ed. and tr. by G.H. Martin (Oxford, 1995), p. 93.

32 *Seipp* 1312.017ss.

33 Fortescue, *DNLN* Part I, c. 30, p. 223. On medieval thought and gender fluidity, see Dyan Elliot, 'The Three Ages of Joan Scott', *AHR* 113 (2008), 1390–403, p. 1390; Caroline Walker Bynum, *Jesus as Mother: Studies in the Spirituality of the High Middle Ages* (Berkeley, CA, 1982).

from the same milieu, the all-male, close-knit world of the leading legal professionals, pleaders and judges. Professor Baker expressed disappointment at finding misogyny in a common law reading, and defended 'the common law mentality' from charges of misogyny.[34] It would be odd, however, if common lawyers had not shared in the misogynist discourses of their age, since they were not cut off from the currents of contemporary intellectual life. Historical scholarship has highlighted the range of views expressed by medieval commentators, in the areas of philosophy and theology, political theory, literature, civil law, medical theory and history, many of them focusing on women's inferiority and weakness in physical, intellectual, rational and moral terms, and emphasising the danger to men of this weakness.[35] Misogynist trends in medieval literature cast doubt on women's truthfulness and reliability and asserted their weakness. Classical Roman jurists, in explaining a variety of disqualifications and different treatment for women, had posited both women's bad character (lack of shame, cunning, greed) and also (perhaps rather inconsistently) their lack of capacity (they were weak, infirm, imbecilic, fragile, ignorant).[36] Such insults had a powerful intellectual presence,[37] and clearly made their way into common law sources. There are echoes of ingrained misogyny in common lawyers' reported jokes about consummation of marriage with a young girl, rape and women's foolishness (at best) in relation to sex and virginity, and in their comments portraying women as blameworthily weak-willed, sexually disloyal or 'shrewish'.[38] A stratum of lawyers' remarks likened women to animals. Thus, sisterly relations were described in bestial terms in one royal enactment, which stated that making elder sisters guardians of younger sisters 'would be to

34 132 *SS*, pp. lxx, lxxi.

35 See, e.g., Carla Casagrande, The Protected Woman', in *A History of Women II*, ed. by Klapisch-Zuber, pp. 70–104, 86, 92, 103; *Women Defamed and Women Defended: An Anthology of Medieval Texts*, ed. and tr. by Alcuin Blamires, Karen Pratt and C.W. Marx (Oxford, 1992); R. Howard Bloch, 'Medieval Misogyny', *Representations* 20 (1987), 1–24; Cadden, *Meanings of Sex Difference*, c 4; René Metz, 'Le statut de la femme en droit canonique médiéval', *Recueils de la societé Jean Bodin* 12 (1962), 9–82.

36 Joëlle Beaucamp, 'Le vocabulaire de la faiblesse féminine dans les textes juridiques romains du IIe au VIe siècle', *Revue historique du droit français et étranger* 54 (1976), 485–509; Orit Malka, 'Disqualified Witnesses between Tannaitic Halakha and Roman Law: The Archeology of a Legal Institution', *LHR* 37 (2019), 903–36; Suzanne Dixon, 'Infirmitas Sexus: Womanly Weakness in Roman Law', *LHR* 52 (1984), 343–71, 344, 358.

37 Elisabeth van Houts, 'Gender and Authority of Oral Witnesses in Europe (800–1300)', *TRHS* 9 (1999), 201–20, 212; *Woman Defamed*, ed. by Blamires and others.

38 20 *SS* pp. 189, 190 (1310) *John the Cooper of T. v Isolde widow of Richard Ildok* (1312); Brand, 'Inside the courtroom', 11; *Seipp* 1376.012, 1441.032. st. Westminster I (1275) c. 22, *SR* I, p. 33; *Seipp* 1315.046 ss; CP 40/209 m. 136d; *Seipp* 1421.141rog; 1436.047; 1478.026. Raising women's sexual conduct in cases involving land or villeinage claims and defences to trespass, see, e.g., 33 *SS*, p. 188; CP 40/179 m. 21 (IMG 43); CP 40/426 m. 396 (IMG 783); 103 *SS* p. 384. case 34.18; CP 40/443 m. 46d.

commit the lambs to the wolf',[39] and common lawyers had a favourite way of expressing the presumption of legitimacy of a child born within marriage, which compared the wife to a cow.[40] The idea that women might give birth to monsters also, perhaps, plays into this idea of women as less than fully human.[41] Sometimes, using synecdoche, they are reduced, in the context of succession, to 'wombs'.[42] The analogies or juxtapositions used in relation to married women suggest a lack of capacity and the location of control and responsibility in another person: they are considered alongside minors, monks, villeins and those labelled 'idiots'.[43] Limitations on women's capacities and actions appropriate to them are stressed. Thus, widows are told that they should stay at home, caring for their children.[44] Such statements were entertained by, and upheld by, common lawyers, and remain an important part of the legacy of the medieval common law.

Nevertheless, just as it has been shown that there were counter-currents to the prevalent misogyny in medieval thought beyond the common law, with some statements of mental equality of women and men, or praising women or even challenging a complete distinction on the basis of sex,[45] so the records of the common law evince some less negative attitudes towards women. Amongst the misogyny, we also find some positive portrayals: of a wife resisting temptation to stray, or a heroic widow fighting against the odds to bring to justice the jurors who had wrongfully had her husband hanged or a wife wrongfully imprisoned with her husband, escaping and seeking help for him.[46] Common law records include the occasional 'cameo

39 *SR* I, p. 5; *P & M* II, p. 272.

40 *Seipp* 1304.027rs; 1309.129ss 1307.020rs, 1406.013, 1440.003, *P & M* I, p. 422; J.L. Barton, 'Nullity of Marriage and Illegitimacy in the England of the Middle Ages', in *Legal History Studies*, ed. by Dafydd Jenkins (Cardiff, 1975), c. 2, p. 40; P.R. Hyams, 'The Action of Naifty in the Early Common Law', *LQR* 90 (1974), 326–50; *Leges Henrici Primi*, 243, no. 77, 2a. *P and M* II, p. 405.

41 *Bracton* II, p. 31.

42 See, e.g., *Seipp* 1310.136ss; *Litt.*, book 1, c. 1, para. 6–9.

43 See, e.g., st. 3 Edw IV c. 5, *SR* II, p. 399; *Seipp* 1343.257ass. 1413.046; 1466.015; 1478.016; 1311.295ss; 1451.009abr; 1504.015; 1343.257ass; 1413.046; 1425.024; 1451.009abr; 1458.048; *P & M* II. 419; 421. For similar material in readings, see 129 *SS* 129, p. 47, 22. See also *The Old Tenures c. 1515 and The Old Natura Brevium c, 1518*, ed. by Morris S. Arnold (Chicago, IL, 1980) f.10, 25.

44 *Bracton* II, p. 281; Daniel Klerman, 'Women Prosecutors in Thirteenth Century England', *Harvard Journal of Law and the Humanities* 14 (2002), 271–313, 306.

45 See, e.g., Patricia Skinner, *Living with Disfigurement in Early Medieval Europe* (London, 2017), p. 133; John Gillingham, *Conquests, Catastrophe and Recovery: Britain and Ireland 1066–1485* (London, 2014), p. 283; Joy A. Schroeder, *Deborah's Daughters: Gender Politics and Biblical Interpretation* (Oxford, 2014), p. 34; Goodrich, 'Gynaetopia', p. 279; Louise J. Wilkinson, *Women in Thirteenth-Century Lincolnshire* (London, 2007), pp. 3–4; Ceridwen Lloyd-Morgan, 'The querelle des femmes: A Continuing Tradition in Welsh Women's Literature', in *Medieval Women: Texts and Contexts in Late Medieval Britain*, ed. by Jocelyn Wogan-Browne and others (Leiden, 2000), pp. 101–14.

46 *Seipp* 1482.115; *Mirror*, book II, c. 15; KB 9/293 m. 39 (IMG 77).

appearance' from a supernatural woman: thus St Winifred is credited with intervention in an incident of kidnapping and violence in a 1456 King's Bench entry which highlights her help of a Shrewsbury man held captive and tortured by extortioners.[47] The Virgin Mary, as well as Eve, has a place in legal treatises.[48]

Medieval common lawyers seem to have been able to hold conflicting views about women, some more negative than others.[49] They could repeat misogynist tropes and theories to each other, and this might certainly be cumulatively damaging to women, but they also knew that it was not practical to take them to their logical conclusions, nor to act on them in all cases. As well as the opposing views found in other branches of medieval thought, common lawyers were also exposed to other influences which might lead them not always to follow misogynist logic. First of all, and unlike some other medieval thinkers, they often lived with real women: from the fourteenth century in particular, many prominent common lawyers, including judges, were married men. Another important additional source of ideas was their necessary familiarity with other domestic jurisdictions. Common lawyers were, at times, obliged to take into account rules relating to women in local and ecclesiastical jurisdiction, some of which accorded women somewhat greater capacity than did the common law. Their awareness of the existence of alternative rules and views may also have contributed to a picture of women and their appropriate treatment which, as we will see, was far from being simple.

Inclusion, omission and a linguistic 'one sex model'?

Chapter 39 of the *Magna Carta* of 1215 (usually cited by lawyerly legal historians from the version of 1225, as Chapter 29) provided that:

> No free man (*liber homo*) is to be arrested, or imprisoned, or disseised, or outlawed, or exiled, or in any other way ruined. Nor will we go against him or send against him, except by the lawful judgment of his peers, or by the law of the land.[50]

Despite the fame of this provision, its implications for medieval ideas about sex, gender and law are yet to be given full consideration. Likewise, attention to the inclusion, explicit or implicit, of women, or their exclusion, from

47 KB 27/781 m. 115 and 115d (IMG 237 and 572); SC 8/96/4769. Women portrayed actively resisting injustice or crime, see, e.g., SC8/57/2833; SC8/307/15333; SC8/280/13994.

48 See, e.g., Goodrich, 'Gynaetopia', 278; *Bracton* e.g. at II, p. 33 and IV, pp. 193, 361; *Mirror*, book II, c. 1.

49 For this point in relation to French legal writers, see van Houts, 'Gender and Authority', pp. 213–4.

50 *SR* I, pp. 6, 11, 14, 17, 24, 28, 33, 38.

legislative and quasi-legislative materials more widely, could enhance discussions in this area.

The most prominent textbook on English legal history deals with the question of whether or not the safeguards of c. 29 were considered to apply to women in fairly short order, holding that *liber homo* clearly always encompassed women.[51] Elsewhere, its author has treated this matter at greater length, but with the same outcome, and the 'women (obviously) included' reading has also been embraced by prominent medieval historians.[52] While it is clear that the orthodox view amongst later common lawyers came to be that women were covered by *liber homo* in this provision, however, it appears less clear that this was unequivocally the case throughout the medieval period. The issue is complicated by changing views as to the meaning of c. 29 more generally (what was lawful judgment by peers, and what was 'the law of the land') and as to its status, whether confirmatory of common law or an independent source of law.[53] Examination of the issue involves consideration of the interwoven questions of whether the words were understood to apply to women at all, and also what substantive import they might have been understood to have, given the provision's permission to imprison or otherwise disadvantage, if this was permitted by 'the law of the land', when 'the law of the land' allowed significant limitation on the freedom of women.[54]

There have been four main strands to the argument for *liber homo* having always been understood to cover women as well as men. The first has concentrated on the specific phrase, *liber homo*, noting that it was used, in relatively contemporary sources, in contexts suggesting the inclusion of women. The second strand has had a more general linguistic focus, holding *homo* always to have been understood to be a 'one sex' word, including females as well as males. The third strand has stressed the views of post-medieval common lawyers, holding women to be included. Finally, as a fourth strand, there is the evidence of practice, and the apparent use by women of the provision. It is not clear, however, that these strands come together to form a definitive conclusion in favour of women's 'obvious' inclusion throughout the period.

Perhaps the least convincing of the strands is that regarding contemporary use of the words *liber homo*. Employment of these words in earlier and

51 Baker, *Introduction*, p. 499.

52 J.H. Baker, *The Reinvention of Magna Carta* (Cambridge, 2017), especially at pp. 32–4; John Gillingham, 'Back to Runnymede', *London Review of Books* 37:9 (7th May, 2015), https://www.lrb.co.uk/the-paper/v37/n09/letters#172279, Accessed 25th July, 2020; David Carpenter, 'Magna Carta 1215: Its Social and Political Context', in *Magna Carta*, ed. by Lawrence Goldman (London, 2018), c. 2; David Carpenter, *Magna Carta* (London, 2015), p. 101. In contrast, one recent commentator has stated that the provision simply did not cover women: Jocelynne A. Scutt, *Women and Magna Carta: A Treaty for Rights or Wrongs?* (London, 2016), p. 46.

53 Baker, *Reinvention*, pp. 6–7.

54 See Seabourne, *IMW*.

contemporary legal texts shows that it was not an accepted term of art with a meaning including women: it could be inclusive or exclusive of them. One passage from *Glanvill*, referring to legitimate recipients of homage, is cast in terms of '*libero homini* whether male or female', so does show that the formula could be used to cover females as well as males, but elsewhere *Glanvill* also used *liber homo* for males only, and, even within *Magna Carta*, *liber homo* sometimes seems to have a male-only sense.[55] *Liber homo* is also used in some later measures in ways which seem to indicate males only.[56]

The more general linguistic argument, that *homo* would have been understood to include women as well as men, is somewhat stronger,[57] but I would argue that we must class as unproven the existence of a strong rule of interpretation to this effect in the medieval common law. There are Roman law antecedents for the idea that (a word of) 'the masculine sex always contains the feminine sex', occasional uses of *homo* for a woman in legal records, and, for example, *Bracton* divides *homines* into male, female and 'hermaphrodite'.[58] It should be noted, however, that Roman law 'masculine includes feminine' rules do not seem to have been absolutely clear-cut, that not all jurists saw this as an invariable rule of interpretation, and that the French *home* is used in unequivocally exclusive fashion in at least one later thirteenth-century statute.[59]

Later medieval English statutes tended towards clear stipulation of applicability to women as well as men, as we will see below, and contemporary documents from outside the English statutory context could be more explicit. An important canon of 1215, for example, stipulated its application to people 'of both sexes'.[60] Medieval English lawyers drafted writs and private

55 *Glanvill*, IX, 3; cited, e.g., in: Gillingham, *Conquests*, p. 4; Baker, *Reinvention*, p. 184. *Glanvill* VI, 1; XIV, 1. Magna Carta cl. 27 (1215) on the intestacy of 'any *liber homo*' seems appropriate only to male intestates.
Bracton uses *homo* and *liber homo* in inconsistent ways: contrast *Bracton* II, p. 228 (homage, deriving from Glanvill IX,1) and II, p. 265; III, p. 131; III, p. 293; IV, p. 169.

56 *SR* I, p. 21; later 'due process' provisions, using 'home': st. 28 Edw III c.3, *SR* I, p. 345; 37 Edw III, *SR* I. 382. c 18. 'Liber homo' in ale-only contexts: st. Merton c. 10, *SR* I, p. 4; st. Winchester (1285) c. 6, *SR* I, p. 97.

57 Baker, *Reinvention*, p. 34.

58 Judith Evans Grubbs, *Women and the Law in the Roman Empire: A Sourcebook on Marriage, Divorce and Widowhood* (London, 2002), pp. 16–7; *D*. 32.62; *D*. 50.16.1; *D*. 50.16.152; *D*. 50.16.195 pr. See also Sandra Petersson, 'Gender Neutral Drafting: Historical Perspective', *Statute Law Review* 19 (1998), 93–112, 94; 84 *SS*, p. 98 no 3426 (woman called the 'homo' of the canons of Walton, 1208); *Bracton* II, p. 31.

59 Compare *D*. 50.16.152 and *D*. 50.16.1, 50.16.40, 50.16.100, 50.16.116, 50.16.163, 50.16.172, 50.16.195; 50.16.204. John Ayliffe, *A New Pandect of Roman Civil Law* (London, 1734), p. 57: 'The masculine gender *very often* includes the feminine'. st. Gloucester (1278), c.10; *SR* I, p. 49 mentions 'home a sa feme': *home* can only be masculine here.

60 Bronach Kane, *Popular Memory and Gender in Medieval England: Men, Women and Testimony in the Church Courts, c.1200–1500* (Woodbridge, 2019), p. 35; Lateran IV canon 21.

documents using explicit masculine and feminine terms or other, more clearly all-encompassing terms rather than relying on a widespread understanding that *homo* included women, for example, and a warranty might be against 'all men and women', or 'against all people', rather than relying on an inclusive interpretation of *homo*.[61] Such practices also seem to cast some doubt upon a conclusion that *homo* in c. 29 would always and obviously have been seen to apply to women.

The common learning of lawyers, by the sixteenth century, is said to have been that *homo* in c. 29 applied to women.[62] Nevertheless, a mid-sixteenth-century reading on *Magna Carta*, though it says that *home* is to be understood 'in these statutes' to include both male and female, still seems confused about the correct interpretation, at least in relation to the trial of peers.[63] An 'inclusive' view of *homo* was adopted by early modern legal luminaries such as Plowden and Coke, however, and has often been seen thereafter,[64] with a growing assumption that c. 29, as then understood, applied fully to women. Sixteenth- and seventeenth-century writers considered that (aristocratic) women should always have been understood to be covered.[65] This later inclusive interpretation was not based on linguistic considerations alone, however, but also, at least in part, on a construction of *Magna Carta* as an important limiting factor on royal power in the writers' own age, and thus something which should be given an expansive interpretation. Coke, in particular, was keen to promote a broad view of the provision, maximising the limit on royal power.[66] His 'inclusive' reading might be seen in the light of that policy goal. Blackstone's discussion of the exclusion of women from qualification for jury service is equivocal on the issue, since it is framed in

61 See, e.g., acquittance *contra omnes homines*, JUST 1/483 m. 15 (IMG 1990); warranty 'men and women' JUST 1/1245 m. 17d (IMG 6341); 1290–91, JUST 1/1081 m. 7d (IMG 4526); 1293 JUST 1/804 m.3d (IMG 2464); 1306–7 JUST 1/253 m. 7 (IMG 2507); 'people' 'contra omnes gentes' JUST 1/1282 m. 12 (IMG 2878). Registers of writs did not see *liber homo* as covering free women: 87 *SS*, xliv, p. 64 nos 103 and 104: in writs *de libertate probanda*, *Cum liber homo sit* becomes *cum libera femina sit*.

62 132 *SS*, p. lxxi.

63 132 *SS*, p. 384.

64 Edmund Plowden, *The Commentaries or Reports of Edmund Plowden* (London, 1816), 86v; Co. Inst. II, 14, 17, 29; *A Discourse upon the Exposicion and Understandinge of Statutes*, ed. by S.E. Thorne (San Marino, CA, 1942), p. 129. It also features in the works by late nineteenth- and early twentieth-century proponents of women's rights: Charlotte Carmichael Stopes, *British Freewomen: Their Historical Privilege* (London, 1894), c. 1, p. 75; Laura Nym Mayhull, 'Defining Militancy: Radical Protest, the Constitutional Idiom and Women's Suffrage in Britain 1908–9', *JBS* 39 (2000), 340–71, 354–6; Baker, *Reinvention*, p. 186, citing CP 40/1026, m. 556 (1519); CP 40/1102, m. 448 (1539).

65 See, e.g., KB 27/965 m. 25; W. Staunford, *Les Plees del Coron*, ed. by Peter Glazebrook (London, 1971), p. 152d; Co. Inst. II, 1 ff, p. 45 ff; *Countess of Rutland's Case*, 6 Co. Rep. 52b; 132 *SS*, pp. 247, 264, 380, 384. Baker, *Reinvention*, pp. 230, 430–1, 463.

66 Co. Inst. II., 45; *SR* II, p. 321; Staunford, *Les Plees del Coron*, 152d, states that *homo* in this context includes women, but is concerned with the position after the statute of Henry VI.

terms of the qualifying juror as a *liber et legalis homo*. It is clear enough that he was not suggesting that women were excluded because they did not count as *liber*, and he states that *homo* was 'a name common to both sexes', and yet a need is felt to strengthen the exclusion of women by using an additional word, *legalis*, which was presumably regarded as not applying to them, though this is not spelled out.[67] Such later interpretations are not necessarily a reliable basis from which to deduce the medieval understanding of whether or not women were necessarily considered to be included in a provision cast in terms of 'men', and the inclusion, until well into the nineteenth century, of statutory provisions to the effect that masculine terms, in an individual act, 'included the feminine' suggests at least the possibility of doubt having persisted on this issue over a very long period of time.[68]

The best evidence for application to women of the provision, and their inclusion within *homo*, is that of practice and comment from the medieval period itself. This, however, is both sparse and equivocal. There are instances of women of high status apparently appealing to the clause, in petitions of the thirteenth and fourteenth centuries,[69] but no clear endorsement of this as a decisive argument on their behalf. Later common law cases are more explicit in referring to it in relation to less exalted women.[70] Such use is some evidence for the possibility of an inclusive interpretation of *liber homo* during the medieval period. There are, however, also instances of medieval women being confined without judgement, without any suggestion that this was contrary to the provision. It is difficult to discern whether this should be seen as an indication that the clause did not clearly apply to women; that it did apply to women but was disregarded by those with power; or that it applied to women in principle, but was rendered nugatory by a variety of derogations from the rule which operated to allow confinement of women in many circumstances.[71]

In the later fourteenth century, it was claimed on behalf of Alice Perrers that she had been wronged by being expropriated and banished without

67 *Bl. Comm.*, book III c. 23, p. 362.

68 1 Vict. c. 26; Solicitors Act 1843, s. 48; Interpretation Act 1850, 13 & 14 Vict. c. 21. s. 4; Interpretation Act 1889, s. 1; Petersson, 'Gender Neutral Drafting', p. 93; Scutt, *Women and Magna Carta*, p. 14.

69 Cases are often connected to lost property rights rather than confinement. See in particular the1252 case of Isabella, countess of Arundel: Susanna Annesley, 'Isabella, countess of Arundel', http://www.finerollshenry3.org.uk/content/month/fm-08-2009.html. See also *RP*, I, p. 66; SC 8/4/190. Other references by women to *Magna Carta* are less specific: see Baker, *Reinvention*, p. 51, SC 8/11/510. There is mention of due process/personal liberty ideas relating to lack of proper charges in a trial of Isabel, countess of Albermarle (d. 1293), in *Goldington v Bassingburn* 1310), *Seipp* 1310.111ss and 1312.010ss; 20 *SS*, pp. 193–7; *Seipp* 1275.003ss: 1276.009ss, though without explicit mention of *Magna Carta*.

70 Baker, *Reinvention*, p. 184; Juliana Draper's 1502 claim, on c. 29, as a *liber homo*: KB 27/965, m. 25.

71 *IMW* cc. 1–3.

an appropriate trial. The petition in question did not specifically refer to *Magna Carta*, but claimed that 'due process' rules applied to women as well as men. For reasons unconnected to this aspect of the claim, this matter was left unresolved.[72] Doubt as to the applicability to women of c. 29, as then understood, can be seen in some later medieval discussion. Statutory intervention in 1442 extended the guarantee of 'trial by peers' to aristocratic women, stating that women were not mentioned in c. 29, and there were 'doubts and ambiguities' about the matter.[73] Even if this is taken to be narrowly focused on procedure in relation to a small group of women rather than a broader principle relating to all women,[74] it does suggest a consciousness that women were different and could not be fitted into the *liber homo* category without some adjustments. It should be noted also that there was a parallel debate, in the mid-fifteenth century as to whether thirteenth-century provisions, which, on their face, applied to (male) heirs only should be held to apply to women in a similar position, despite the fact that they were not mentioned.[75] Such questions appear still to have been unsettled at the end of the medieval period. The corpus of medieval English statutes and other legislative material suggests the absence of a fixed view on women's inclusion.[76] Some statutory material uses *homo* or even words indicating 'everyone', where in fact women are understood to be excluded, while in other cases *homo* or *home* clearly did also cover women. Thus, various proceedings were to be carried out by 'men', but *mort de home* or *homicide* covered female victims.[77] Sometimes it is simply not clear whether women were intended to be included. This is the case in relation to thirteenth-century provisions relating to *home[s] de religion*, and to the defamation of 'great *homes*'.[78] It would appear that *homo*/*home* could be used to mean 'men' or 'people', at the choice of whoever was in charge of interpretation. This did not make for a clear or secure position for women.

Rather than relying upon an idea that women were understood to be included, even if not mentioned, there seems to have been some increase over the medieval period in the tendency for legislation to include specific

72 See *RP* II, 375; W. Mark Ormrod, 'The Trials of Alice Perrers', *Speculum* 83 (2008), 366–96.

73 st. 20 H VI c. 9, *SR* II, p. 321; *RP*, V, 56b; J.G. Bellamy, *The Law of Treason in England in the Later Middle Ages* (New York, 1970), p. 154.

74 Baker, *Reinvention*, pp. 34, 463; 132 *SS*, pp. 170, 253, 264.

75 *Seipp* 1457.017, note especially the view of Fortescue given here and the explicit inclusion of female heirs elsewhere: 33 *SS*, p. 96: st. Westminster II c. 35.

76 Petersson, 'Gender Neutral Drafting'; see also 132 *SS*, p. xlix. Note the lack of interest in gender in T.F.T. Plucknett, *Legislation of Edward I* (Oxford, 1949), and T.F.T. Plucknett, *Statutes and Their Interpretation in the First Half of the Fourteenth Century* (Cambridge, 1922).

77 See, e.g., Charter of the Forest 1217/1224–5, *SR* I, p. 26, st. Merton c. 3, *SR* 1, p. 2; st. Westminster I (1275) c. 11, *SR* I, p. 29; st. Marlborough (1267) c. 24, *SR* I, p. 25.

78 Provisions of 43 H III c. 19, *SR* I, p. 10; st. Westminster I (1275) c. 1, *SR* I, p. 27. On *Scandalum Magnatum* provisions expressed as relating to 'great *homes*', see below, Chapter 5

mention of women. Early legislation might not mention them at all, even when the area with which the enactment dealt was relevant to them. Thus, the Statute of Merton of 1236, dealing with aspects of wardship, discussed the limits of this arrangement with reference to male age of majority only, though wardship also applied to heiresses, and it seems that there was a different age of majority for them.[79] When it was to royal advantage, legislation could be more specific, as in the Statute of the Jewry 1275 provision on taxation of every Jew, which provided that it was to be understood to apply to women as well as men.[80] Later in the period, and particularly from the mid-fourteenth century onwards, explicit mention of women became more common. Women as well as men were mentioned in wage and labour regulation and sumptuary legislation, and explicit application to both men and women became normal.[81] Increasing legislative attention and intervention in relation to women in the post-Black Death period would fit in with views which see this as a general point of departure from one 'Legal System' in the common law to the next, with the new era reinforcing traditional hierarchical obligations.[82] The increased tendency to mention women may have been the result of a more general pattern of increasing specificity in drafting, a trend noted by T.F.T. Plucknett,[83] and there is some inconsistency in any case. Thus, for example, the legislation on silk crafts is inconsistent as to whether women are mentioned or not, and sumptuary legislation varies in terms of the way in which women are treated, sometimes being set out in terms of 'men and women', sometimes in terms of ranked men and their wives, daughters, children.[84] Nevertheless, it is arguable that the overall tendency to more frequent mention of women may also be taken to show increased notice of and heightened concern about women by law-makers

79 c. 6 on marriage of wards uses only 'male' ages of majority: *SR* I, p. 2. See Seabourne, *IMW*, p. 116.

80 *SR* 1, p. 222.

81 Labour regulation mentioning both men and women: st. 12 Ric II c. 5, *SR* II, p. 54; *SR* I, pp. 307, 311; *SR* II, p. 57 st. 12 Ric II c. 4; *SR* II, p. 337; st. 23 H 6 c. 12. st 4 Edw IV c. 1 *SR* II, p. 406; st. 11 H 7 c. 22, *SR* II, p. 585; st. 12 H 7 c. 3, *SR* II, p. 637; st. 7 H IV c. 17 *SR* II, p. 158; *SR* II, p. 248. Female workers dealt with specifically: st. 37 Edw III c. 6, *SR* I, pp. 379–80. Men and women allowed to send children to school: st. 7 Hen. IV c. 17, *SR* II, p. 158. See also Jonathan Rose, *Maintenance in Medieval England* (Cambridge, 2017), p. 218, noting a suggested definition of maintenance of 1388, including 'any lady' or 'woman of religion': *The Westminster Chronicle 1381–1394*, ed. by L.C. Hector and Barbara Harvey (Oxford, 1982), pp. 358–9. 'Ladies' included: st. 8 Hen. VI, c. 4 (1429), *SR* II, pp. 240–1. st. 8 Edw. IV, c. 2, *SR* II, pp. 426–9 prefers the language of 'persons'.

82 See Palmer, *ELABD*, Phifer, 'Property, Power and Patriarchy', p. 15.

83 Rules in other jurisdictions had been expressed to apply to women as well men at an earlier date: 18 *SS*, p. 99 (Waterford, c. 1300); JUST 1/1206 m. 21 (IMG 1951) (Nottingham custom on testation). Plucknett, *Statutes*, pp. 65, 86–7.

84 st. 33 Hen. 6 c. 5, *SR* II, p. 375; st. 22 Edw. IV c. 3, *SR* II, p. 42; st. 1 Ric. III c. 10, *SR* II, p. 493; st. 1 Hen. VII c. 9, *SR* II, p. 506. st.11 Edw III, *SR* I, p. 280; st. 37 Edw III c. 6, c. 8–15, *SR* I, pp. 379–80; st 3 Edw IV c. 5, *SR* II, p. 399; st. 22 Edw IV c. 1, *SR* II, p. 468.

and the common law – whether or not connected to a need to reinforce hierarchies after the Black Death – treating them as worthy and in need of separate attention.

Women: sub-categories of special concern

Though there might be debate as to the inclusion of women in general in legislative measures, attention was paid, by legislators and common lawyers, often and from an early time, to particular subsets of women. Wives and widows received most consideration, with exploration of the nature and consequences of the relationship between husband and wife, and the extent to which the law should 'favour' widows. Sisters were considered in relation to jointly held land, heiresses in relation to rights which others had over them and their land, pregnant women in relation to 'criminal' responsibility and succession to land. These areas of concern and legal approaches to them will be discussed in the next chapter. Some attention was also paid to other sub-groups of women, which will be mentioned briefly here.

Special provision was found necessary and appropriate in relation to queens and nuns. Before the fourteenth century, the legal position of the queen consort developed without much specific legal discussion. *Bracton* had noted some disconnected advantages: queens had priority in relation to attachments (along with the king) and (perhaps) the right to the tail of whales.[85] They acquired some advantages with regard to dower, enforcement of rights, access to courts, privileges in litigation and a degree of independence in litigation and landholding not enjoyed by other married women.[86] They were accorded specific protection through treason laws from the mid-fourteenth century, and it is from a similar period that discussion of the queen's position becomes more common in law reports, debating whether she held a special status or was to be treated in the same way as other married women.[87] Coke would treat the issue as if it had been settled

85 *Bracton* IV, p. 377; II, p. 340; *Fleta* book 1, c. 44, is more certain on the whale question.

86 Lisa. Benz St John, *Three Medieval Queens: Queenship and the Crown in Fourteenth Century England* (New York, 2012), p. 90; John Carmi Parsons, *Eleanor of Castile: Queen and Society in Thirteenth-Century England* (London, 1998), p. 70; Helen M. Cam, 'Cases of Novel Disseisin in the Eyre of London 1321', in *Law Finders and Law Makers in Medieval England*, ed. by Helen M. Cam (London, 1962), pp. 95–105, 104; G. Post, 'Status, id est, magistratus' l'Etat c'est moi and Status regis, the 'Estate Royal' 1100–1322', *Studies in Medieval and Renaissance History* I (1964), 3–103, 55–61, 74–53.

87 25 Edw III st. 5, c. 2, *SR* I, p. 319; Benz St John, *Three Medieval Queens*, c. 4. See also Michael K. Jones and Malcolm G. Underwood, *The King's Mother: Lady Margaret Beaufort Countess of Richmond and Surrey* (Cambridge, 1992), p. 98: *RP* VI, 284, 311–2; J.L. Laynesmith, *The Last Medieval Queens: English Queenship 1445–1503* (Oxford, 2004), p. 237; *Ch. R 1427–1516*, pp. 207–10, 217–8; Howell, *Eleanor of Provence*, p. 112. For debates on the queen's position in litigation and her property, see, e.g., *Seipp* 1344.006rs; 1346.254rs; *Seipp* 1347.057; 1350.183, 1350.184, 1350.098; 1350.210; 1375.007, 1346.237rs;

long before his time, but the fact that a report of a 1487 case was still discussing whether the Queen was a sole person by common law shows that there remained uncertainty at the end of the medieval period.[88] Nuns received attention earlier. They were considered in some medieval legal sources, partly as a matter of showing concern for their secure enclosure and vulnerability to abduction and partly because they might be in an anomalous position, enclosed, metaphorically 'dead to the world', and yet needing to involve themselves in litigation to protect the economic well-being of their houses.[89] Nuns might need special accommodation, for example in terms of being allowed legal representation.[90] Issues on entry into convents also needed special attention, since the question whether a girl or woman had become a nun might be important in land and debt actions, and involuntary confinement in a convent was seen as a plausible tactic of relations or guardians who wished to gain a proprietary advantage by having a girl or woman leave the secular world.[91] After the Protestant Reformation, unlike queens, nuns had, of course, disappeared as a live concern in legal practice in England, so that there was no need for later legal commentators to systematise or simplify the law in this area.

Some subsets of women – particularly villeins and 'foreign' and Jewish women – were subject to additional disadvantages, when compared to other women, and to some extent placed outside the regime of the common law.[92]

1321.185ss; SC8/15/745; SC8/48/2368. For other high-ranking women, see 6 Ric. II st 1 c. 6, *SR* II, p. 27; st. 3 Hen. VII c. 2, *SR* II, p. 512; st. 20 Hen. VI c. 9, *SR* II, p. 321.

88 *Seipp* 1487.053; Co. Litt. Book 2 c. 11 s. 200 a. Note the debate as to the special status of noblewomen with regard to legal process: see *Seipp* 1409.045; 1425.067; 1436.057 and KB 27/594 m. 105 (IMG 236); KB 27/597 m. 102 (IMG 218); KB 27/598 m.d (IMG 474).

89 st. Westminster II c. 34, *SR* I, p. 87; st. of Wales c. 4, *SR* I, p. 58. *Mirror*, book I c. 10, book IV c. 13.

90 33 *SS*, p. 211; Elizabeth Makowski, *English Nuns and the Law in the Middle Ages: Cloistered Nuns and Their Lawyers 1293–1540* (Woodbridge, 2012), p. 63; *Seipp* 1455.023; essoin of confined prioress: 1369.024. Female heads of house in litigation: see, e.g., *Seipp* 1334.063; 1269.002ss; 1334.063, 1347.081.

91 See, e.g., *CRR XVIII, 1243–5* pp. 180–1. SC8/41/2012; Eileen Power, *Medieval English Nunneries*, pp. 35, 37–8; *Seipp* 1276.015ss; 1312.140ss; 1347.156; 1347.202; 1347.229ass; 1364.173ass; 1384.041am; 1384.042am; 1465.031; *CRR V*, pp. 171, 183–66, 162, 280, 293; *CRR VII*, pp. 108–9, 180, 246; *CRR IX* pp. 222, 241, 381–2, 385 58. JUST 1/1055 m. 65d (IMG 3325); *Seipp* 1276.015ss; 1464.049; 388.086 am, CP 40/511 m.521d. For lawyers' discussions of nuns, see, e.g., 105 SS, p. 140; 132 SS p. 100; *Seipp* 1312.140ss.

92 On villeinage, see, e.g., Mark Bailey, *The Decline of Serfdom in Late Medieval England: From Bondage to Freedom* (Woodbridge, 2014), p. 4; Baker, *OHLE* VI, p. 599; Eleanor Searle, 'Seigneurial Control of Women's Marriage: The Antecedents and Function of Merchet in England', *P & P* lxxxii (1979), 3–43, 6, 20–1; P.A. Brand and P.R. Hyams, 'Debate: Seigneurial Control of Women's Marriage', *P & P* lxxxii (1979), 123–33, 130–1. For comparatively late references to 'bondwomen', see st. 3 Hen. VII c. 2, SR II, p. 512. Discussion of villeinage and false imprisonment: JUST 1/1084 m. 27 (IMG 4671); CP 40/423 m. 231d (IMG 1318), assault JUST 1/483 m. d (IMG 2262). On lawyers' concern with marriages between villeins and free people, see, e.g., *Bracton* II, pp. 30, 31, III,

Women with particular conditions or disabilities, such as those classed as 'lepers', might also face legal disadvantage.[93] The groups which the common law identified for different treatment were not always identical to those which concerned other bodies of law or thought. Thus, 'concubines', an interest of *Bracton*, do feature in common law records, but are not the subject of particular, different rules based on this categorisation.[94] Women engaging in sex work, who feature heavily in discussions of other jurisdictions, are mentioned in legal records, under various labels, but were of less concern to the common law, which generally left attempts to stamp out or regulate prostitution to urban authorities and the church.[95]

The discussion up to this point has assumed that classification of women into different sub-groups was relatively straightforward, but that was not necessarily the case, and it is worthy of note that the establishment of clear

---

pp. 92, 96; *Fleta*, book 1 cc. 3 and 4. On the disadvantages of being 'foreign', see, e.g., Seipp 1425.092. W. Mark Ormrod, Bart Lambert and Jonathan Mackman, *Immigrant England 1300–1550* (Manchester, 2019), pp. 24–5, 45–6, 176; SC 8/25/1216; SC 8/26/1253, SC 8/26/1279; *SR*, I, 310: Paul Brand, 'The Origins of 'Alien Status' in the English Common Law', *JLH* 39 (2018), 18–28. On Welsh and Scotswomen, see *SR* I, pp. 56, 61, 67–8, c. 13; *SR* II, p. 140 st. 4 H IV c. 26, c 34; *CPR 1467–77*, 50; *Seipp* 1483.010, KB 27/885 m. 39d (IMG 290). For Jewish women, see, e.g., Victoria Hoyle, 'The Bonds that Bind: Money-Lending between Anglo-Jewish and Christian Women in the Plea Rolls of the Exchequer of the Jews, 1218–80', *JMH* 34 (2008), 119–29; Adrienne Williams Boyarin, 'Medieval Anglo-Jewish Women at Court', in *Women Intellectuals and Leaders in the Middle Ages*, ed. by Kathryn Kerby-Fulton, Katie Anne-Marie Bugyis and John Van Engen (Woodbridge, 2020), pp. 55–70; Paul Brand, 'Jews and the Law in England, 1275–1290', *EHR* 115 (2000), 1138–58; 15 SS, pp. 131–2.

93 On 'lepers': 62 *SS*, p. 372; *CRR* VII, p. 199: objection, to a woman's appeal in 1214 that she was a 'leper' (so should be excluded from the community).

94 *Bracton* II, pp. 54, 95–6, 187; III, p. 1, 231, 271; Ruth Mazo Karras 'Marriage, Concubinage, and the Law', in *Law and the Illicit*, c. 9. In case records, it is often used of a woman living with a priest. See, e.g., JUST 1/365 m.24d (IMG 4064); JUST 1/1237 m. 11 (IMG 4969); JUST 1/210 m. 26d (IMG 5091); JUST 1/569A m. 20d (IMG 8233); KB 27/597 m. 2 (IMG 0232); KB 27/537 m. (IMG 8910); KB 27/294 m. 3 (IMG 359); JUST 3/1/7 m. 11d (IMG 0323). JUST 3/50/4 m. 33 (IMG 144). SC 8/34/1659 apparent laymen. C 1/99/3 1486–93.

95 For exceptions, see Chapter 6. For prostitution/sex work, see Ruth Mazo Karras, *Common Women: Prostitution and Sexuality in Medieval England* (New York and Oxford, 1996); *Mirror*, book 4 c. 16; 100 *SS*, 19; *Seipp* 1308.003ss; *Bracton* II, p. 415. For the appellation 'strumpet' or 'common strumpet', see, e.g., KB 27/638 m. 19 (IMG 285); KB 27/718 m. 14 (IMG 302). For 'common meretrices', see, e.g., KB 27/585 Rex m.17d (IMG 485). See also J.B. Post, 'A Fifteenth-Century Customary of the Southwark Stews', *Journal of the Society of Archivists* (1977), 418–28; Ruth Mazo Karras, 'Regulation of Brothels', *Signs* 14 (1989), 399–433. Lease terms: *Onyng v Morys and Others* Ames YB 1 (1929), CP 40/517 m. 440 (IMG 968), *Seipp* 1456.122abr. For royal action: C 16/489 m. 13d, CPR H 6, 6:610. (Southwark, 1391 and 1437): SC8/73/3626 SC 8/27/1309; indictments, e.g. KB 9/389 mm. 48, 49, 49d (IMG 86, 98, 99). Ruth Mazo Karras, *Sexuality in Medieval Europe: Doing unto Others*, 2nd edn (London and New York, 2005), p. 123; J.M. Bennett, 'Writing Fornication: Medieval Leyrwite and Its Historians', *TRHS* 6 ser 13 (2003), 131–62; S.K. Cohn, *Popular Protest in Late Medieval English Towns* (Cambridge, 2013), p. 251.

rules defining some sub-groups of women was slower than was the case for comparable classification of males. This applies in particular to the important point at which an heiress moved from 'minority' to 'majority' for the purposes of property-holding and the end of wardship. *Bracton* pointed out vagueness in relation to the rules on heiresses' ages of majority in relation to military fees, and debate as to whether a lord lost his wardship rights over an heiress once she married.[96] Later in the thirteenth century, there seems to have been some greater clarity for heiresses, with *Fleta* replacing *Bracton*'s 'functional' test for majority for the heiresses of sokemen, which involved ability to run a house, with a simpler age test, in which both males and females were of age at 15.[97] This suggests a slower rate of firming-up of classification, and clarification of rights, in relation to females than was the case with males. When considering majority and inheritance of land, it would seem that the thoughts of those working in the common law went first to male heirs. That they were the paradigm and the greater concern is nicely illustrated by *Bracton*'s description of proof of age by bodily appearance, which refers to beard growth.[98] There was still some disagreement in the mid-fifteenth century, in relation to majority of heiresses holding land by different tenures, but Littleton's *Tenures*, towards the end of the period under consideration, did not see the age of majority for the end of wardship as uncertain at all.[99]

There were other areas in which reaching certainty on age criteria for girls and women seemed to be difficult for common lawyers. In dower, for example, where a criterion of age or perceived readiness for sexual relations came to be used as a qualifying test from the latter half of the thirteenth century, there was some debate and disagreement about the critical age boundary, and some movement between the reason for the age limit being capacity to endure penetration and capacity to conceive.[100] The medieval common law seemed to tolerate a greater degree of uncertainty in relation

96 Seabourne, *IMW*, pp. 115–6; *Bracton* II, pp. 251, 257.

97 *Bracton* II, 251; *Fleta*, book I c. 11; *Seipp* 1310.004ss (14 as age of majority of heiress in chivalry). *P & M* II, p. 300; st. Westminster I c. 22: marriage with the lord's consent ended her wardship. *Bracton* II, p. 250; John Bedell, 'Memory and Proof of Age in England 1272–1327', *P & P* 162 (1999), 3–27, 6.

98 *Bracton* IV, pp. 319–20.

99 Doubts: *Seipp* 1457.002; 1457.017, 51 *SS* pp. 138–43, 132–7; 132 *SS*, 372; SC8/28/1398 (1460). Certainty: Littleton, *Tenures*, book II, c. 4, no. 104.

100 Paul Brand, 'Deserving and Undeserving Wives: Earning and Forfeiting Dower in Medieval England', *JLH* 22 (2001), 1–20; 132 *SS*, p. 41. Age of widows for dower, disagreement: *Seipp* 1410.127. *Bracton* III, p. 372; *Fleta* book 5, c. 27, suggests below 9½ was too young for a girl to 'fulfil her obligations to her husband' and so qualify. The age of raped girls is noted, presumably as aggravation, indicating incapacity, see, e.g., JUST 3/167 m. 23d (IMG 198), JUST 3/201 m. 5d (IMG 792); KB 27/351 m. 22 (IMG 1960). On the contested borderline between 'girl' and 'woman', see, e.g., Kim M. Phillips, *Medieval Maidens: Young Women and Gender in England c. 1270–c. 1540* (Manchester, 2003). For assessment of the age of females by inspection, see: 98 *SS*, p. 521; *Seipp* 1340.265rs; 1376.012; 1401.035.

to the classification of women than it did in relation to men.[101] Clearly, some divisions or definitions of subsets of women were simpler than others, but the fact that there were blurred borders in some cases should be something of a corrective to too great an insistence on placing subsets of women in the foreground and relegating 'women' to an inferior position in legal historical analysis.

Conclusion

Sexual difference was by no means the only criterion for the distribution of common law rights. Thus, in relation to rights to succession in land, proximity of relationship to the deceased person was also important, and in relation to wardship, comparison of the age of seisin was a rival principle to that of favouring the male line over the female.[102] Nevertheless, differentiation between men and women was a fundamental part of common law thinking. In their treatment of 'women' as a category, common law sources show strong reliance on a two sex model. If the records of the common law seem more rigidly attached to a male-female binary than do some other areas of medieval intellectual endeavour and culture, that is unsurprising in view of the law's particular need for certainty of concepts from which to set out to resolve disputes and to determine entitlements to land in particular: common lawyers did not have as much room for imaginative manoeuvre in their work or their records as did writers of romance. Despite the acceptance of the fundamental nature of women's difference, however, prescriptive sources did not always explicitly take them into account, causing some disagreements and uncertainty amongst common lawyers themselves, when trying to decide whether and how to apply to women rules which might be expressed in terms which were either masculine or only arguably inclusive of women. There appears to have been a move towards greater differentiation and specificity in prescriptive sources over the medieval period, but not a simple move from a 'one sex' model (with *homo* unequivocally covering both men and women) to a 'two sex' model, with clear statements of application to women as well as men. Differentiation within the category of women was already present in the earliest years of the common law, and lawyers singled out some groups for separate attention. Their conception of women was never monolithic, and they were perfectly capable of seeing 'women' as both an overarching category and also a collection of sub-groups which might require separate consideration and regulation. These sub-groups were not only based upon marital status, might not be clearly differentiated and a woman might be a member of more than one category, classed as

101 Seabourne, *IMW*, pp. 115–6. For vagueness in defining groups of women outside the common law, see, e.g., 'whores', Karras, *Common Women*, pp. 16–7.

102 Plucknett, *Legislation of Edward I*, c. 5 The Family, p. 113; for debate on this, see 58 *SS*, pp. 158–60.

both a *nativa* and servant or a daughter and servant, for example.[103] It was recognised by common lawyers that minority, marital status and wardship might interact to cause difficulties.[104] Marital status and employment status might also clash under the labour legislation of the mid-fourteenth century onwards. An interesting illustration of movement over time with regard to categorisation of women is the long-term process by which a statute about women in general, which listed several different categories, came to be described simply as concerning *ancille*. Many fifteenth-century records refer to a 'recent' statute *de raptu ancille*.[105] It seems however that the statute being referred to was, in fact, the 1275 statute of Westminster I, c. 13. The *Statutes of the Realm* version of this does not mention servants,[106] but the statute is referred to in an entry of 1450 as the foundation for actions in this area.[107] The steps by which the change of interpretation occurred are yet to be determined, but apparently the *damoysele* of earlier iterations had by this time come to be read as *ancilla*, and this sub-group had come to be seen as its main focus.

Furthermore, common law thinking about particular groups or categories themselves was not necessarily consistent or simple, as will be seen in the following chapter, which discusses some of the ways in which related ideas of union and separation ran through the common law's treatment of the most significant subsets of women.

103 CP 40/426 m. 415 (IMG 821); KB 27/401 m. 69 (IMG 6086).

104 See the complex scenarios in 105 *SS*, cxxviii.

105 (1450) KB 27/758 m. 17 (IMG 210); (1460) KB 27/798 m. 18 (IMG 257).

106 *SR* I, p. 29.

107 KB 27/758 m. 3d (IMG 413).

2 Unstable constructions

Unity, disunity, property and favour in common law thought on women

The subsets of women most regularly discussed in common law sources and later commentary on medieval law were married women and widows. Those looking backwards – whether as lawyers or as historians – have often attributed to medieval common law's treatment of women three particular constructions: the married woman as united to her husband under the 'doctrine of coverture', married (and some other) women as the property of men and favour or generosity towards women. While these constructions are interesting, both individually and in combination, and while they are not without basis in medieval legal materials, they are not the whole story, and over-emphasis on them can, at times, have a distorting effect. All depend to some extent on 'reading back' later ideas, later certainties. It is necessary to acknowledge that medieval common law thought in this area was considerably more fluid and multi-layered than emphasis on such ideas, or any one of them, would suggest.

Flesh, blood, souls and rods: 'coverture' considered

By the mid-eighteenth century, the law relating to husband and wife was presented as a coherent 'doctrine of coverture', organised around an idea of marital unity. This is exemplified by the familiar statement from Blackstone's *Commentaries* that '[b]y marriage, the husband and wife are one person in law: ...[She] is ... called in our law-French a feme-covert; is said to be covert-baron, ... and her condition during her marriage is called her coverture.'[1] The terms '*feme covert*' and 'coverture' may certainly be found in medieval common law sources, but their medieval meanings and implications should not be read back from later sources.[2] The medieval

1 *Bl. Comm.*, book 1, c. 15, 1; Co. Litt., book 2, c. 168 p. 112.

2 See *Married Women and the Law: Coverture in England and the Common Law World*, ed. by Tim Stretton and Krista J. Kesselring (Montreal, 2013); Tim Stretton, 'Coverture and Unity of Person in Blackstone's *Commentaries*', in *Blackstone and His Commentaries, Biography, Law, History*, ed. Wilfrid Prest (Oxford, 2009), pp. 111–28, 127; Sara M. Butler, 'Discourse on the Nature of Coverture in the Later Medieval Courtroom', in *Married*

position was not so simple, nor so monolithic, as that put forward by later commentators.

The words *coverture* and *covert* themselves give mixed messages: the idea of a husband 'covering' his wife suggests meanings ranging from protection, through containment or concealment, to a livestock-related sexual idea.[3] Such was the words' lack of an anchor in one definite idea that Fortescue could discuss coverture in the context of women covering their heads.[4] The words do not obviously indicate complete union of personality, entire submerging of the woman in the man's identity, such as would later be taken to be central. Logically, for one thing to cover another, it is necessary to retain the understanding that they remain separate. The relationship of 'coverture' and 'unity' is thus rather complex. There are examples of the language of unity in medieval sources relating to husband and wife,[5] but this remains in tension with constructions of the marital relationship which require an idea of separation. Furthermore, where 'unity' occurs, it bears differing meanings or nuances: medieval statements suggesting unity of the spouses range from an idea of them being 'one flesh and one blood', through the idea of unity within one body, the male as head and the female as the rest of the body, to more abstract, less physical, ideas of the spouses as 'one person (in law)' or leading 'conjoined lives', and the same text may contain more than one of these ideas.[6] A degree of separation is acknowledged in statements which emphasise not unity but the husband's power and domination over the wife. This domination is sometimes symbolised by the idea of the wife being 'under the husband's rod', an image itself saturated with meanings, the rod acting as a symbol of authority, of domination through the power to chastise and also of sexual domination, through the association between rod and penis.[7] An interesting variation can be seen in a register of writs from the late thirteenth century, which suggests that the husband – or the condition of marriage – has a smothering effect on the wife, taking away her

Women, ed. by Stretton and Kesselring, c. 2, pp. 15, 25; Klerman, 'Women Prosecutors', p. 7; Cannon, 'Rights', p. 159.

3 *OED* II. s.v. cover; *P & M* II, p. 403.

4 Fortescue, *DNLN* Part 2, c. 56, p. 319.

5 See, e.g., *Anon v Musket* (1313–14) 27 *SS*, p. 45.

6 See, e.g., *Dialogus de Scacc.*, pp. 83, 114; *Bracton* III, p. 363; IV, pp. 330, 335; *Fleta*, book V, c. 25; *Placita Corone*, xxviii; Fortescue, *De Laudibus Legum Angliae*, ed. by F. Gregor and A. Amos (Cincinnati, 1874) c. 42; *Seipp* 1407.040, 1413.017; 1414.014; 1426.034, 1431.168, 1444.006, 1461.008, 1470.029ss; J.G. Bellamy, *The Criminal Trial in Later Medieval England: Felony before the Courts from Edward I to the Sixteenth Century* (Toronto, 1998), p. 8.

7 See, e.g., *LHP*, 45, 3; *Bracton* II, p. 36; *Fleta*, book 1, c. 9; *Glanvill*, Prologue, p. 1; *Britton*, book 3, c. 2, no. 12; Litt., book 1, c. 10; Kane, *Popular Memory*, p. 120; Pedersen, 'Privates on parade', p. 81. More general ideas of dominance: *Glanvill*, VI, p. 3; *Bracton* IV, p. 335; *P & M* II, p. 402. Coss, *Lady*, p. 123; Paul Brand, 'Family and Inheritance: Women and Children', in *An Illustrated History of Late Medieval England* ed. by Chris Given Wilson (Manchester, 1996), p. 63. For ideas of subjection of wives, see *Seipp* 1376.028.

voice: when joined to a husband, she 'has no voice to act by herself without [him]'.[8]

Maitland called the unity of person's idea 'impossible dogma', rejecting its practical influence in twelfth- and thirteenth-century common law.[9] Rather than seeing it as a dogma which was ignored, however, it is probably more accurate to see the unity idea as a familiar metaphor or, as C.S. Kenny preferred, a 'legal fiction': something which could be used if desired, as an origin story for particular rules, but which did not necessarily indicate a clear response in the practical world of common law.[10] There are certainly indications that medieval lawyers were fully conscious that their references to unity between husband and wife were not to be seen as central truths, in the passages in *Bracton* and the Year Books which qualify unity statements with 'as it were' or 'so to speak' additions,[11] evincing a subtlety not always present in later presentations of the common law, and in the mid-fifteenth century statement of Prisot J. that the 'husband and wife are one person in law, in some respects it is so and in some respects not'.[12] In recent work on coverture ideas over a longer period, Stretton has noted a move in the role of 'coverture' from limited fiction to metaphor to doctrine.[13] This is a perceptive analysis, though perhaps rather than seeing a progression between the first two stages, the medieval common law position should be seen to comprise both limited fiction and metaphor.

Fiction, metaphor and analogy were common modes of exploring concepts in medieval scholarly and literary thought, and were also much in evidence in legal thought. In legal sources, we see, for example, birth metaphors for rights acquired through long possession and actions arising from obligations, hospitals described as 'dead things', the Church or king described as a minor and analogies being drawn between bondmen and animals.[14] Littleton's *Tenures* likens different property interests to ingredients in a 'puddyng', and the growing idea of the corporation also required a certain degree of metaphorical thinking.[15] The use of these techniques indicates

8 87 *SS*, p. 85 no 170b: *ea coniuncta viro sue vocem agendi non habet per se sine viro ....*

9 *P & M* II, p. 402.

10 Kenny, *Effects of Marriage*, pp. 13, 14, 120.

11 *Bracton* III, p. 30; *Seipp* 1330.823ss; *Britton*, book 5, c. 1.1.

12 *Seipp* 1456.058, cited in Butler, 'Discourse', pp. 15, 29–30.

13 Stretton, 'Coverture and Unity', p. 127.

14 *Bracton* II, pp. 36, 157, 284; 8 *SS*, p. 141, *Mirror*, book III, c. 26; *Seipp* 1334.231ass *Seipp* 1293.102rs; 1313.680ss *Seipp* 1319.101ss; 1306.123rs; 1317.014ss; 1317.026ss; 1317.097ss; 1332.179; 1309.209ss.

15 *Litt.*, book III, c. 2, no. 267; Andreea D. Beboc, 'Theorizing Legal Personhood in Late Medieval England', in *Theorizing Legal Personhood in Late Medieval England*, ed. by Andreea D. Beboc (Leiden and Boston, MA, 2015), pp. 1–28, Gaines Post, *Studies in Medieval Legal Thought: Public Law and the State 1100–1322* (Princeton, NJ, 1964), p. 30; David Seipp, 'Formalism and Realism in Fifteenth-Century English Law: Bodies Corporate and Bodies Natural', in *Judges and Judging in the History of the Common Law*

an attempt to explain a situation which is difficult, novel or non-standard, and needs to be elucidated by reference to other, more familiar situations. Married women were a derogation from the normal subject of the medieval common law – the autonomous, free, man – and dealing with them encouraged such creative thinking. Other situations involving women had also called forth from common lawyers a metaphorical response. This can be seen in relation to sisters, where a unity concept was used, though only in relation to land and inheritance. Before the reign of Henry II, it had been settled that, if a man died leaving only daughters, they would share the land rather than primogeniture applying, as it would have done for males.[16] The separate rules to deal with the implications of this tenure by 'coparcenry' were discussed in cases and lawyers' educational scenarios, such discussion developing ideas and vocabulary of unity and fractional personality.[17] This was a knowingly metaphorical mode of discourse: nobody actually thought that one of three inheriting sisters was a third of a person. In addition, we see the idea that nuns were 'dead to the world' or 'dead in law', but, as with other metaphors, it was neither undisputed nor carried through to the hilt.[18]

There were medieval attempts to show the derivation of rules relating to wives from an idea of unity, but these were not particularly successful, as can be seen from a passage in *Bracton*, endeavouring to decide how a husband and wife should perform wager of law, and wondering whether the idea of the spouses as 'one flesh' means that they must defend themselves together or whether they can do so separately.[19] Some rules relating to spouses were explained on other grounds. For example, some treatments of the invalidity of their gifts to one another explain this not in terms of unity, but rather on the basis of a suspicion that unhealthy lust and affection might cause such transfers.[20] Unity was stated as the reason for some legal rules in cases and treatises from the fourteenth and fifteenth centuries, but there remained consciousness of the limits to the utility of unity ideas in terms of providing a clear answer in concrete cases.[21] Separate identity continued to be assumed

---

and Civil Law from Antiquity to Modern Times, ed. by Paul Brand and Joshua Getzler (Cambridge, 2012), pp. 44–55.

16 J.C. Holt, 'Feudal Society and the Family in Early Medieval England: IV. The Heiress and the Alien', *TRHS* 35 (1985), 1–28, 2.

17 *Seipp* 1285.008ss; 1286.017ss; 1293.025rs; 1318.001ss; 1329.153; 1293.132rs; 1306.133rs; 1311.166ss, 1311.173ss; 1311.261ss; 1314.059ss (aid of parceners); 105 *SS* clv, cli, cliii, clxxxiii 12; 67, 70, 248, 249. 320. For the eldest sister's enhanced role, see *P & M* II, p. 272; *Glanvill* VII, 3; *Bracton* II, pp. 218, 222–3, 226, *Britton*, book III c. 4 no. 7, no. 23. Littleton constructs sister-coparceners as one person: *Litt.* book III, c 1. *Bracton* II, p. 227 guardianship, *Cal. Cl. Rolls, 1234–37*, 375–6 (1236).

18 *Bracton* IV, p. 311; *Seipp* 1388.086am; 1324.174; 1335.114; 1312.140ss.

19 *Bracton* IV, p. 164.

20 *Bracton* II, pp. 56, 97; *Fleta* book III, c. 3; *D.* 24.1.1.

21 Argument that because H and W are 'as one person', H must answer for W's deeds: 34 *SS* case 41. Judge using unity as purported source for rules: Butler, 'Discourse', pp. 15, 28; *Litt.* book II, c. 10, no 168.

and acknowledged, for example in the use of the language of domination and in expressions of uncertainty or insecurity about husbands' control of wives, which might claim that women were less amenable to husbands than in the past, and (perhaps humorous) suggestions that a woman might be the master or jailer of her husband.[22] A domination analogy is also used in the comparison of the relationship of husband and wife to that of religious superior and inferior (such as abbot and monk) or that of lord and villein.[23]

The varying constructions of women's place in the marital relationship suggest that there was not, in the medieval common law, a unified and coherent 'doctrine of coverture' on the later model. We will see in Chapters 5 and 6 that unity ideas did not rule in relation to responsibility for 'tort' and 'crime'.[24] Husbandly dominance also had its limits. Thus, a wife could obtain sureties of the peace against her husband, a husband could not, according to law, kill his wife with impunity (and nor would the wife-slayer be conceived of as guilty of 'self killing').[25] A woman was not always regarded as being under the control of her husband without a will of her own.[26] A husband could 'receive' his wife.[27] We come closest to what looks like a doctrine of coverture, organised around a hybrid concept of 'male-dominated unity', in the realms of real property and litigation. Such an idea seems to be embodied in basic rules such as the husband's control over land and personal property – what Plucknett described as the 'exorbitant rights of husbands over the real and personal property of their wives'.[28] This is suggested, for example, by a statement in a case from 1196 that a woman could not have bought land in her own right, because 'she could have no chattels for herself in the time of her husband which were not her husband's', and by the necessity of the participation of a husband in legal actions brought by or relating to the wife, upheld with very few exceptions throughout the period.[29] It is

22 W's acts 'done for dread of her husband': *Seipp* 1467.038; Elizabeth Fowler, 'Civil Death and the Maiden: Agency and the Conditions of Contract in Piers Plowman', *Speculum* 70 (1995), 760–92, 771. *Seipp* 1336.045; *Seipp* 1345.104rs. 129 *SS*, p. 31. *Seipp* 1307.041rs; *Seipp* 1311.219ss. For use in a case of 'inter brachia viri sui' in this context, see JUST 1/303 m. 21 (IMG 8680). 1306.193rs; *Bracton* II, p. 419.

23 See, e.g., *Seipp* 1399.004; 1400.026; 1401.049; 1430.050; 1458.048; 1464.049; 129 *SS*, p. 52; *Seipp* 1464.049. For comparisons of women and their legal disabilities to groups, from children to bastards, see 129 *SS*, pp. 22, 47. See also *Old Tenures, The Old Natura Brevium*, f. 10, 25.

24 These are anachronistic but efficient labels for wrongs deserving of punishment or redress at common law.

25 *P & M* II, pp. 422, 436; Baker, *OHLE* VI, p. 621.

26 See Chapter 6.

27 See, e.g., JUST 3/136 m. 14 (IMG 25).

28 Plucknett, *Legislation of Edward I*, p. 128.

29 *Pipe Roll Society* vol. xxiv, p. 232; S.J. Bailey, 'The Countless Gundred's Lands', *CLJ* 10 (1948), 84–103, 91; Plucknett, *Legislation*, p. 128. J.S. Loengard, 'What Did Magna Carta Mean to Widows?', in *Magna Carta and the England of King John* ed. by J.S. Loengard (Woodbridge, 2010), pp. 134–50, 137; Hudson, *OHLE II*, p. 680; *P & M* II, pp. 404–7, 420,

interesting to note however that even within the areas of litigation and property, there are signs that the hold of any unity metaphor was incomplete. Thus, for example, in records of litigation involving spouses from the later thirteenth century, sometimes an attorney was designated 'their' attorney, but he might rather be designated the attorney of the wife or the husband alone.[30] Separate attorneys were possible in the fourteenth century, and it was envisaged that they might not act in a co-operative manner.[31] It was certainly possible for spouses to act as attorneys for each other or for one to appear in person and the other by attorney, all of which suggests that some degree of theoretical separation was accepted, even in 'legal personality'.[32]

In relation to property, sometimes laypeople talked about land or chattels as if they belonged to a married woman.[33] A good example of this is seen in a King's Bench plea roll entry of 1483, recording that jurors at a sheriff's tourn presented that a cleric entered Robert Skynner's house with force and arms, assaulted his wife and feloniously took away 4 *d.*, which was the wife's money. In the King's Bench, the defendant argued successfully that the indictment was insufficient to put him to answer, because it did not accord with the law of the land in relation to property and marriage.[34] Nevertheless, the initial formulation showed that not everyone instinctively saw the wife as incapable of having her own money. In addition, medieval common lawyers themselves accepted that the interests of husband and wife were not entirely merged, and that there was a need for processes to limit the idea of husbandly control of property in some circumstances. Thus, the idea of 'paraphernalia' – personal property regarded as belonging to the wife – emerged to mitigate the effects of the growing idea that a wife could not own chattels,[35] and some provisions were made to counter the possibility of husbands pressuring wives to part with property, or transferring 'their' land

427–34; *Seipp* 1454.040; *Dialogus de Scacc.*, p. 114; 100 *SS*, p. 152 case 13.27, KB 27/401 m. 49. Exceptional liability of woman to pay a debt incurred whilst married, as H and W had quarrelled and lived apart: *BNB* pl. 568.

30 KB 26/206 m. 1 (IMG 2839); KB 26/206 mm. 5, 7 (IMG 2847, 2851); KB27/66 m. 18d (IMG 210); CP 40/104 m. 40 (IMG 85).

31 *Seipp* 1313.041ss, 1332.058 (Ds).

32 See, e.g., *Seipp* 1306.012rs; 1339.063rs; 1306.012rs; 1321.026. See also the differing spousal positions in *Seipp* 1340.203rs and 1340.265rs.

33 See, e.g., KB 27/401 m. 27 (IMG 6001).

34 KB 27/888 m. 12d (IMG 62).

35 Janet Loengard, 'Which May be Said to be her Own': Widows and Goods in Late Medieval England', in *Medieval Domesticity: Home, Housing and Household in Medieval England*, ed. by M. Kowaleski and P.J.P. Goldberg (Cambridge, 2008), pp. 162–76, 163–4, notes policing of the boundaries of 'paraphernalia' and *Seipp* 1454.041 suggests a lack of generosity to women. See also *Seipp* 1497.006; 1302.030rs; 1318.092ss; 1428.015. *P & M* II, pp. 101–2, 409; *SR* I, p. 214; st. 4 H VII c. 24; *SR* II, p. 547; *Bracton* IV, pp. 30–9; 102 *SS*, p. 106; Baker, *Introduction*, p. 524; Yates, 'Married Women and Their Landholdings', p. 167; st. 34 Edward III, c. 16; *Abstracts of Surrey Feet of Fines, 1509–1558*, ed. by C.A.F. Meekings (Frome and London, 1946), pp. xxv–xxvii. Statute of Fines, 4 Henry VII, c. 24. See, e.g.,

(though, despite *Bracton*'s optimism that procedures for the examination in court of a wife about to agree to the transfer of 'her' land would rule out untoward pressure by husbands, it is unlikely that such procedures sufficed to ensure that no wife would be so pressured, and their principal use may well have been as a protection for purchasers)[36] or failing to act to protect their interests.[37] No idea of unity or coverture was allowed to get in the way of royal interests: for example, the fact that the king had banished a woman's husband did not stop the king suing her without him.[38] There are also signals of an awareness that, while a court might feel constrained to deem a wife's actions those of her husband, its members did not actually regard that as the truth of the matter. For example, a report of a 1306 case shows a judge holding that if the husband was absent when his wife made a transaction, it still counted as his deed.[39] Other questions which lawyers found not to be solved by a unity doctrine, and which were, consequently, in need of debate, included: whether goods could be left 'to the use of' a married woman; whether she could have a bailiff or take profits, bail money to her own use or be attached by 'her own' property, the status of a gift between two parties who subsequently married, the wife's 'contractual' dealings or wrongs to her goods prior to her marriage, the effect of one spouse's felony or treason on the property rights of the other and the problems for women's litigation which might be caused by disappearing husbands.[40] Matters such as whether a wife could steal from her husband, or whether spouses could conspire together, were clearly regarded by lawyers as tricky rather than obviously answered by application of a unity doctrine.[41] Likewise, creativity, rather than easy application of a unity doctrine, was to the fore in adaptations to procedures in the case of homage by married joint tenants: a late fifteenth-century law report suggests that the homage to the lord would be

---

Seipp 1313.489ss; 1312.137ss; 1330.574ss; 1330.640ss; 1344.137rs, 1346.095rs; 1421.111rog; 1429.094.

36 For a wife's refusal to participate in a transfer, see Janet Loengard, 'What Is a Nice (Thirteenth-Century) Englishwoman Doing in the King's Courts?', in *The Ties That Bind: Essays in Medieval British History in Honor of Barbara Hanawalt*, ed. by Linda E. Mitchell, Katherine L. French and Douglas L. Biggs (London, 2010), pp. 55–70, 64. *Bracton*, IV, 31; Cannon, 'Rights', p. 159; *P & M* II, 407. *Cui in vita* discussed, e.g., *Seipp* 1306.193rs; 1346.110rs; 1351.084; 1405.007; 1494.058; Joseph Biancalana, 'The Origin and Early History of the Writs of Entry', *LHR* 25 (2007), 513–56, 519, 523–4.

37 st. Westminster II c. 3, 40, 41, *SR* I, 73; *SR* I, 50; *SR* I, 91, *P & M* II, 404, 407.

38 *Seipp* 1399.002; 1336.182.

39 *Seipp* 1306.193rs.

40 100 *SS*, p. 161; *Seipp* 1412.032abr; 1431.168; 1461.008; 1440.006; 1428.015; 1312.094ss; 1337.011rs; 1292.124rs 1443.016. Spousal offences, property implications: *Bracton* II, p. 367; *P & M* II, p. 404; *Seipp* 1313.351ss. 1272.007ss; 1275.012ss; 1268.008ss; 1457.022; 105 *SS*, 29, p. 123; 129 *SS* p. 3; 102 *SS*, 135; 1347.199; *Seipp* 1302.203rs; 1339.050rs. Problems of absent men, proof of death: *Seipp* 1309.054ss; 1309.188ss; 1310.032ss; 1362.005ass; 1362.005ass; 1313.628ss; 1346.011rs; 1478.026.

41 *Seipp* 1345.188rs; 1364.012, 1443.119abr; Rose, *Maintenance*, pp. 144, 160.

performed by the husband, and he would transmit it to his wife by kissing her.[42]

In sum, it is clear that there was no deep conceptual coherence in relation to the way in which married women were accommodated in the various different areas of common law activity. There is a striking similarity between the ability of medieval common lawyers to accommodate several cohabiting interpretations of the relationship between spouses and the conclusion of Seipp's analysis of common law ideas of corporate personality, which noted that rather than 'distinctive, consistent individual judicial philosophies' on this matter, there seemed to have been 'a consistent collective judicial commitment to preservation of conflicting philosophies and conflicting approaches'.[43]

One factor which stood in the way of formulating within the medieval common law the sort of monolithic theory of the effects of marriage on women's legal rights which is shown in Blackstone's famous statement is that medieval common lawyers had to fit their conception of women's place within marriage into what was in some ways a more complex legal landscape. They had to consider the inter-relationship between the different classifications which might apply to one woman, to take an interest in the complexities which could arise when the rules about married women collided with villeinage, religious status, wardship, minority, employment status.[44] Medieval treatises, reports, readings and moot cases showed a strong concern for the interface between villeinage and the rules concerning married women, exploring the status implications of a bondwoman marrying a free man.[45] Cases from educational exercises featured free women marrying villeins, one particularly knotty scenario involving two villein brothers, a woman who marries them both, a lord, a secret pregnancy, twins, clergy and land rights.[46] In this context, we might not be surprised that there was a less dogmatic and monolithic view on women's status within marriage than would later be the case: the husband did not stand alone as the sole relevant authority figure in a woman's life, in relation to whom she must be defined. In addition, medieval common lawyers clearly needed to be aware of the existence of alternative rules, local and ecclesiastical, which affected women, and would see that these sometimes allowed wives greater possibilities of independent action than they had in the common law.[47] A world

42 *Seipp* 1478.026.

43 Seipp, 'Formalism and Realism', p. 51.

44 H arguing he could remove W from employment, e.g., *Seipp* 1464.049; 1355.245ass; 100 *SS*, xliv; CP 40/550 m. 173d.

45 *Seipp* 1302.103rs. Married women and property considered in readings: 129 *SS*, e.g. pp. 99, 102, 105.

46 See the fifteenth-century examples in 105 *SS*, e.g. pp. clii, clxi, clxxiii, 28, 32, 14 ff; 5, 5a–b.

47 On chattels, see, e.g., CP 40/719 m. 120d (IMG 1545), 85 *SS*, lxxi; Michael M. Sheehan, *Marriage, Family and Law in Medieval Europe: Collected Studies*, ed. by James K. Farge (Toronto, 1997), pp. 25–9; *Glanvill* VII, 5; *Bracton* II, p. 180, *Fleta* book II, c. 57, *P & M* II,

in which the common law courts had not yet achieved the predominance of the eighteenth-century institutions was not one in which a monolithic idea of 'coverture', on Blackstone's lines, could hold sway. In addition, it is relevant that whether or not two people were in fact married was open to greater potential dispute in (say) 1300 than in Blackstone's day (following the Hardwicke Marriage Act of 1753). Medieval plea rolls and law reports included many cases and hypotheticals concerning the implications for property or contractual actions, or trespass, of the existence or timing of marriage or divorce.[48] Whether or not two people were married could be a matter of disagreement, and canon law might hold valid some 'marriages' which would be insufficient to 'count' at common law, for the purposes of actions for property rights (including women's dower rights). Common lawyers showed an awareness of possible differences between jurisdictions, for example in the discussion in a dower case, *Thornsett v. Whaite*, in 1311.[49] An example of a marriage which would probably have been valid as far as the Church was concerned, but which was not considered good enough to act as the foundation for rights to a dead man's land under certain common law procedures, can be seen in a novel disseisin case of 1306: according to the jurors' special verdict, there had been a sickbed marriage between a dying man and his 'concubine', without mass, without formal espousals. This, it was concluded, was insufficient to allow the couple's son to take advantage of the assize.[50] Canon law and common law had different concerns when answering questions about the validity of marriage. Common law procedure used a variety of methods to obtain an answer as to whether or not there had been a marriage, including sending questions to the ecclesiastical authorities, or asking for the decision of jurors, who might comment on the validity of a marriage based on whether a couple regarded themselves as married, or upon the information of their neighbours.[51] We might conclude

351–2, 420, 428–9; 100 *SS* 100, p. 131 case 13.8. Debate: *Seipp* 1311.295ss; Cordelia Beattie, 'Married Women's Wills: Probate, Property, and Piety in Later Medieval England', *LHR* 37 (2019), 29–60; 18 *SS*, pp. 227, 2291; Hull; Marjorie K. McIntosh, 'The Benefits and Drawbacks of Femme Sole Status', *JBS* 44 (2005), 410–38; 82 *SS*, p. 131, local custom allowing married women to alienate acquisitions. 21 *SS*, pp. 102–6.

48 See, e.g., *Seipp* 1289.003ss; 1311.139ss; 1330.002; 1330.460ss; 1338.270ass; 1342.169rs; 1345.059rs, 1365.111; 1365.138ass; 1312.116ss; 1312.133ss; 1370.044; 1405.078; 1406.070;1440.003; 1495.002; JUST 1/642 m. 7 (IMG 2297); KB 27/176 m. 83 (IMG 5285); JUST 1/367 m. 36d (IMG 241); *Seipp* 1365.111. JUST 1/1066 m. 6 (IMG 3708); JUST 1/956 m. (IMG 7898). Statement on divorce rules: *Seipp* 1373.092.

49 31 *SS*, xvi, p. 38 no. 9.

50 *P & M* II, p. 381; CP 40/160 m. 203 (AALT IMG 433). See also CP 40/45 m. 23 (IMG 5884), JUST 1/1113 m. 36 (IMG 9344). On deathbed transactions, see *Glanvill* VII, 1. JUST 1/881 m. 2 (IMG 444). See, e.g., *cui in vita* action: JUST 1/367 m. 33d (IMG 236); JUST 1/955 m. 13 (IMG 7593).

51 *Bracton* III, p. 37. Questions sent to the ecclesiastical authorities, e.g., JUST 1/367 m. 5 (IMG 12); KB 27/558 m. 22, m. 22d (IMG 46, 275). Disputed marriages, e.g., JUST 1/367 m. 36d (IMG 241); *Seipp* 1365.111. JUST 1/1066 m. 6 (IMG 3708); JUST 1/956 m. (IMG 7898);

that the existence of the possibility of different answers to this fundamental question and different processes for answering it would tend to militate against a thoroughgoing and unassailable doctrine of coverture-as-unity, even if medieval common lawyers had been determined to insist upon it.

There is a good case for seeing an overall 'doctrine of coverture' as an explanation after the fact, itself a 'cover' for a fairly disparate and sometimes inconsistent body of rules, liabilities and disabilities relating to married women. It is important to recognise this, so as to avoid an over-simplified *longue durée* view of conceptions of women's position in marriage as one of linear progress away from an all-encompassing idea of coverture-as-unity in the medieval period, to a set of rules which moved increasingly towards treating married women as full individual legal subjects. Another consequence of seeing that there was not a straightforward, monolithic doctrine or understanding of coverture in the medieval common law is that it should give commentators on legal history, or history more widely, pause for thought before resorting to a 'strict law v. more positive practice' binary in the discussion of this particular aspect of the treatment of medieval women.

Property

The late nineteenth-century legal historian Courtney Kenny borrowed a phrase from Shakespeare's *Taming of the Shrew* to describe the husband's right over the wife in medieval common law in terms of ownership and property: she was his 'goods', 'chattels', 'house', 'household stuff', 'field', 'barn', 'horse', 'ox', 'ass', his 'anything'.[52] Medieval women are also sometimes described in more modern works as having been the 'property' (or the 'fragile property') of male kin or husbands, implying their assimilation to chattels.[53] Given their subordinate position and the extensive rights over their bodies accorded to certain males, this is understandable, but there are limits to its utility.[54] A very basic issue with such a claim lies with the idea of 'property' itself. It has been demonstrated that the place of 'property' and 'ownership' ideas in the medieval common law was not straightforward, nor easily to be assimilated to more modern understandings of these concepts (themselves controversial).[55] If we can get past that difficulty, there is the problem of

JUST 1/1325 m. 60 (IMG 1202). Jurors' narratives of disputes about marriage, e.g., JUST 1/1055 m. 15d (IMG 3232); KB 27/558 m. 22 (IMG 46); *Seipp* 1405.078.

52 Kenny, *Effects of Marriage*, p. 12, citing William Shakespeare, *Taming of the Shrew* Act III scene iii.

53 See, e.g., Scutt, *Women and Magna Carta*, p. 9; Cannon, 'Rights of Medieval English Women', p. 173; Bardsley, *Women's Roles*, p. 140.

54 Emma Hawkes, '"She Was Ravished against Her Will, What So Ever She Say": Female Consent in Rape and Ravishment in Late-Medieval England', *Limina* 1 (1995), 47–54, 48, 51–2; Susan Brownmiller, *Against our Will, Men Women and Rape* (New York, 1975), p. 18.

55 Seipp, 'Concept of Property', p. 31. See also *Legalisms*, ed. by Kantor, Lambert and Skoda; T. Johnson, 'Legal History and the Material Turn', in *Oxford Handbook of Legal History*,

evidence of the use of 'property-like' language in relation to women. The language of chattels occurs occasionally in contemporary documents, such as the *Mirror*'s description of the abduction of nuns as 'larceny', but medieval women were not treated fully as chattels so as to be dealt with under procedures associated with movable goods.[56] The idea of 'people as property' has been considered in the context of medieval English villeins, another area in which there are occasional uses of property language, suggesting a conception of the villein as chattel, or at least something appropriately considered in 'property' terms, but the 'clear limitations' of such an analysis has also been noted.[57] Such criticism applies at least as much in the case of women. Seipp notes that common lawyers do not mention 'property' in one's own person, or in a spouse or child, prior to the seventeenth century.[58] In addition, while another 'property-inflected' word, 'seisin', is used in relation to a man being married to a woman, women are also described in equally 'property-like' terms as being 'in possession of' a husband.[59] Without going into linguistic analysis for which I am unqualified, I make the tentative suggestion that the import of at least some of this 'property talk' (such as the 'seisin/possession' example) is the expression of a general idea of proximity or belonging rather than a subordinating, subject-object, relationship. The better view of the use of apparently 'proprietary' language of this sort is that it should not be taken to assimilate medieval interpersonal relationships with popular modern ideas of property or ownership.

Favour

The rhetoric of 'favour' to women is found in the work of later commentators on the common law, and of historians, ranging from Blackstone's claim

ed. by Tompkins and Dubber, c. 27, p. 502; McSweeney, *Priests of the Law*, c. 3; Thomas J. McSweeney, 'Property before Property: Romanising the English Law of Land', *Buffalo Law Review* 60 (2012), 1139–99, 1143–4; Susan Reynolds, 'Tenure and Property in Medieval England', *HR* 88 (2015), 563–75.

56 *Mirror*, book I, c. 10, book II, c. 26; Garthine Walker, *Crime, Gender and Social Order in Early Modern England* (Cambridge, 2003), p. 140. There may be a slip into calling a wife a husband's chattel in *Seipp* 1409.049 and 1440.077, though the wording is ambiguous. On the 'women as property' categorisation, see Emma Hawkes, 'Preliminary Notes on Consent in the 1382 Rape and Ravishment Laws of Richard II', *Legal History* 11 (2007), 117–32, 131.

57 Seipp, 'Concept', p. 51; Paul Hyams, *Kings, Lords and Peasants in Medieval England: The Common Law of Villeinage in the Twelfth and Thirteenth Centuries* (New York, 1980), pp. 1–2; *Dialogus de Scacc*, pp. 56, 101, 112, sets out the lord's rights of control over his villeins and rights to their chattels, but stops short of explicitly designating the villeins themselves as chattels. *Britton*, book 1, c. 32 no. 5, however, does describe the villein himself as *purement le chatel son seignur*. Butler has rightly noted the use of the language of chattels and procedures of chattel recovery in relation to villeins. Sara M. Butler, https://legalhistorymiscellany.com/2019/08/15/how-to-tell-a-serf-from-a-slave-in-medieval-england/.

58 Seipp, 'Concept of Property', pp. 50, 85; *Barham v. Dennis*, Cro. Eliz. 770, 78 ER 1001 (1601).

59 *CRR* XX (1250), p. 263; *Seipp* 1310.117ss; *P & M* II, p. 146.

that 'the female sex' was and had been a 'great ... favourite' of the laws of England,[60] and his statement that apparent limitations on (married) women were in fact a sign of 'favour', to modern historians' emphasis on the generosity to widows of medieval dower.[61] Statements of 'favour' to (some) women (and in some circumstances) do occur in medieval common law sources, but the reality of this favour and the assumptions lying behind assertions of favour must be interrogated. Such 'favour talk' is most commonly encountered in medieval common law sources in relation to the widow seeking dower.[62] *Bracton* expresses the idea that 'dower should be free', the *Mirror* states that it should not be delayed, and emphasises its 'tender nature', and favouring dower is suggested on a number of other occasions.[63] Changes made in the 1236 Provisions of Merton, dealing with problems in obtaining dower and the subject matter of dower, were portrayed as pro-widow reforms and the expansion of dower into Wales was depicted as a favour to Welsh women.[64] Dower was portrayed in the late twelfth-century *Dialogus de Scaccario* as a reward for the widow's modesty or chastity.[65] Some common law comment on the need to help widows also echoes wider ideas of a duty to protect and succour such 'miserable persons', with an emphasis on pity for the stereotypically miserable widow in some sources.[66] Such claims of protection or favour are not always present, however. Thus, common lawyers' readings on the seventh chapter of *Magna Carta*, concerning widows, dower, quarantine

60 Cannon, 'Rights', p. 158; *Bl. Comm.*, book I, c. 15. See also, e.g., *Somersetshire Pleas*, p. xxiii.

61 Favour to married women was not accepted by all. See, e.g., Cleveland, *Woman under English Law*, p. 161.

62 Note, however, a report of a homicide case stressing generosity to women: *Seipp* 1321.124ss. For the developing rules of dower, see, e.g., Janet S. Loengard, '"Of the Gift of her Husband": English Dower and Its Consequences in the Year 1200', in *Women of the Medieval World*, ed. by Julius Kirshner and Suzanne P. Wemple (Oxford, 1985), pp. 214–55; *Magna Carta and the England of King John*, ed. by Janet S. Loengard (Woodbridge, 2010), 134 ff; Joseph Biancalana, 'Widows at Common Law: The Evolution of Common Law Dower', *Irish Jurist* 23 (1988), 255–329; Hudson, *OHLE* II, pp. 366, 447; *Glanvill* book VI; *Bracton* II, pp. 265–80, III, pp. 357–412. *Britton*, vol. Ii, p. xli, book 5 cc. 1–13. *Litt.* book I, c. V. Brand, '"Deserving" and "undeserving" wives'; Plucknett, *Legislation*, p. 121.

63 See, e.g., *Bracton* II, p. 179; *Fleta* book 2, c. 35; *Britton* book 5 c. 5, 2, c. 7, 4; *Seipp* 1292.080rs; 1342.040rs; 1310.108ss; 1310.222ss; 1307.063rs;1310.108ss; 1483.011; *Bracton* IV, p. 313, the special privilege of dower (*favorem dotis*). Dower is favoured: *Fleta*, book 5, c. 22; *Seipp* 1486.032; 1302.017rs: 1307.063rs. For rhetoric about (ineffective) pity for a poor woman, see *Seipp* 1310.144ss.

64 *SR* I, p. 1; *Bracton* II, p. 179; *Fleta* book II, c. 57. *SR* I, pp. 61, 67.

65 '*Premium pudoris*': *Dialogus de Scacc.* book II, c. 18, p. 173. Its special status (and connection to sexual purity) can, perhaps, also be read in the late fourteenth- and early fifteenth-century description of England as the Virgin Mary's *dos*. Nigel Saul, *Richard II* (New Haven, CT, 1999), p. 307, uses 'dowry' to translate *dos* here, but 'dower' also seems possible.

66 *Seipp* 1410.127, Cokayn JCP, 'the law is favorable to wives who ask dower, because ... it is meant to be their living and sustenance' *P & M* I, p. 110; Sheehan, *Marriage, Family and Law*, pp. 18, 23. 87 *SS*, p. 235 no 549.

and remarriage, are in general not in the language of favour, but of correcting particular mischiefs, derogations from what was seen to be the common law.[67] There is some slight suggestion of favour as the justification for (some aspects of) dower in a mid-fifteenth-century reading dealing with a (socially elevated) widow's right to a castle after her husband's death. This right is stated to be given to her 'in honour of matrimony', or perhaps in relation to the 'burden of childbirth'.[68]

Despite suggestions of generosity and connections to exalted constructions of widows, legal intervention in relation to them was clearly not focused only on maximising their interests. Early central intervention had often been connected to the king's legal and financial rights in relation to widows, and when the common law's focus broadened, also making rules for the property rights of widows without a direct relationship with the king, helping the widow as such was not the only concern.[69] Assisting a widow to obtain her dower provided a benefit to later husbands. *Fleta* and *Britton* suggest a concern to make women well disposed to marriage as a reason for a 'favourable' approach to dower.[70] A strategy of configuring the law on dower so as to encourage women to marry or remarry may not have been directed entirely to their happiness, but also to the economic well-being of those who might marry them.

There was never, in any case, a thoroughgoing commitment by the common law to furthering the interests of the widow. Common law and legislative sources show that at times the dowager or would-be dowager was to be helped, but at other times, the guiding principle seems to have been control and reduction of her rights.[71] There was recognition that widows were vulnerable to a husband's negligence or collusion with regard to potential dower lands.[72] Nevertheless there were conflicting concerns that the widow was capable of misbehaving and causing trouble for the heir and others, by making a false claim of pregnancy, alienating the land, eloigning the heir, claiming too much land or failing to look after it, and fears that women would acquire a windfall by marrying a man who was close to death, or that those who had not been old enough or who had abandoned a husband for a lover, would claim dower.[73] A lack

67 132 *SS*, pp. 20–90.

68 132 *SS*, 31 *propter honorem matrimonii et onus infantis*.

69 *SR* I, pp. 1, 6, 226, 233, 239; Hudson, *OHLE* II, p. 234; Widows as possible abductees: Seabourne, *IMW*, c. 4.

70 *Fleta* book 5, c. 22; *Britton* book 5, c. 1.1.

71 See, e.g., Loengard, 'Rationabilis Dos', p. 72; 'What did Magna Carta Mean to Widows?'; Coss, *Lady*, p. 144.

72 *Bracton* III, p. 392; *SR* I, pp. 74, 77; *SR* II, p. 583.

73 *Glanvill* VI, 18; *Bracton* II, pp. 103, 268; III, pp. 360, 395, 396, 400, 404–5. See also *Fleta* book V cc. 25–33; *Litt.*, book 1, c. 5, 9; st. Merton c. 2, *SR* I, p. 276; st. Gloucester, 6 Edw. 1, Chapter 5; st. Westminster II cc. 4, 7, 14, 34, *SR* I, pp. 74, 77; st. 11 Hen. VII, c. 20, *SR* II, p. 583; *BNB*, i, xix, 89; *Seipp* 1314.002ss; 1314.119ss; 1334.191; 1307.058rs, 1330.204ss,

of 'favour' might be detected in the insistence that entitlement to an action depended on a formal marriage, of the sort which could be certified by a bishop – perhaps showing a more stringent attitude than that seen in relation to those claiming as heirs, whose parents' marriage was disputed; thus a secret marriage might work for succession but not dower.[74] Also not obviously favoured were those whose husbands had been found to be outlaws, felons, traitors or villeins, those 'widowed' by a husband's decision to become a monk and those widowed and dowered during their minority.[75] An entitlement to dower did not mean that widows would obtain it without difficulty, or keep it.[76] Common lawyers knew of and were interested in variations in award or exclusion from dower based on local custom or the alternative common law schemes of fixing dower.[77] Choices were being made as to generosity or its lack in common law, though the reasoning behind them is seldom articulated.[78] Sometimes reporters and lawyers disagreed with judges about dower, though with no clear pro- or anti-widow policy discernible.[79] Overall, while there are statements of a

---

1368.003. 1312.149ss; 1406.037; 1410.127; 1486.032. Brand, 'Deserving'; Mitchell, *Portraits*, 8; Seabourne, 'Copulative Complexities'; Admeasurement and Waste: see, e.g., 33 *SS*, p. 104 no 616; 132 *SS*, p. 85.

74 *Bracton* II, p. 266; *Britton*, book V, c. 7, 5. Elaboration of defences: 'not married', e.g., CP 40/423 m. 74 (IMG 149); JUST 1/408 m. 64 (IMG 733); 'husband is alive': see, e.g., JUST 1/826 m. 1 (IMG 5016); CP 40/287 m. 469 (IMG 952). 'P is excommunicate': CP 40/193 m. 82d (IMG 167); 'you made a fine', CP 40/287 m. 196 (IMG 396); 'elopement with adulterer': JUST 1/416 m. 2 (IMG 7); CP 40/305 m. 216 (IMG 432); Wmr II c. 34; Seabourne, 'Copulative Complexities'. 'Coke, the Statute', Brand, 'Deserving'; 6 Ric. II st. 1 c. 6; Walker, 'Punishing Convicted Ravishers', 237; J. Post, 'Sir Thomas West and the Statute of Rapes 1382', *Bulletin of the Institute of Historical Research*, 53 (1980), 24–30; Hawkes, 'Preliminary Notes'. CP 40/195A m. 364 (IMG 735); CP 40/195B m. 24 (IMG 41). This is 1312.186ss. Treason/felony objections, e.g., *Bracton* II, p. 367; *Seipp* 1327.091; CP 40/164 m. 251 (IMG 512); JUST 1/457 m. 22 (IMG 4818); JUST 1/956 m. 22d (IMG 7919).

75 Forfeiture for H's felony/treason: *Bracton* II, p. 367; Archer, 'Rich Old Ladies', 20. See, below at XXX and, e.g., *Seipp* 1327.091; CP 40/164 m. 251 (IMG 512); JUST 1/457 m. 22 (IMG 4818); JUST 1/956 m. 23d (IMG 7919). 19 SS 131. *Seipp* 1344.136rs, CP 40/339 m. 448: no favour for a woman unhappy at dower accepted for her when she was a minor, though the idea of 'favour' for dower was brought up on her behalf.

76 See, e.g., 33 *SS* p. 104 no 616.

77 *Seipp* 1346.238rs; 1309.079ss. Possibly more generous: customs of Kent: *SR* I, pp. 223, 227. *Seipp* 1292.045rs; 1306.127rs; 1313.101ss; 1314.054ss; 1330.080; 1333.021; 1339.236rs; 1345.077rs; 1342.203rs; 1465.126:1330.689ss (of whole). *Seipp* 1305.116rs; 1330.585ss; 1289.032ss (doubt, MC); 1366.108; 1285.014ss; 1304.178rs; 1309.074ss; 1309.164ss; 1332.127; 1339.109rs; 1480.031. Peter L. Larson, 'Widow-right in Durham, England (1349–1660)', *Continuity and Change* 33 (2018), 173–201, 173; 114 SS, cxxi–cxxvii; Smith, 'Women's Property Rights', pp. 181–6 and 'Coping with Uncertainty: Women's Tenure of Customary Land in England c. 1370–1430', in *Enterprise and Individuals in Fifteenth-Century England*, ed. by Jennifer Kermode (Stroud, 1991), pp. 43–67.

78 Cokayn JCP in *Seipp* 1410.127: dower was for support for the widow, not connected with issue.

79 *Seipp* 1311.016ss; 1312.009ss; 1329.090.

general idea of favouring dower, the rules do not give a strong message of practical application of that idea.

Influential historians, looking at dower from the perspective of (male) heirs who might be affected by it, have emphasised the idea of its generosity to women. For example, a notable article on dower in the fifteenth century, despite admitting that '[n]o record survives of contemporary opinion on the existence of dowagers and their effect on succession', describes dower as 'one of the ... most destructive of baronial incidents', treating dowagers as a problem, and as causing 'havoc' in the normal course of succession and a particular dowager as keeping a 'stranglehold' on estates.[80] It should, however, be remembered that there are other possible perspectives, and the assumption that there was a simple policy or model of inheritance from which dower was a troubling derogation needs some reassessment.[81] Although we can attribute to medieval men in a position to dictate rules and their application a preference for male privilege and power through landownership, and although there was an impetus towards keeping family land together, and dynastic consolidation, that does not mean that there were no other factors seen as worthy of consideration. There seems no need to rule out the existence of feelings of duty and affection in medieval men towards their female kin, nor is there a need to assume the absence of a perception of the desirability of assisting those of their own number who might marry widows. There were situations in which heirs might bridle at the longevity of a dowager, but the assumption that this was normal is unwarranted. In addition, more exaggerated ideas of favour to women in relation to dower are certainly at odds with the statistics which have been taken from legal historians' painstaking study of common law records, which suggest a clear pattern of decline in the fifteenth century.[82] The work of legal experts outside the courtroom, from the medieval period onwards, cut down the dominance of dower in relation to provision of land for widows, and newer modes of securing their support did not replicate even the rhetoric of favour.[83] When one moves beyond their landed provision, through the vehicle of dower, the

80 Rowena E. Archer, 'Rich Old Ladies: The Problem of Late Medieval Dowagers', in *Property and Politics: Essays in Later Medieval English History,* ed. by T. Pollard (Gloucester, 1984), pp. 15–35, 16, 22, 26, 28; Dower as 'an irregularity in the feudal system'; Mitchell, *Portraits*, pp. 58, 131; K.B. McFarlane, *The Nobility of Late Medieval England* (Oxford, 1973), p. 66. The idea that courts' time was occupied, implicitly unduly, by 'litigious widows' can be seen in Hall's comments in *Glanvill*, p. 184.

81 See Eileen Spring, 'The Heiress-at-Law: English Real Property Law from a New Point of View', *LHR* 8 (1990), 273–96; Eileen Spring, *Law, Land and Family: Aristocratic Inheritance in England 1300–1800* (Chapel Hill, 1993); Joel T. Rosenthal, *Patriarchy and Families of Privilege in Fifteenth Century England* (Philadelphia, 1992), p. 198.

82 See Michael Phifer, 'Property, Power and Patriarchy: The Decline of Women's Property Right in England after the Black Death', Ph.D. dissertation (University of Houston, 2014), especially at pp. 81, 166 and c. 6.

83 Baker, *Introduction*, p. 290; Loengard, 'What Is a Nice ... Englishwoman Doing', p. 69; Linda E. Mitchell, 'Maud Marshall and Margaret Marshall: Two Viragos Extraordinaire', in *The Ties That Bind*, ed. by Mitchell and others, pp. 121–42, 140. Changing scope of

common law showed considerably less interest in widows. In relation to the widow's entitlement to personal property on the husband's death, there was a retreat from common law from intervention to enforce provision via the 'widow's part': men's control over chattels and freedom of testation, subject only to local custom, came to the fore from the later fourteenth century.[84] Favour to widows was not a clear priority.

While there is at least some rhetorical claim of favour to widows, the sources of medieval common law make no claim at all that women in general were 'great favourites'. Later chapters will expand upon some of the claims which have been made in relation to supposed 'indulgence' of women in relation to culpability for offences, and why they may now be regarded as exaggerated.[85] Claims of generosity to women in other contexts may be equally unconvincing. Thus the requirements for the physical presence of wives, and their affirmation of agreement for transfers of land which might be against their interests, presented as checks that their participation was willing were probably more useful in protecting the position of third party acquirers of land they were in ensuring genuine consent on the part of the woman, and are likely to have allowed through some cases of forced or fraudulent transfer.[86] Pity for women may be mentioned in reports, but it did not always result in generous treatment.[87]

Tudor legal theorists would suggest as a maxim the law's favour towards pregnant women,[88] but this cannot be seen as having been the organising principle of medieval common law in relation to their treatment. As will be discussed in Chapter 6, there was a long-standing policy delaying the execution of pregnant felons until after their delivery, but this is to be understood as a 'favour' to the foetus, and the avoidance of guilt for the wrongful ending

dower: Linda E. Mitchell, *Portraits of Medieval Women: Family, Marriage and Politics in England 1225–1350* (New York, 2003), pp. 126, 131; Coss, *Lady*, p. 146.

84 Women and wills: *Bracton* II, pp. 178–80; *Glanvill*, vii, 5; *SR* I, p. 1: *Magna Carta* 1215, c. 26; Hudson *OHLE* II, p. 378; *P & M* II, pp. 347–50, 404–5; 427–34; R. H, Helmholz, 'Married Women's Wills in Later Medieval England', in *Wife and Widow*, ed. by Walker, c. 7. pp. 165–82. R.H. Helmholz, 'Legitim in English Legal History', *University of Illinois Law Review* 3 (1984), 659–74; Hyams, 'Maitland', p. 227. Loengard, 'Rationalbilis dos', p. 62. Some fourteenth- and fifteenth-century cases affirm the widow's part, though there are contrary statements: *P & M* II, pp. 347, 352–3; *Seipp* 1308.026ss, 1311.295ss, 1324.062. 1356.097; 109 *SS*, p. 108; *Seipp* 1366.095; CP 40/198 m. 82 d (IMG 184) (1313, mentioning Magna Carta). *Mirror* book V, c. 2, implies that the action *de rationabili parte bonorum* should but does not currently accrue to a man's widow and children. *Bracton* suggested that stricter regimes might be appropriate in London, 'for a citizen will hardly amass wealth if he is bound to leave it to an ill-deserving wife or to idle and uninstructed children': II, p. 180.

85 See Chapter 6.

86 Hyams, 'Maitland', p. 225. See, e.g., a woman disputing that she agreed to a transfer by fine: JUST 1/302 m. 24 (IMG 8235). On the requirement that women surrender land in person, not by attorney: *Seipp* 1330.764ss.

87 Reporters noting judicial pity: *Seipp* 1353.165ass. Pity but no help: *Seipp* 1310.144ss. Reference to a deceased woman's poverty: *Eyre of London 1244*, Case 100.

88 Baker, *OHLE VI*, pp. 778–9.

of a (potential) life for those sentencing and carrying out the execution, rather than as a favour to the woman. A reduction in punishment for pregnant women was mandated by statute in one case, and there were examples of kinder than necessary provision for pregnant women prisoners, and some accommodation for their participation in litigation.[89] Nevertheless, there is little support for an idea that there was, or it was thought appropriate for there to be, particularly generous overall treatment of pregnant women. There was no apparent inhibition on much non-capital punishment, and plea rolls contain complaints suggesting that pregnant women might be closely confined, placed in stocks, or subjected to corporal punishment, which could lead to severe injury to woman mother and foetus, or even to death, as was alleged in the case of a pregnant Sussex brewster, who, having broken the assize of ale, was said to have been punished and beaten to such a degree that she and the child died.[90] Pregnancy might be also regarded as a legitimate reason to terminate employment.[91] At times, the common law's attitude to the pregnant woman seems closer to suspicion than favour, with accusations of deceit against those women claiming to be pregnant with a husband's posthumous child, and a procedure for checking this, couched in terms not of possible understandable error but of deliberate dishonesty.[92] So common was suspicion of women's chastity and so frequently was it impugned in relation to succession that the common law developed presumptions to deal with questions of legitimacy and bastardy. There is some arguable generosity to women in this area, in that some statements and case records seem to allow fairly slim chances of legitimate impregnation by a husband to determine in favour of legitimacy: for example, in a situation in which a husband had been away

89 See, e.g., Butler, 'Pleading', pp. 144–5; *CPR 1436–41*, pp. 225, 472; *CCR* 1346–9, 609. Pregnancy as a reason for non-appearance (dower case defendant): CP 40/154 m. 92d (IMG 773). Compensation for having been cited in court Christian over a debt and made to pay for a respite while pregnant: JUST 1/573 m. 107d (IMG 843). *SR* II, p. 637 19 H VII c. 12, c. 8; Baker, *OHLE* VI, pp. 778–9. Indignation at alleged mistreatment of pregnant women: *RP* V, 476. Report noting a judicial trip to the bedside of a pregnant widow bringing an appeal of homicide, to learn whether she wished to press for capital punishment of the offender. *Dialogus de Scacc.*, p. 83; *Seipp* 1402.045; 1430.058, 1440.115; 1443.060. 1481.125; KB 27/248 m. 8d (IMG 193).

90 JUST 1/926 m. 17 (IMG 4351) (acquitted). See also KB 27/469 m. 14d (IMG 301). Miscarriages allegedly caused by ecclesiastical punishment: Goldberg, *Women in England*, pp. 118; JUST 1/111 m. 28d (IMG 3822).

91 CP 40/645 m. 39 (IMG 611).

92 *Bracton* II, pp. 201–2, 204; *Fleta* book 1 c. 15; *Britton* book II cc. 7–19; book 3 c. 2 no 13–15; *Maud wife of Thomas of Dunster v. Isabel widow of Walter of Upham*): C 245/1, no. 23, Michaelmas 1279', in *PROME*. Common law cases: 60 *SS*, cliii; *BNB* pleas 1503, 1605. Retrospective questioning about a former pregnancy: *Seipp* 1367.029, CP 40/427 m. 408. 37 *SS*, p. 220, states that a widow falsely claiming pregnancy by H will lose her dower: 1314M. See the case of Joan, widow of Bogo le Veel, accused of having withheld the heir to her deceased husband, the child, allegedly at that point unborn: CP 40/195A m. 364 (IMG 735); CP 40/195B m. 24 (IMG 41); *Seipp* 1312.186ss.

from his home for three years and his wife bore a child during this absence, the child might be deemed legitimate, on the basis that it was possible that the husband might have sneaked back to father it.[93] Apparently excessive gestation periods may not have been allowed to 'bastardise' the child of a widow (and thus condemn the widow's reputation) quite so easily as later accounts, such as that by Coke, might claim.[94] An example of the process of later simplification of a more complex medieval position can be seen in the treatment of a 1287 case *John de Radewell v Henry son of Beatrix, Ralph Pyrot et al.*[95] This involved a dispute as to whether X was the son and heir to a landholder Y. Doubt had been raised about this based on the length of time from Y's death to X's birth, which was 40 weeks and 11 days, as well as Y's absence and poor health at the end of his life. The calculation about legitimacy here was not just about time, but an assessment of the possibility of procreation in all of the circumstances. Nevertheless, it was later simplified to a 40-week rule: Coke presented the simplified rule, and this became the common understanding of what had been the medieval position.[96] There might therefore have been more generosity in such cases in the medieval period than in some later periods, but it should be noted first that legal discourse in this area has many prurient and bawdy elements and seems to be founded on a poor opinion of women's morality, and second that any generosity in such decisions is at least as much concerned with reluctance to 'bastardise' heirs as it is with favour to pregnant or recently delivered women.

Conclusion

Women were subjects of the common law and subjects of interest for common lawyers. They were seen both as a united group, part of a generally unquestioned, two sex model, and also, at times, as separate subsets. Discussion of the law's relationship to categories of women, and, in particular, wives and widows, itself shows rich veins of thought about unity and division, sometimes making use of metaphors to explain rules, but not (yet) presenting a narrative of being ruled by such metaphors. Legal discussion suggests intellectual interest and a desire to vaunt the common law's favour towards particular groups of women, but this does not translate into a general policy of furthering their interests, and nor would this have been understood to be a necessary or appropriate aspiration.

93 *Bracton* II, 35, 186; *Britton* book III, c. 2, 14–15; *BNB* pl. 1229; *P & M* II, pp. 398–9.

94 *Bracton* II, pp. 204–5; III, p. 311; *Fleta* book 5 c. 6; book 1 c. 6, *Seipp* 1421.081rog, CP 40/642, m. 439 and d (IMG 892 and 1929), *Machon v Holt* 50 *SS* pp. 24–30. Serjeant Rolf's idea that pregnancy could last seven years: *Seipp* 1422.042ss.

95 58 *SS*, p. 29; JUST 1/11 m.10d (IMG 115); KB 27/124 m. 13d, m. 14 (IMG 7660, 7475); KB 27/142 m. 26, m. 27, m. 26d (IMG 3008, 3010, 3137).

96 *Plac. Abbrev.*, p. 221, notes only that gestation has exceeded 40 weeks, but at p. 234 notes lack of access.

Part II

Audible and inaudible; credible and not credible

Women in the legal process

F.W. Maitland felt able and inclined to summarise medieval women's role in relation to the common law in very few words, stating that, while, as far as 'private rights' were concerned, they were 'on the same level as men, though postponed in the canons of inheritance', they lacked 'public functions'. This lack was summarised with customary elegance: 'In the camp, at the council board, on the bench, in the jury box there is no place for them'.[1] A 'sure instinct' had brought the law to this position by the reign of Edward I, and continuities in the situation of women 'until our own time' were emphasised.[2] In this summary, a questionably simple distinction between private rights and public functions was employed. Roman law had used such terminology, and it is sometimes seen in medieval legal sources, but neither the Roman distinction nor the modern version maps well onto medieval legal practice.[3] Modern legal scholarship has routinely questioned the extent to which 'the public/private distinction' represents a clear dividing line,[4] and historical scholarship has also come to adopt a critical attitude to it, especially in relation to the lives of noblewomen and queens.[5] Studies of medieval

1 *P & M*, I, p. 468, my italics. This is echoed, for example, in Chadwick-Healey's introduction to *Somersetshire Pleas* (1897), pp. xxii–xxiii.

2 *P & M*, I, p. 468.

3 *D*. 1.1.2; *Bracton* II, pp. 25–6; 8 *SS*, pp. 29–30, 32. For the lack of distinction between property and public law in medieval England, see, e.g., Mitchell, *Portraits*, p. 12; Seipp, 'Concept of Property', p. 80; Robin Chapman Stacey, *Law and the Imagination in Medieval Wales* (Philadelphia, 2018), p. 135. For an early modern distinction between *ius privatum*, 'the sinews of property', and *ius publicum*, the 'sinews of government', see F. Bacon, *A Preparation toward the Union of Laws* (London, 1641) in *The Works of Francis Bacon* ed. by James Spedding and others (London, 1872), pp. 731, 733.

4 See, e.g., *Lloyd's Introduction to Jurisprudence* 14-00; *Jason N.E. Varuhas and Shona Wilson Stark, The Frontiers of Public Law (Oxford, 2020) especially Part III and c.* 14: Carol Harlow, 'Public and Private Law: A Redundant Divide'.

5 See, e.g., Emma. Hawkes, 'Judging Female Judges', pp. 93, 101–2; Jane Tibbets Schulenburg, 'Female Sanctity: Public and Private Roles, c. 500–1100', in *Women and Power in the Middle Ages*, ed. by Mary Erler and Maryanne Kowaleski (Athens, GA, 1988), 102–25, p. 105. Everard, 'Public Authority', p. 125; Erler and Kowaleski, *Gendering the Master Narrative*.

queens, in particular, have shown the difficulty of drawing a clear boundary between 'public' and 'private'. Is Edward II's queen, Isabella of France, discussing the rights of her husband with members of her French family, to be considered to be acting in a 'public' or a 'private' capacity, for example?[6]

Maitland's statement also tends to tidy up and render timeless women's role in the common law, the stark negatives of the second half of the sentence 'balanced' by the strained positives of the first part, and 'the law' is itself presented as a gender-neutral force. Despite the passing of more than a century of women's participation as non-party 'officials' in the legal system since the time *Pollock and Maitland* was written, and despite copious scholarship from legal academics and historians on women, gender and law in the interim, later legal historians have not always ventured far from Maitland's summary.[7] This section of the book will argue that there is more to say and to ask about medieval women's 'non-party' involvement in common law litigation. A history of common law should include a consideration of women's presence and absence in those 'public' functions relating to law. It should be acknowledged that '[a]s might be expected, the position of woman as a citizen was not very exactly defined',[8] but, though evidence may be particularly sparse and 'definite answers' on several points may be difficult to obtain, this should not lead to avoidance of the issue.

Chapter 3 will consider women's participation and exclusion from participation in what might, with a degree of approximation, be described as the 'public functions' relating to common law cases: judge, lawyer, witness and juror. There is some artificiality in separating these functions from those of some litigants, who might be seen, or might present themselves, as acting for the king's peace or the public good, but for the sake of convenience and the avoidance of excessively unwieldy chapters, consideration of women's participation 'as parties' will be deferred until the third part of the book, and will be considered in Chapters 4–6.

6 For Isabella's role, see, e.g., J.R.S. Phillips, *Edward II* (New Haven, CT and London, 2010), pp. 221, 471; E.A.R. Brown, 'Diplomacy, Adultery and Domestic Politics at the Court of Philip the Fair', in *Documenting the Past*, ed. by J.S. Hamilton and P.J. Bradley (Woodbridge, 1989), pp. 62–5. For temporary 'public' roles of queens, including regency, see, e.g., W. Mark Ormrod, *Edward III* (New Haven, CT and London, 2011), pp. 47–8; Benz, *Queen Consort, Queen Mother*, pp. 195–7, 205–18. The idea of a female monarch was not out of the question for Edward I, who entertained the possibility of one of his daughters succeeding him: Phillips, *Edward II*, p. 41.

7 See, e.g., Baker, *Introduction*, p. 499.

8 Cleveland, *Woman under the English Law*, p. 71.

3 'By the mouth of man'

Women as non-party actors in litigation

The report of a dower case of 1342, probably that brought by Edith, widow of William Oky, against Henry son of Roger Oky, includes discussion of how to resolve the question of whether or not a man, on whose death depended entitlements to land, was actually dead. The reporter noted that there had been an attempt by the claimant to use documentary evidence – which was specified as a certificate from the civic authorities of Bristol – to prove that the husband had died. Pleading this, however, was not regarded as an appropriate move. According to the court, the matter had to be proved 'by the mouth of man': '*Il coveynt en tiel cas qe la chose soit prove par bouche de home*'.[9] The main point being made was one about the importance of orality and the physical presence of those testifying, but the use of *home*, uncertain, as I have argued, in its position with regard to the inclusion of women, highlights a tendency which will be seen more than once in this chapter. Where non-party participation in litigation at common law is concerned, the possible inclusion of women is frequently left ambiguous, whether by the use of words which might be taken in different ways, as here, or by non-exhaustive (or contradicted) statements of exclusion or by apparent silence. Coupled with the existence of a range of misogynist judgements on women's character and capacity, ready to be adopted from wider intellectual traditions and used in the common law, this meant that the door was left open either to inclusion or to exclusion of women as it seemed appropriate to those with the power to decide. In this chapter, we will see both the reality of exclusion of women from non-party roles as authoritative speakers, witnesses and decision makers in common law litigation and also the possibility of their inclusion, in limited circumstances, dictated or accepted by (male) authorities. The 'mouth of man' in the courtroom might or might not speak with the voice of a woman.

9 'In such a case, the matter must be proved by mouth of man': *Seipp* 1342.124rs; probable record is CP 40/330 m. 284 (IMG 581), though note the geographical variations.

Judging: *viros sapientes et timentes deum*[10]

Though ideas of 'judging' and 'judicial functions' are not immutable, varying with the scope of the legal system, and the distribution of tasks and decisions between judges and others such as juries, in general, the most important of the authoritative speakers of the law in the medieval courtroom was the judge, and amongst judges, those at the peak of importance in the common law were the judges of the superior courts at Westminster and other royal tribunals.[11] The identities of these judges are well documented in plea rolls and in commissions. These documents show that there was indeed, as Maitland stated, 'no place' for women on their benches. Rather than leaving the matter there, however, perhaps dismissing it as being 'obvious' and therefore uninteresting, it is appropriate for a modern account of the history of the common law to consider the nature of and reasons for the exclusion of women from judicial functions.

While there were statements in Roman law and canon law sources of a ban on women acting in a judicial capacity,[12] there are few comments on this in medieval common law sources. Such occasional justifications or discussions as there are show differing views as to the rationale and the extent of exclusion of women. The late thirteenth-century *Mirror of Justices* did state an explicit prohibition on women acting as judges. It explained this by reference to Scripture, centring the objection on women's sinful nature, which rendered them unqualified to judge others, and on the inappropriateness of the occupation of God's seat by a woman.[13] Apart from this statement, there is little discussion of the matter in the common law context thereafter, until the fifteenth-century judge Sir John Fortescue's *De Natura Legis Naturae*, written in the mid-1460s, included a more elaborate argument against women's suitability as judges. This was a step in his 'Lancastrian' argument that women could not reign, so that claims to the throne traced through women were invalid, a convenient blow to the claims of the House of York (though potentially troublesome in terms of the English claim to France).[14] Despite his political agenda, Fortescue's views on women and judging are of

10 'Wise and God-fearing men': *Bracton* II, p. 306.

11 On judges and their functions, see Paul Brand, 'Judges and Judging, 1176–1307', in *Judges and Judging*, ed. by Brand and Getzler, pp. 16–43; McSweeney, *Priests of the Law*.

12 *D.* 5.1.12; 50.17.2; Eltjo Schrage, 'Women Do Not Sit as Judges, or Do They – The Office of Judge in Vincentius Bellovacensis' Speculum', *Fundamina* 16 (2010), 377–89; Goodrich, 'Gynaetopia', p. 278; R.H. Helmholz, 'Judges and Trials in the English Ecclesiastical Courts', in *Judicial Tribunals*, ed. by Mulholland and Pullin (Manchester: Manchester University Press, 2003), pp. 102–16, 110–11; Emma Hawkes, 'Judging Female Judges: Sir John Fortescue's Vision of Women as Judges in *De Natura Legis Naturae*', *Limina* 8 (2002), 93–112.

13 *Mirror*, book 2 c 2, c. 3.

14 Fortescue, *DNLN*; Margaret Kekewich, *Sir John Fortescue and the Governance of England* (Woodbridge, 2019), p. 188. See also Goodrich, 'Gynaetopia', p. 281; Hawkes, 'Judging Female Judges', p. 93.

interest here in that they were presumably such as he considered would be regarded by his audience as plausible. They were presented in an imaginary court case, a three-way dispute about succession to a kingdom, between a king's daughter, her son and the king's brother. The 'anti-women' side in the case, split between the voices of the king's grandson and his brother, was shown drawing on civil law, Biblical and historical examples, and Aristotelian ideas to argue that women were not suitable as (superior) judges because of their essential subordinate and irrational nature, which fitted them only for 'humbler' and more domestic tasks.[15] They also stressed women's supposed reluctance to impose the death penalty as a reason against them acting as judges.[16] The King's daughter was allowed to suggest that the Biblical restrictions were to be understood as falling upon married women – not women in general – that they were not eternal and essential, and that not all women were less capable than all men, but of course none of these points prevailed.[17]

In this work, *Justice* is portrayed as female. Fortescue gave short shrift to any idea that a judicial role for women was supported by this womanly presentation of *Justice*, however, playing down this gendered representation as a grammatical accident: *justitia* is a feminine noun in Latin.[18] The text does, however, go further than simply reflecting the gendered nature of Latin, including clear and sometimes elaborate metaphors of justice, and different sorts of law, as female, and showing these female presences in an authoritative, judicial role.[19] It has been argued that such portrayals suggest a less-than-totally negative attitude to the possibility of female judging. A somewhat similar argument has been made in relation to the appearance of female judging in literary works relating to 'Courts of Love', suggesting that this undermines any pose of being unable to contemplate a female judge. While we may consider that the female adjudication in the 'Courts of Love' was probably assumed to be a fanciful idea, serving to enforce rather than undermining the understanding that women could not judge, the more serious tone and purpose of Fortescue's work means it can less easily be dismissed as part of a carnivalesque tradition.[20] Nevertheless,

15 Hawkes 'Judging Female Judges', pp. 95–7; Fortescue, *DNLN*, e.g. Part I c. 3, p. 192, Part II cc. 3, 8–9, 62.

16 Hawkes, 'Judging Female Judges', pp. 37, 98; Fortescue, *DNLN*, Part II c. 3.

17 Hawkes 'Judging Female Judges', pp. 94–6, 98; Fortescue *DNLN* Part II cc. 39–40.

18 Hawkes 'Judging Female Judges', pp. 105–6; Marina Warner, *Monuments and Maidens: The Allegory of the Female Form* (London, 1985), pp. 63–70, 146–76; Fortescue, *DNLN*, Part 2 c. 1, p. 249.

19 *DNLN*, Preface, Part I c. 42, p. 239; Part I cc. 10, 15, 20, 29, 45, p. 200.

20 *Andreas Capellanus on Love*, tr. by P.G. Walsh (London, 1982); Peter Goodrich, 'Law in the Courts of Love: Andreas Capellanus and the Judgments of Love', *Stanford Law Review* 48 (1996), 633–75, 673; Goodrich, 'Gynaetopia', p. 282; McSweeney, *Priests of the Law*, pp. 194–5. 'The Court of Love', in *The Chaucerian Apocrypha, a Selection*, ed. by K. Forni (Kalamazoo, 2005), pp. 7–58 (l. 118); Van Houts, 'Gender', p. 213; H.L.

Fortescue's metaphorical usages can hardly be thought to outweigh the negative view of female judging which he presses.

Potentially more troubling to any claim that there was a blanket rule against women acting as judges were the scriptural, historical and contemporary examples of women having some judicial role. Fortescue felt obliged to engage with the scriptural examples, and, like earlier commentators, concluded that Biblical support for women's judging should not be held to provide a valid precedent for contemporary practice.[21] Less attention was paid to the historical examples, from England or elsewhere, of rulers' wives acting in a judicial capacity. Earlier English queens had in fact been accepted in broadly judicial roles, whether or not formally recognised as regent.[22] Since the holding of certain roles and jurisdiction was considered to 'run with' land, other women might also inherit some judicial roles.[23] As Maitland pointed out, some women had rights over manor courts or, at an early period, had succeeded to hereditary shrievalties, which included a judicial function.[24] Perhaps the most interesting example of this is that of the Clifford heiresses in the late thirteenth century, who succeeded to a shrievalty and apparently took some action in person to head off jurisdictional incursions, though the legal functions associated with the role were generally delegated to men.[25] Fortescue dealt with women succeeding to a father who was a duke, earl or marquis, and thus having the right and responsibility to judge their subordinates. He attempted to draw the sting

---

Bordier, *Philippe de Remi, sire de Beaumanoir: jurisconsulte et poëte national du Beauvaisis 1246–1296* (Paris, 1869), pp. 268–70. See also Geoffrey Chaucer, 'Wife of Bath's Tale', especially lines 888–918.

21 *Judges* 4:5; Joy A. Schroeder, *Deborah's Daughters: Gender Politics and Biblical Interpretation* (Oxford, 2014); Gratian, *Decretum*, C. 15, q. 3. *Corpus Iuris Canonici*, Vol. I, ed. by Emil Friedberg (Graz, 1959), p. 750; *Summa Parisiensis*, C. 33, q. 5, c. 17, ed. by Terence P. McLaughlin (Toronto, 1952), p. 255; Schrage, p. 387; Van Houts, 'Gender', p. 217.

22 Van Houts, 'Gender', pp. 201, 217; *P & M* I, p. 466; Hudson, *OHLE* II, pp. 274, 500, 521; *The Brut*, ed. by F.W.D. Brie II, pp. 239; Benz, *Queen Consorts*, pp. 185, 188–9, 195; D.D.R. Owen, *Eleanor of Aquitaine: Queen and Legend* (Oxford, 2000), p. 45; Howell, *Eleanor of Provence*:, pp. 112–24; Elizabeth M. Hallam, *The Itinerary of Edward II and His Household, 1307–1328*, List and Index Society, 211 (London, 1984), p. 7; Maxwell-Lyte, Historical Notes, pp. 295–6; Maurer, *Margaret of Anjou: Queenship and Power*, p. 100. For French examples, see Alan Harding, *Medieval Law and the Foundations of the State* (Oxford, 2001), p. 114; Van Houts, 'Gender', p. 217; Metz, 'Le statut de la femme', p. 104; Schrage, 'Women', p. 386. For courts of queens and noble ladies, see e.g. CP 40/193 m.208 (IMG 419); *Seipp* 1324.053, 1328.077; 1343.230rs; 1353.073; 1425.007; 1448.025; 1456.019; SC 8/213/10642.

23 *Bracton* II, p. 281.

24 *P & M* I, p. 466; Baker, *Introduction*, p. 500; Louise Wilkinson, 'Women as Sheriff', in *English Governance in the Thirteenth Century*, ed. by Adrian Jobson (Woodbridge, 2004), pp. 111–24; Hawkes, 'Judging Female Judges', pp. 99–100.

25 Douglas C. Jansen, 'Women and Public Authority in the Thirteenth Century', in *Queens, Regents and Potentates, Women of Power I*, ed. by Theresa M. Vann (Woodbridge, 1993), pp. 91–105, 91, 96; KB 27/104 m. 11.

of this possibility, for his purposes, by portraying such female jurisdiction as acceptable, because the women in question were still subject to superior male rule in the shape of the king's justice.[26] While there were indeed ways in which common law courts could correct perceived mistakes or injustices in lower-level courts,[27] however, there were limits to such processes, so that considerable power to judge was left to these courts. Fortescue's explanation is not a strong one.

On top of his partisan purpose in writing critically about women's capabilities, we should note that Fortescue did in fact recant from his overall judgment on the issue of women reigning in his 'Declaration on Writings from Scotland', when the second triumph of Edward IV made it necessary to find an accommodation with the new regime.[28] While showing that he was not prepared to run the risk of execution over the issue of women's rule, however, this does not suggest a genuine change of heart, and nor does it detract from the fact that the misogynist views he put in the mouths of his characters in the earlier work must have been regarded as plausible and familiar to common lawyers.[29] It is clear that the implications of his new view – that women could rule because, as it had now occurred to him, they were in fact always under the authority of a man, i.e. the Pope – were not followed through to a conclusion with regard to their judging capabilities.

It is interesting to note that it would appear that the idea of female involvement in judicial functions was not wholly out of the question; what was unacceptable was their presence in higher, common law, judicial roles. These were part of a masculine domain.[30] Less of a problem appears to have been seen with either the holding of roles which might involve some incidental lower-level judging, or the granting to women of responsibilities which might be seen as adjacent to or connected with judging. Thus, they might be ordered to apprehend 'criminals', they might certainly hold the right to have the instruments of justice, gallows and tumbrel, and might keep a gaol, and they also occasionally occupied quasi-judicial roles in arbitration or mediation.[31]

26 Fortescue, *DNLN*, Part 2 c. 15 and c. 23; Hawkes, 'Judging Female Judges', pp. 101–2. J. Everard, 'Public Authority and Private Rights: Women in the English Royal Courts of Justice, 1196–1250', in *Sexuality and Gender in History: Selected Essays*, ed. by Penelope Hetherington and Philippa Maddern (Western Australia, 1993), p. 129.

27 Baker, *Introduction*, p. 147.

28 *The Works of Sir John Fortescue*, ed. by T. Fortescue (2 vols, London, 1869), p. 535; *CPR 1467–77*, p. 296.

29 See John Fortescue, Francis Gregor, et al., *De Laudibus Legum Angliae: A Treatise in Commendation of the Laws of England* (Cincinnati, OH, 1874), pp. xxxvii, xxxix.

30 Sixteenth-century suggestions that women could be judges in a wider range of jurisdictions: 132 *SS*, p. lxxi.

31 *CPR 1321–24* p 350; Mitchell, *Portraits*, p. 116. See, e.g. 103 *SS* Case 34.5; KB 27/214 m. 73d; Seabourne, *IMW*, pp. 172–7; SC 1/23/27. Nuns running sanctuaries or as temporary

Lawyers: *hommes de la ley*

As is well known, the common law came to be dominated by professional lawyers over the course of the medieval period.[32] Within this developing, professionalising world, the names and nature of roles were not static. Thus, for example, although there were some women acting in a role labelled 'attorney' in medieval records, or being put in the place of an absent person in litigation or standing in for a husband who was incapacitated, this did not denote the 'professional' role which it would later signify.[33] Although, as a recent edited collection has highlighted, there were many ways in which women might participate in intellectual pursuits and in leadership, there is no sign of women making a living as *hommes de la ley* or *sage de la ley* in the medieval common law: they were not 'legal professionals' in the sense of being legal clerks, serjeants at law or apprentices.[34] Medieval women might certainly have a functional – perhaps in some cases a sophisticated – knowledge of the law relating to themselves and their families,[35] but they had no opportunity to learn and practise the increasingly specialised skills of the common lawyer. Generally, this went without saying, but the same two sources mentioned above in relation to their views on women as judges also had something to say on women as lawyers. The *Mirror of Justices* expressed a view that women should not be pleaders, essoiners or attorneys, and Fortescue's *De Natura Legis Naturae* also ruled out their participation as legal representatives.[36] One might infer from this exclusion an assessment of women as incapable of performing the intellectual work required, an objection to their speaking in public and perhaps a particular feeling of the inappropriateness of their speaking for a man.[37]

---

gaolers: SC 8/224/11191; KB 27/491 m.22d (IMG 393). *Seipp* 1468.042; van Houts, 'Gender', p. 212, *Coutumes de Beauvaisis*, c. 41, paras. 1287–8.

32 See, e.g., Baker, *Introduction*, c. 10.

33 *P & M* I, pp. 192, 212, 218; YB 13 Edw. 3, Rolls Series, p. 186 (1339); Year Book 18 Edw. 3, Rolls Series, Introduction by Luke Owen Pike, p. xxxviii.; 3 *SS*, p. 56, pl. 141; Hudson *OHLE* II, p. 587; *CRR XV 1233–7*, p. 172 no 820 (W attorney for H). and p. 63 no 287; Loengard, 'What Is a Nice … Englishwoman Doing', p. 56 notes that the 1242–5 Curia Regis Rolls have only one woman attorney for her husband, in a plea of land: no. 1475 (1244). See also 30 *SS*, p. 158; *Seipp* 1321.226ss; SC 8/31/1504; SC 8/303/15130.

34 *Women Intellectuals*, ed. Kerby-Fulton and others. See Anthony Musson, 'The Role of Amateur and Professional Judges in the Royal Courts of Late Medieval England', in *Judicial Tribunals*, ed. by Mulholland, vol 1, pp. 37–57, 38.

35 See, e.g., Amanda Bohne, 'Networks of Influence: Widows, Sole Administration, and Unconventional Relationships in Thirteenth-Century London', in *Women Intellectuals*, ed. by Kerby-Fulton and others (Woodbridge: D.S. Brewer, 2020), c. 13.

36 *Mirror*, book II, cc. 4, 5, 30, 31; Hawkes, 'Judging', p. 93. Co. Litt. 128a, book II, c. 11 s. 196, book II, c. 3 p. 45.

37 1 *Tim*. 2:11–12; *D* 3.1.5; *D*.16.2.5. On women's incompetence in court, see Fortescue, *DNLN*, p. 302 Part 2 cc. 3, 13, 41 (ignorance of law, 'simplicity', excessive emotion).

There was a sense in which women's ability to perform the task of legal representation was indeed limited, not as a result of any innate lack of capacity, but because of the way in which the legal profession developed and the choices made in the course of this development. Increasing professionalisation of legal process in common law courts including the move to (French/Latin) written record served to increase and formalise exclusion of women.[38] Likewise, the structuring of the legal profession around the Inns of Court, deliberately and exclusively male institutions, served to entrench the shutting out of women. All of this apparently made it unimaginable for a woman to become a professional lawyer. Women were sometimes given a semi-representative role, for example, being deputed by co-executors to render charters on behalf of them all, but not a 'professional' one.[39] The fact of the Inns' exclusively male atmosphere and the specific forms of masculinity they embodied has been emphasised in recent historical scholarship.[40] Both the masculinity of such legal institutions and the concomitant absence of women have, however, been of less interest to classical legal history, even after a century of moves towards inclusion of women within the legal profession in England and Wales. Discussions of the 'rise' of the legal profession, which have been at the heart of the mission of classical English legal history in the twentieth century and beyond have tended not to note the simple point that such 'progress' is not necessarily a positive matter for all.[41] More sociologically inflected ideas which see both sides of professionalism have not found a place in this legal history.[42] From one point of view, it is 'stating the obvious' to say that professionalisation means shutting out the unprofessional, but failing to give weight to this fact of exclusion perpetuates it within our legal historical narratives.

38 On professionalisation and 'secularisation' of the judiciary, see Brand, 'The Age of Bracton', in *The History of English Law*, ed. by Hudson, pp. 65–89; Paul Brand, *The Making of the Common Law* (London, 1992), cc. 1, 3. On the masculine nature of the professions, see *BMOC*. On women's lesser literacy and exclusion from academia, see Wilkinson, *Women*, p. 11.

39 In 26 *SS*, p. 14, case 11, *Montfort v. Basset*, CP 40/184 m. 52d.

40 E. Amanda McVitty, 'Engendering Erudition: Masculinity and Legal Authority at England's Medieval Inns of Court', *Gender and History* 32 (2020), 447–64.

41 See, e.g., Paul Brand, *The Origins of the English Legal Profession* (Oxford, 1992); J.H. Baker, *The Legal Profession and the Common Law* (London, 1986). For 'rise' images, see, e.g., W. Hill, 'The Rise of the English Legal Profession', *TRHS* 3 (1874), 98–162; Roscoe Pound, 'What Is a Profession? The Rise of the Legal Profession in Antiquity', *Notre Dame Law Review* 19 (1944), 203–28; W. Prest, *The Rise of the Barristers: A Social History of the English Bar 1590–1640* (Oxford, 1996). For fines for having women in the Inn, see *Records of the Honorable Society of Lincoln's Inn: The Black Books*, ed. by William Paley Baildon, James D. Walker and Ronald Roxburgh (London, 1897), IV, pp. 66, 89 (though note the society laundress: vol 1, p. xxi).

42 For more modern contexts, see Kate Leader, 'From Bear Gardens to the County Court: Creating the Litigant in Person', *CLJ* 79 (2020), 260–87; Chris Brooks, *Lawyers, Litigation and English Society since 1450* (London and Rio Grande, 1998), p. 186.

Medieval women's own views on the developing and specialising practice of common law are mostly beyond recovery, as is their engagement with legal sources. It would be very interesting to know of precursors to the law-book ownership of Winifred, mother of Sir Edward Coke, but studies of women's book ownership do not seem to have tackled this issue yet.[43] No doubt, on the whole, women had no choice but to accept and submit to the institutions around them, but it does not seem impossible that some might have taken a similar view to that of Margaret Starre, present in the marketplace of Cambridge in 1381 as charters were burned, who is said to have 'gathered the ashes of the burning documents, scattered them to the winds', exclaiming 'Away with the skill of the clerks, away with it!'[44] No records disclose signs of women attempting to enter legal professions: the story appears to be less like that of the guilds of relatively 'mechanical' medical men in France, who struggled to keep out women when the latter tried to practice, and more like the situation of the academically trained and highly literate medical specialists described in Green's study of 'women's medicine', whose monopoly of the requisite education meant that their role was entirely secure from female incursions.[45] In the case of common lawyers, centuries of male exclusivity would follow, with the legal professions even slower than the medics to open their doors to English women.

Jurors, witnesses and other creditworthy speakers

As well as judges and legal professionals, the legal system of medieval England relied on the participation of a group of 'lay' individuals whose function involved speaking the truth. We may conveniently label them with familiar terms, 'jurors' and 'witnesses', though we should not assume that the modern function of 'juror' or 'witness' can be found unproblematically in the medieval common law system. There has been a long discussion of the extent to which the function of 'juror' in the medieval common law overlapped with what a modern observer would class as that of 'witness', i.e. the extent to which a juror came to court to impart matters seen or known as opposed to coming to be informed by others.[46] The 'modern' distinction

43 Allen D. Boyer, 'Sir Edward Coke 1552–1634)', *ODNB*; ... *alle the bokes that I haue of latyn, englisch, and frensch*: 'laywomen and their books in late medieval England', in *Women and Literature in Britain, 1150–1500*, ed. C.M. Meale (1993), pp. 159–82.

44 C.H. Cooper, *Annals of Cambridge*, vol. 1 (Cambridge, 1842), p. 121.

45 Geneviève Dumas, 'Les femmes et les pratiques de la santé dans le 'Registre des plaidoiries du Parlement de Paris, 1364–1427', *Canadian Bulletin of Medical History* 13 (1996), 3–27; Monica H. Green, *Making Women's Medicine Masculine: The Rise of Male Authority in Pre-Modern Gynaecology* (Oxford, 2008), pp. xiii–xiv.

46 Daniel Klerman, 'Was the Jury Ever Self Informing?', in *Judicial Tribunals in England and Europe, 1200–1700*, ed. by Maureen Mulholland and Brian Pullan (Manchester, 2003), pp. 58–9; Anthony Musson, 'Twelve Good Men and True? The Character of Early Fourteenth-Century Juries', *LHR* 15 (1997), 115–44, 126; Edward Powell, 'Jury Trial at Gaol Delivery in the Late Middle Ages: The Midland Circuit, 1400–29', in *Twelve Good Men and True: The Criminal Trial Jury in England, 1200–1800*, ed. by J.S. Cockburn and Thomas A. Green (Princeton, NJ, 1988), pp. 78–116, 115. Green, 'Retrospective on

between courtroom witnesses (providers of evidence) and jurors (makers of decisions based on evidence from others) was not clearly present until at least the sixteenth century.[47] In addition, the modern lawyer's conception of 'acting as a witness' amalgamates a number of functions – giving sworn testimony in court, being examined and cross-examined by lawyers and having the testimony weighed up and applied or discounted in reaching a verdict – which were not necessarily seen as pertaining to one role, with a single set of rules, in the medieval common law.[48] Scholars have noted the lack of existing contemporary accounts of criminal procedure and of such matters as the use of witnesses, and there is equally little on the provenance of evidence in 'civil' cases.[49] Despite these layers of uncertainty, however, there are some discernible facts and enough evidence to make some general suggestions about women's role in these areas.

Women were not jurors, in the sense of being summoned to 'try' the issue in the normal course of procedure in land cases or other 'civil' cases at common law, nor were they petty or presentment jurors in 'criminal' cases.[50] The one female institution described as a jury – the 'jury of matrons' for assessing whether or not a woman was pregnant with a 'quick' foetus – is important, but limited in its scope, not being given the task of deciding on the substance of a case in the 'criminal' sphere and often being subject to male supervision in its 'civil' incarnation, at least in the thirteenth century. It is dealt with below. The *Mirror of Justices* states a prohibition on women jurors in the general sense, but a specific attempt at explanation of their exclusion from jury service is not easily to be found before Blackstone's intellectually unsatisfying statement that they are ineligible *propter defectum sexus*.[51] Medieval statutory provisions relating to jury qualification have nothing to say about women: their concern is ensuring the presence of enough jurors of sufficient property and proximity.[52] Over the course of the medieval period, a larger body of males may have become possible jurors: the 'democratizing' of the

---

the Criminal Trial Jury', pp. 370–4; Baker, *OHLE VI*, pp. 361–2; David J. Seipp, 'Jurors, Evidences and the Tempest of 1499', in *The Dearest Birth Right of the People of England: The Jury in the History of the Common Law*, ed. by J.W. Cairns and G. McLeod, (Oxford: Hart, 2002) c. 5.

47 Barbara J. Shapiro, 'Oaths, Credibility and the Legal Process in Early Modern England: Part One', *Law and Humanities* 6 (2012), 145–78, 153.

48 See, e.g., 21 *SS*, pp. xxx–xxxii; Jenkins, 'Towards the Jury', p. 27.

49 Bellamy, *Criminal Trial*, p. 8. Fortescue's criticism of civilian systems' use of witnesses (rather than juries), *Fortescue, De Laudibus Legum Angliae* cc. 21, 31.

50 *Fleta* book II c. 12: if needed, villeins could be on coroners' juries, but no suggestion women could be.

51 *Mirror* book I c. 17; *Bl. Comm.* book III, c. 23; Judy M. Cornett, 'Hoodwink'd by Custom: The Exclusion of Women from Juries in Eighteenth-Century English Law and Literature', *William & Mary Journal of Women & Law* 4 (1997), 1–89, 15.

52 See, e.g., st. Westminster II c. 38, *SR* 1, p. 89; st. 21 Edw. I (1293), *SR* I, 113; st. 28 Edw. I, c. 9, *SR* I, p. 139; st. 34 Edw. III c. 4, *SR* I, p. 365; st. 42 Edw. III c. 11, *SR* I, p. 389; st. 2 Hen. V c. 3, *SR* II, p. 188, st. 1 Ric. III c. 4, *SR* II, p. 479; st. 11 Hen. VII c. 26, *SR* II, 590; Masschaele *Jury* 130.

criminal trial jury has been noted.[53] This could only widen the gap between the participation of men and women in the legal process, since there was never any suggestion of women serving as trial jurors. We should not see the exclusion only through the lens of modern ideals of civic participation, since there are many indications that being a juror in medieval England was burdensome and possibly risky, and that not being put on a jury was seen in some quarters as a favour.[54] Nevertheless, given the increase in scope of the activities of the jury (or jury-like institutions) throughout the medieval period, drawing significant and increasing parts of the male population into contact with government and law while excluding women meant that there was an increasing gap between male and female engagement with the machinery of the legal process, making participation in the common law in a 'non-party' way increasingly more masculine.[55]

Medieval common law did not leave a definitive account of suitable and unsuitable witnesses,[56] so that it is difficult to assess with any specificity the thinking behind rules or conventions as to qualification for the role.[57] Early royal inquiries might sometimes have used female witnesses. Evidence deriving from women was accepted, in the Domesday inquests and in twelfth-century inquiries into widows and children over whom the king had rights.[58] Common law records of the later medieval period did not generally include comment on witnesses, if they were present. Reports may give fleeting references to witnessing. For example, a 1315 dower case referred to the need for 'witnesses present at a marriage'. No qualifications beyond presence at the marriage were mentioned, but in fact only men were recorded as having been used.[59] Elsewhere, the emphasis is on witnesses being a certain age and having assets by which they might be distrained.[60] Given prevailing property regimes, the latter of these criteria favoured male witnesses. Jury lists, where these exist (and except in those relating to the 'jury of matrons', who might be classed, in modern terms, as witnesses as much as jurors), feature only men.[61]

53 Green, *Verdict*, p. 22. Clearly, only men were included.

54 See, e.g., Hyams, 'Maitland and the Rest of Us', p. 227, *P & M* I, pp. 483–4.

55 Masschaele, *Jury*, c. 5.

56 See: Helmholz *OHLE* I, c. 5 and pp. 604–25; Mike Macnair, 'Vicinage and the Antecedents of the Jury', *LHR* 17 (1999), 537–90, 554, and Klerman, 'Was the Jury Ever Self-Informing', p. 74.

57 Bellamy, *Criminal Trial*, p. 25. Note also that the common law idea of 'testimony' was not only a human process, records 'testify to' facts: *Seipp* 1309.124ss; 1309.180ss; 1311.020ss.

58 Van Houts, 'Gender', 208; Robin Fleming, *Domesday Book and the Law. Society and Legal Custom in Early Medieval England* (Cambridge, 1998), p. 260, no. 1658; p. 45, n. 66; *Rotuli de Dominabus et Pueris et Puellis de XII Comitatibus*, ed. by J.H. Round (London, 1913).

59 *Seipp* 1315.064ss; CP 40/211 m. 75 (IMG 150).

60 *Seipp* 1342.124rs (querying of underage witness). Distraint: *Seipp* 1318.021ss; 1334.065 st. 12 Edw. II, c. 2, *SR* I, p. 177. The requirement for landownership emphasised in relation to jurors: *Seipp* 1309.137ss.

61 Men disqualified from legal process because of misbehaviour as jurors: *Glanvill* II, 19; *Seipp* 1350.147, 1332.204ass; 1356.139ass; Jonathan Rose, 'Litigation and Political

The common law did not articulate whether and when women could be witnesses.[62] Medieval 'learned laws', which had a more clear-cut 'witness' function, included more overt statements. Canon law sources stated a prohibition, based on the barring of women from acting in 'civil or public functions'.[63] Even here, however, there is not one simple attitude to women's participation. There were statements against women witnessing on grounds of overall weakness or mental inconstancy, but the matter was not beyond argument, and civil and canon law sources often set out exclusions, only to give copious exceptions to them, and to assume that women would in fact give evidence at times, since the weight of their evidence was also discussed.[64] English church court material shows that women did perform witnessing functions in ecclesiastical legal process, including making depositions, and occasionally acting as a sort of 'expert witness', examining men's bodies, in cases in which impotence was alleged, and those of women, in relation to virginity.[65] In making any comparison with the common law, it should be borne in mind that 'witnessing' here might be done outside the court setting, and so, while concerns about women's character and capacities might apply in both jurisdictions, concerns about authoritiative public speech did not.[66] Other bodies of 'secular' law show both explicit exclusion of women from witness roles and also a range of

Conflict in Fifteenth-Century East Anglia: Conspiracy and Attaint Actions and Sir John Fastolf', *JLH* 27 (2006), 53–80, 61–2; 58 *SS*, liv–lxxi; David Millon, 'Positivism and Historiography of the Common Law', *Wisconsin Law Review* (1989), 684–700, 686.

62 Butler, *Forensic Medicine*, pp. 130–1. *P & M* 1, p. 467 (suit).

63 Van Houts, 'Gender', pp. 201–20, 202–3; Gratian, *Decretum*, Part ii, Causa 33, question 5, no. xvii (*Corpus Iuris Canonici*, ed. A. Friedberg (Leipzig, 1879), p. 1255; women should not act as witnesses, even in marriage litigation; if they did so, their evidence should be treated with scepticism. Roman law implicitly countenanced the idea of female witness at a trial: *D.* 50, 17, 2; *D.* 22.5.4; 22.5.18.

64 James Brundage, 'Juridical Space: Female Witnesses in Canon Law', *Dumbarton Oaks Papers* 52 (1998), 147–56; Helmholz, *OHLE* I, pp. 339–40; C. Donahue, 'Proof by Witnesses in the Church Courts of Medieval England: An Imperfect Reception of the Learned Law', in *On the Laws and Customs*, ed. by Arnold, (Chapel Hill, NC: University of North Carolina Press, 1981), pp. 127–58, 130; G.R. Evans, *Law and Theology* (London, 2002), p. 149; Sarah B. White, 'The Procedure and Practice of Witness Testimony in English Ecclesiastical Courts, c.1193–1300', *Studies in Church History* 56 (2020), 114–30; Kane, *Popular Memory*, p. 49; Walter Ullman, 'Medieval Principles of Evidence', *LQR* 62 (1946), 77–87, 81 (civilian sources). Note the greater value given to male than to female testimony in the case of a clash: Donahue, 'Proof by Witnesses', p. 131, Tancred, *Ordo*, 3.12. On decreasing use of women's testimony: Kane, *Popular Memory*, p. 50; Goldberg, *Women in England*, p. 38.

65 Donahue, 'Proof by Witnesses', pp. 151–2; Goldberg, *Women in England*, pp. 58–80, 103–17, 156; Kim M. Phillips, 'The Breasts of Virgins: Sexual Reputation and Young Women's Bodies in Medieval Culture and Society', *Cultural and Social History* 15 (2018), 1–19, 10; Bronach Kane, *Impotence and Virginity in the Late Medieval Ecclesiastical Court of York* (York, 2008).

66 Helmholz, *OHLE* I, p. 338; White, 'Procedure and Practice', p. 117.

explicitly 'allowed female witnessing areas'.[67] Norman and Welsh law sources, for example, both included explicit limitations on women's capacity to act as a witness and explicit permission for them to act in this way in particular circumstances: in cases concerning pregnancy, 'deflowering', live birth, marriage and proof of age in the case of Normandy and in relation to virginity, but explicitly not as surety or testifier in relation to a man, or as compurgators in cases of theft or for homicide in the case of Wales.[68] Sources relating to practice in Brittany have been taken to suggest acceptance of women if no man was available,[69] and Beaumanoir's late thirteenth-century *Coutumes de Beauvaisis* grudgingly accepted the value of women's testimony as confirmation of male testimony or where there was no male testimony available, and considered the special issues relating to the credibility of women's testimony with regard to a husband or kinsman.[70] English manorial courts also gave women a considerably lesser role than men.[71]

Common law treatises, to the extent that they discuss witnesses and evidence, usually assume masculine subjects, and rarely have anything to say about women in this context.[72] *Bracton*'s expression of concern about poor sources of information for juries, for example, relates to credence being given to the words of those who are unworthy, not to the words of a woman.[73] Reports of medieval common law cases occasionally mention female evidence being taken, in the sense of women being questioned in relation to information they might be able to give about an offence. In a case of homicide from 1235, the record suggests that witnesses were examined one by one, and notes that these included 'two women and a girl'.[74] Appeal cases involved women in telling sometimes lengthy stories, and show some blurring of the 'witness' and 'accuser' roles, especially in relation to widows' appeals

67 Van Houts, 'Gender', pp. 210–11; *Coutumes de Beauvaisis*, c. 40, para. 1259, c. 5, para 185; c. 29, para. 815; ch. 39, paras 1175–6, 1182; Walter Ullman, 'Defence of the Accused in the Medieval Inquisition', *Law and Jurisdiction in the Middle Ages*, ed. by G. Garnett (Aldershot: Ashgate, 1988), no. xv, 481–9, at 486.

68 *Le Grand Coutumier de Normandie*, ed. by Judith Everard (Jersey, 2009), cc. 41, 66, 121, 123, 125. Jenkins, *Hywel Dda, The Law*, pp. 49, 57, 60. See also Christine Ekholst, *A Punishment for each Crime: Gender and Crime in Swedish Medieval Law* (Boston, MA, 2014), p. 21: general exclusion, exceptions including live birth.

69 Judith Everard, 'Sworn Testimony and Memory of the Past in Brittany c. 1100–1250', in *Medieval Memories: Men, Women and the Past, 700–1300*, ed. by Elisabeth van Houts (London and New York, 2013), c. 4.

70 Elisabeth van Houts, 'Introduction', in *Medieval Memories*, p. 6; *The Coutumes of Philippe de Beaumanoir*, tr. by F.R.P. Akehurst (Philadelphia, PA, 1992), Chapter 39, no. 1197, p. 433; *Coutumes de Beauvaisis*, Chapter 39, para. 1182.

71 Wilkinson, *Women*, p. 139.

72 *Glanvill* VII, 6 (wills). Note the similar lack of clarity in relation to young witnesses: *Seipp* 1342.124rs; CP 40/330 m. 284 (IMG 581). *Bracton* IV, p. 248, rules out members of one household, but says nothing about sex.

73 Kamali, *Felony*, p. 261; *Bracton* II, p. 404. The passage uses masculine plurals.

74 F.W. *Maitland*, 'The Murder of Henry Clement', *EHR* 10 (1895), 294–7; *Somersetshire Pleas*, p. 21.

for the death of their husbands. Thus, for example, Alice, wife of Ellis of Ipswich, showed that, as she was on her way to market, she heard men plotting her husband's death, then saw the attack and death.[75] In this context, as we will see in Chapter 5, it was, until the fourteenth century, necessary for women to cast themselves in the role of eye-witness to the offence or demise. Other areas of legal practice show regular use of male witnesses only; for example, although the procedure varies in some ways, records of witnesses to deal with disputes as to whether somebody is in fact alive or dead in dower and some other land cases appear to include male witnesses only.[76] Whether or not there was thought to be a rule against women witnesses, there might well be good tactical reasons not to use women as witnesses, if their evidence was liable to be disbelieved, in the event of a clash with that of men.

There are some discussions of women bearing witness – and their rejection in this capacity – in relation to the proof of the villein status of men. In a case in the plea roll of the Lincolnshire eyre of 1271–2, men claimed as villeins are shown objecting to two women (their sisters) being used to prove their villein status.[77] Records and reports of *Ralph of Lamplugh v. Thomas Bowman*, a dispute as to an individual's free or villein status, from the 1279 eyre of Northumberland, pronounced that women were excluded from being witnesses in such cases. It gave two purported justifications for this: the 'facts' that women are of a 'more delicate nature than men' and that 'the male ... is more worthy than the woman'.[78] The reports do not suggest a full ban on female evidence in all cases, however. It is acknowledged that female witness might be heard in matrimonial disputes. It also appears that there was perceived to be a particular problem with women contributing to a decision regarding a man,[79] because men (and 'men's blood') were inherently superior to them and theirs.[80] *Fleta* too stressed the fact that the inappropriateness of female participation was in relation to male status.[81] Such an idea seems to have been influential elsewhere,[82] and seems to combine two

75 62 *SS*, p. 305, *CRR VII*, pp. 49–50.

76 See, e.g., JUST 1/1045 m. 44d (IMG 1635); JUST 1/60 m. 4 (IMG 1561); CP 40/92 m. 138d (IMG 735); 59 *SS* no 192.

77 The objection is not decisive, and the case is tried by jury. JUST 1/483 m. 3 (IMG 1965).

78 JUST 1/648 m. 7 (IMG 2718); JUST 1/ 645 m. 3 (IMG 2444); JUST 1/1059 m. 47 (IMG 4485); *Seipp* 1279.005ss. See 122 *SS* pp. 67–70; *P & M* II, p. 668.

79 122 *SS* pp. 67–70; *P & M* II, p. 668. JUST 1/648 m. 7 (IMG 2718) and JUST1/1059 m. 47 (IMG 4485); JUST 1/645 m. 3 (IMG 2444); *Seipp* 1279.005ss.

80 *Seipp* 1279.005ss. On 'greater worthiness' of male blood (with regard to inheritance): *Seipp* 1306.136rs.

81 *Fleta* book 2, c. 51; *Britton* book 1, c. 32 no. 20.

82 *Welsh Law of Women*, p. 19; Jenkins, 'Towards the Jury in Medieval Wales', in *Dearest Birth Right*, ed. by Cairns and G. McLeod, c. 2, p. 37. Goldberg, *Women in England*, pp. 123, 185 (purgation). Local jurisdictions: 18 *SS* pp. 185–6, 196, 21 *SS* p. xxx. *P & M* I, pp. 467–8; *RP* I, 146–7. (canonical purgation). *P & M* loc. cit state that 'apparently in the king's court a woman had to find male oath-helpers', citing *BNB*, pl. 7: the latter shows that a woman did use men, though it is not clear that she was obliged to do so.

separate strands: the inferiority of women and the particular lack of 'fit' of their pronouncing upon men.[83] Possible support for female witness with regard to status of men may, however, be found in the case of John Powderham, a man claiming to be (or to be related to) Edward II, who was executed in 1318. One of the chronicle sources dealing with the episode states that both his father and his mother were brought to court to swear to his origins, at his trial before the king and council. Clearly this was not a normal common law proceeding, and it was presumably the fact that the mother would be best placed to know that she, and not a royal lady, had given birth to John which led to her inclusion rather than a general concession as to the credibility of female witness, but it does show some worth being placed upon female testimony in this area, despite expressions of reluctance to use it which can be seen elsewhere.[84] There is also occasional discussion and evidence of women as witnesses in relation to reproduction, pregnancy or gynaecological state of other women, presentment of Englishry and the *murdrum* fine.

There is interesting evidence about women's witness in connection with an aspect of the property rights of men: tenancy 'by the curtesy of England'. A man claiming this right to hold his wife's lands for life was required to have produced a live child with her during their marriage.[85] If there was a dispute as to whether a baby, now dead, had ever lived, would the word of women, likely, in many cases, to be the only first-hand and immediate witnesses of life or its absence, be acceptable?[86] There are statements from reports of cases in the 1270s and 1280s which suggest the exclusion of women's testimony, and perhaps the exclusion of evidence derived from women, in curtesy cases:

> [W]omen are not received by inquisitions in the king's court ..., nor can it be established to the court whether there was a child born alive or not, unless it has been by men either seen or heard to cry by them ...[87]
>
> Women are not admitted to proof in the king's court in such a case.[88]

These statements do not suffice to show timeless hostility to the idea of female witness in such cases, however. They may represent a new and

83 Everard, 'Public Authority', p. 127; *LHP* p. 135; *Magna Carta* 1215 c. 39.
84 Childs, 'Welcome My Brother', p. 152.
85 Baker, *Introduction*, pp. 290–1; Hudson, *OHLE* II p. 788; Glanvill VII, 18; Gwen Seabourne, 'It is necessary that the issue be heard to cry or squall within the four [walls]: Qualifying for Tenancy by the Curtesy of England in the Reign of Edward I', *JLH* 40 (2019), 44–68.
86 See Seabourne, 'It is Necessary', pp. 62–7. On men's exclusion (or not) from childbirth, see Monica H. Green, '"Diseases of Women" to "Secrets of Women": The Transformation of Gynecological Literature in the Later Middle Ages', *Journal of Medieval and Early Modern Studies* 30 (2000), 5–39; Green, *Making Women's Medicine Masculine*; F. Harris-Stoertz, 'Pregnancy and Childbirth in Twelfth-and Thirteenth-Century French and English Law', *Journal of the History of Sexuality* 21 (2012), 263–81, 263.
87 Extract from *John Cantilupe's Case*, 1276–77 in *P & M* II, pp. 412–18, 416; *Placitorum Abbreviatio* (1811), p. 267. See also KB 27/29 m. 1. (IMG 8053) KB 27/30 m. 2 (IMG 8197).
88 JUST 1/1245 m. 95d (IMG 6462) (1284).

short-lived initiative in the reign of Edward I, and appear to relate only to women giving evidence in court proceedings themselves, as opposed to providing information which could be used in legal proceedings. Even in the later thirteenth century, there are cases which show some credence for female evidence in this context. Assuming that there was not a man present at the birth, at least some consultation of females is implied when jurors are recorded to have mentioned that a child was born dead, or moved, then died soon after birth.[89] Acceptance and reliance on the evidence of women whilst excluding them as legitimate and authoritative speakers in court is also apparent in records of 'proof of age' inquests, to determine whether an heir is of age, in which only males are recorded as witnesses to the inquest, but no secret is made of the fact that some of their testimony is derived from information supplied by a woman.[90]

Though *Bracton* and other sources reproduce old ideas that midwives or other women might be deceitful with regard to reports of births,[91] no rule against women's evidence in curtesy/life cases is mentioned in any of the treatise or Year Book formulations. Nor do most of the later sources suggest a general contemporary idea that women's accounts should be excluded in this context.[92] That the very idea of taking women's evidence seriously was not rejected can also be seen in a 1259 Kent case relating to a widow's rights in land, governed by local/manorial law, but brought to the attention of royal justices.[93] The plea roll notes an assize which was summoned to ask whether John de Watton and four other men had unjustly disseised Denise of Wormdale of land. John and the others denied wrongdoing, their story being that Denise had held the land by way of freebench (roughly equivalent to dower), but had lost this right by court order (so not unjustly) because she had been found by the court of Milton Regis to have had a baby during her

89 See, e.g., (1251) JUST 1/1046 m. 10d (IMG 1843); (1276) JUST 1/663 m. 3 (IMG 3688); (1279–81) JUST 1/1055 m. 9 (IMG 2989); (1288) JUST 1/1281A m. 7 (IMG 2707); *JUST 1/1294 m.8d (IMG 3893) (*1290–1); 1292 JUST 1/985 m. (IMG 917); (1292) JUST 1/302 m. 3d (IMG 8243); JUST 1/303 m. 6 (IMG 8644); (1295) JUST 1/625 m.35 (IMG 290); KB 27/29 m. 1 (IMG 8053).

90 Lee, 'A Company of Women and Men', p. 93; Sue Sheridan Walker, 'Proof of Age of Feudal Heirs in Medieval England', *Mediaeval Studies* 35 (1973), 306–23, at pp. 308, 314.

91 *Bracton* IV, p. 361; *Fleta* book VI, c. 55; W.R. Childs, '"Welcome My Brother": Edward II, John of Powderham and the Chronicles, 1318', *Church and Chronicle in the Middle Ages: Essays Presented to John Taylor*, ed. by I. Wood and G.A. Loud (London, 1991), p. 151. Harris-Stoertz, 'Pregnancy and Childbirth', p. 265; *Bracton* II, pp. 201–7, IV, p. 299; III, p. 311; *Fleta*, book I, c. 15.

92 21 *SS*, p. 112, *Le Grand Coutumier de Normandie*, ed. by Everard, pp. 546, 548, 578, 586; cc. 123, 125; E.V. Tardif ed *Coutumes de Normandie* (2 vols, Rouen, 1896) vol. 2 p. 307 c. CXIX. No discussion of women's exclusion: *Litt.*, book I, c. 4; 8 Co Rep 34a; Co. Litt. book 1 c. 4 s. 35.

93 Andrew Hershey, *An Introduction to and Edition of the Hugh Bigod Eyre Rolls, June 1258–February 1259: P.R.O. Just 1/1187 & Just 1/873.* B266.(T), B290.[Kent] B266. JUST 1/873 mm.14 and 16 (IMG 9276, 9279).

widowhood, and since it was the custom there that this ended freebench, the land had been taken by court order.[94] At the court of Milton Regis, the evidence leading to Denise's loss of the land had come from two women, who said that they were present when Denise gave birth in a cellar in Wormdale. Their testimony was taken to be worthy of weight. An idea that there was a strong and long-standing rule of exclusion of women's evidence in relation to live birth would not sit well with women's particularly prominent role in proof in relation to other matters of reproduction, to which we will turn next. When legal proceedings needed to resolve a question as to the pregnancy or virginity of a woman, or whether she had given birth recently, the common law, like other systems, was prepared to give women a role.[95] The need for a decision as to whether or not a woman was pregnant came up in two main contexts: succession to land and felony.[96]

A disputed claim of pregnancy could cast property rights into uncertainty for a considerable time. A good example of this can be seen in relation to the situation following the death of Gilbert de Clare at Bannockburn, when the possible pregnancy of his widow, Maud de Burgh, delayed the distribution of his lands between his sisters.[97] From an early period, there are examples in the records of disputes over whether or not a widow was pregnant with her husband's child. Such a child might displace the heir apparent (often a brother of the husband). There was a need to determine whether there was a pregnancy (as well, at times, as a need to deal with a challenge to a baby's legitimacy). In a disputed parentage case of 1211, enquiry as to whether a child was the biological child of those claiming to be its parents was at least partly 'by lawful men and women'.[98] This case was looking backwards, to a

94 Hershey, *Introduction*, B266.(T). On the custom of losing freebench in this way, see T. Robinson, *The Common Law of Kent or the Customs of Gavelkind* (1788), 162–4 1st edn 1741, 162–7; and CP 40/14 m. 21d (IMG 4782); JUST 1/1255 m. 11d (IMG 73); KB 27/333 m. 32 (IMG 65); JUST 1/1412 m. 1 (0791).

95 For 'legal matrons' in Normandy from at least the late twelfth century, see Van Houts, 'Gender', p. 204.

96 See, in particular, J.C. Oldham, 'On "Pleading the Belly": A Concise History of the Jury of Matrons', *Criminal Justice History* 6 (1985), 1–64; Sara M. Butler, 'Pleading the Belly: A Sparing Plea? Pregnant Convicts and the Courts in Medieval England', in *Crossing Borders*, ed. by Butler and Kesselring (Leiden: Brill, 2018), pp. 131–52; Sara M. Butler, 'More than Mothers: Juries of Matrons and Pleas of the Belly in Medieval England', *LHR* 37 (2019), 1–44; Harris-Stoertz, 'Pregnancy and Childbirth'; F. Harris-Stoertz, 'Midwives in the Middle Ages: Birth Attendants 600–1300', in *Medicine and the Law in the Middle Ages*, ed. by W.J. Turner and S.M. Butler (Leiden, 2014), pp. 58–871; *Bracton* II, pp. 201–3; *Fleta* book 1 c. 31. For impotence, female evidence: Helmholz: *OHLE* I, pp. 549–50, Jacqueline Murray, 'On the Origins and Role of 'Wise Women' in Causes for Annulment on the Grounds of Male Impotence', *JMH* 16 (1990), 235–49.

97 J.R.S. Phillips, *Edward II* (New Haven, CT and London, 2010), pp. 243, 269; Michael Altschul, 'Clare, Gilbert de, eighth earl of Gloucester and seventh earl of Hertford (1291–1314) *ODNB*.

98 Masschaele, *Jury*, p. 31; *CRR* VI, p. 169 (1211).

pregnancy no longer persisting. From the reign of Henry III onwards, there is evidence of a more formal procedure, under the writ *de ventre inspiciendo*, for women claiming to be pregnant at the time of the dispute.[99] The role of women in this procedure was prominent, though there are interesting traces of a perceived need for male supervision, perhaps reflecting the suspicion shown in treatises and narrative sources that false claims would be made to keep heirs out of 'their' land.[100] There might be a requirement that the examination was to be conducted by women, but with some form of male involvement.[101] Some versions of the writ suggest that examining groups should include men, but other accounts suggest women acting alone as examiners.[102] The *de ventre insipiciendo* procedure continued to be valid in and beyond the fifteenth century.[103]

In addition to the land-related cases, women were used to determine whether a woman was pregnant, when she had been convicted of felony and sentenced to death. There are recorded instances of this procedure from the early fourteenth century onwards, and the likelihood is that this was also the practice at an earlier date, since groups of women, or groups including women, were being used for other inquiries relating to pregnancy and rape in the thirteenth century.[104] The terminology encountered in relation to these women is not constant. They may be called 'women', 'matrons', or 'midwives', and described in terms of good standing and character ('lawful', discreet', 'creditworthy', 'wise') or age (presumably importing an idea of experience).[105] There has been discussion of which women were regarded as appropriate to make these determinations, or serve on 'juries of

99 60 *SS*, pp. clii. The *de ventre inspiciendo* procedure used or ordered: *CPR 1247–58* p. 222; *CRR XX (1250)* p. 141 no 844; *CRR XVII 1242–3* pp. 30–1 no 121. *Britton*, book III c. 2 no. 13 – oath, articles, presentment. *CRR IV* p. 212 (1206): four married couples to see whether a woman was pregnant or had borne a child by her husband.

100 *Bracton* II, p. 201; *Fleta*, book I c. 15; *P & M* I, pp. 381, 389; C 245/1, no. 23. *Britton* book 3 c. 2 no 13–15. *CRR XVII 1242–3* pp. 30–1, no 121, orders inspection by women in the presence of men.

101 See the 1221 case in 60 *SS*, pp. cliii – *BNB* 1503; pl 1605, pl 137; *Bracton* II, p. 203.

102 See, e.g., *CRR IV* 212 (1206); *BNB* pl. 137, 198, 1503, 1605; 87 *SS*, p. 75; *CPR 1247–58* p. 222; *Fleta* book 1 c. 15; *Seipp* 1422.042ss; 50 *SS* pp. 24–7.

103 *Seipp* 1422.042ss; 50 *SS* pp. 24–7; mention of the writ, 1503: 116 *SS* p. 420.

104 Butler, 'More than Mothers', p. 14, JUST 3/104, m. 15d. Butler, 'Pleading the Belly', p. 138, notes 1220s use of women to examine rape victim: *Pleas of the Crown for the Hundred of Swineshead and Township of Bristol*, ed. by E.J. Watson (Bristol, 1902), pp. 133–4, no 15. Rape complainants examined by a mixed group (1241) by a jury of women, whose verdict was to be confirmed by a male jury (1282): JUST 1/359 m.35d (IMG 3219); JUST 3/35B m. 38. For thirteenth century, 'mixed juries' of examination of women claiming pregnancy or male supervision, see Masschaele *Jury* c. 4, p. 130; *CRR* XVII, pp. 30–1; *BNB* no 1605; *CRR* IV, p. 212. Sometimes (male) jurors are required to pronounce upon the existence of a past pregnancy: CP 40/179 m. (IMG 43).

105 *Bracton* II, p. 202 (civil context); JUST 1/966 m. 7 (IMG 8917); *CPR 1436–41*, 357. Maddern, *Violence and Social Order,* p. 71; JUST 3/210 m. 16r (IMG 35); JUST 3.137A m 23 (1352) (IMG 49); Butler, 'More than Mothers', p. 18; JUST 3/45/1, m. 5 (1332); *CPR*

matrons', with consideration of the level of expertise expected, and whether this may have changed with changing ideas about the value and appropriate treatment of the foetus.[106] The idea of constructing and labelling the inspecting women as a 'jury' was present in the early fourteenth century, and by the late fourteenth century, documents describe it, and suggest it was chosen in a way which increasingly resembles the (male) petty jury.[107] Records occasionally say a little more about how the matrons proceeded – e.g. palpation of the belly, examination of the breasts and questioning – or how their participation is regarded.[108] Despite suggestions that juries of matrons colluded in fictitious findings of pregnancy in order to spare other women execution, it has been demonstrated that this is not substantiated for the medieval and early modern period. By no means all who claimed pregnancy were found to be pregnant, sometimes there is a confirmatory record that women found pregnant did in fact give birth, and people did not behave as if a positive finding was guaranteed: claims of pregnancy were not universal.[109] No doubt there were mistakes, but these were not necessarily all in one direction.

The use of women in determinations of pregnancy or non-pregnancy for legal purposes had Roman law antecedents, and one might deduce rationales for it based on expertise (assumed or actual) or on perceived inappropriateness of males making such investigations in relation to birth and women's bodies.[110] To a certain extent, common lawyers displayed a disinclination to involve themselves in the area of female reproductive matters. They were uncertain – or affected uncertainty – about some aspects of pregnancy.[111] The work of the matrons was described in mysterious terms, as looking for 'private signs' of pregnancy, and doubt was expressed in the fifteenth-century courtroom about the duration of pregnancy (one fifteenth-century serjeant memorably suggesting that it might last seven years).[112] Earlier

1436–41, p. 356. The terminology resembles canon law's 'honest and prudent matrons', used to discern the fact of a woman's virginity. Helmholz, *OHLE* 1 p. 337.

106 Oldham, 'On Pleading', p. 15; *Bl. Comm.* book IV c. 31; Butler, 'Pleading', p. 138; Butler 'More than Mothers'.

107 Butler, 'Pleading', p. 138; JUST 3/174 m. 2 (1387); JUST 3/178 m. 9d (1393) JUST 3.177 m. 101 (1396). See also JUST 3/188 m. 25 (IMG 70) and m. 89 (IMG 219); JUST 3/177 m. 49.

108 JUST 3/189 m. 5 (IMG 13); CPR 1436–41, 357. Maddern, *Violence and Social Order*, p. 71; JUST 3/210 m. 16r (IMG 35), matrons to inspect her body and 'secrets'.

109 See Chapter 6. Successful pleas, e.g., JUST 3/113 m. 6d (IMG 27); unsuccessful, e.g., JUST 3/220 m.182 (IMG 243); JUST 3/173 m. 26 (IMG 61). Birth noted, e.g., JUST 3/36/1 m. 7 (IMG 17).

110 Oldham, 'On Pleading the Belly', p. 2; *D.* 25.4.5.10.

111 For disagreement about the consequences of exceeding the gestation period in legitimacy cases, see Harris Stoertz, 'Pregnancy and Childbirth', p. 280; *Bracton* II, pp. 203–4.

112 Butler, 'More than Mothers', p. 28; *Seipp* 1422.042ss. The expression is 'par vii ans', which is translated in 50 SS p. 25 as 'after seven years of age', but the context suggests length of gestation rather than maternal age. It is tempting to speculate as to whether this statement represents humour, the adoption of a 'tall tale' of lengthy gestation, or a corruption

treatises did not seem as uncertain, however, positing a fairly accurate gestation period,[113] and jurors did not necessarily shrink back from answering questions on women's pregnancies and the circumstances in which they began. A good example may be seen in a 1314 assize case turning on the legitimacy of one Agnes. The jurors said that she had been born one year and three weeks after her putative father's death, that the mother had not seemed pregnant straight after this death, 'had told neighbours that she was not pregnant, and she was seen and examined by those neighbours and found not pregnant'. They were asked about opinion as to the mother's 'incontinence' after her husband's death, and felt able to answer that another man was reputed to be Agnes's father and the spouses had no surviving child.[114] Examination of women was not always seen as something inappropriate or impossible for men. In the case of a woman making an essoin of ill-health, i.e. claiming to be unable to attend court because she was too ill, the procedure was apparently inspection by knights, as with men, and there is evidence that this was carried out. Thus, for example, in 1194, four knights viewed and confirmed the sickness of a woman, Margaret, wife of David of Peachley, and even a prioress might be inspected in this way.[115] Judges also made an assessment of the maturity of girls or young women in some cases, considering themselves perfectly capable of judging their age through physical inspection.[116] The state of medieval common lawyers' knowledge – or admitted knowledge – about women's bodies and their reproductive capacities is a matter of some uncertainty.

Proof of pregnancy might rely on the 'matrons', but in some cases, at least in cases of proving the absence of pregnancy, the common law used other mechanisms. The woman's own word might be given some weight, as might a more general inspection. In an assize case of 1287, the parties were in dispute as to whether John (brother of Robert) or Henry (perhaps his posthumous child) was entitled to the land formerly held by Robert from Ralph. Henry was born 40 weeks and 11 days after Robert's death, and considerably longer after the point at which it was likely that Robert could have impregnated Henry's mother, Beatrix. Ralph was stated to have acted upon Beatrix's sworn statement that she was pregnant with Robert's child. The jurors, however, stated that after Robert's death, Ralph had held an

of a statement about the possibility of deeming H2 to be the father of a child born at seven *months* into a marriage, which had been entered into straight after the death of H1.

113 *Bracton* II, 203; *Britton*, book 3, c. 2 no. 15 (40-week presumption).

114 JUST 1/1350 m. 995d (IMG 995).

115 67 *SS*, p. 161; *Rot. Cur. Reg.* vol 1 p. 29; 53 *SS* plea 467. On the prioress, whose inspection confirmed illness, see 67 *SS*, p. 113 and below p. XXX. On this process, see *Fleta* book VI c 99; st. Westminster II (1285) c. 17. Male inspectors are expected in writs in 87 SS pp. 27–8, no 38–9; pp. 10–11, no 29; p. 42 nos 26–8, and are seen being sent or reporting on the health of a woman claimed to be 'languid' in, e.g., 60 *SS* p. 58 no 37, *CRR* 88 (1225) m 36; 53 *SS* p. 352 no 715 (1219); 84 *SS* p. 222 no 4239 (1209).

116 See, e.g., *Seipp* 1344.154rs, 1367.041, 1401.035.

inquisition to find out who was Robert's heir. Beatrix was present and was asked whether she was pregnant or not. She swore that she was not, removed her outer clothing, and it was apparently regarded as clear that she was not (visibly) pregnant. On the strength of this, Ralph had initially received John as Robert's heir. In both versions, credence was apparently given to the assertion of Beatrix.[117]

The witness of women to birth might be accepted in other ways. They may have given evidence in some sense in 'neonaticide' cases. Thus, a Norfolk gaol delivery roll of 1381 contains an indictment of a woman who had allegedly given birth alone, killed her baby and concealed the body, evidence of this having come from a midwife and other women. The accused was acquitted, but the evidence of the women seems to have been taken seriously.[118] Women's witness to death also had some relevance, in relation to the appeals of married women, in respect of the killing of their husbands. As will be discussed in Chapter 5, for the earlier part of the period under consideration, some weight was given to the presence or witnessing of the event by the widow bringing the appeal. In relation to women's own violent death, there is an indication that in cases of death which was not immediate, their identification of the killer might be taken seriously in common law processes, as was apparently the case in the reign of Henry III, when a coroner's roll of 1269 recorded that a woman, fatally wounded in an attack on her family, had identified some of the culprits before she died.[119]

The presentment of Englishry process was a required step in dealing with suspicious deaths in parts of England in the first half of the period of this book, finally being abolished in 1340. In the period and places in which this process applied, communities were required to affirm that a dead person was 'English', or not Norman, on pain of a financial penalty.[120] In some counties, but not all, women might be used to present Englishry.[121] Rules are often stated in terms of the side of the family from which the witnesses originate (i.e. that they come from the father's side or mother's side) rather than their own sex. Equality of 'sides' is common, though some county rules favoured witnesses from the father's side, or the 'birds of a feather flock together' idea of female witnesses for female corpses, male witnesses for

117 JUST 1/11 m. 10d (IMG 115); *Plac. Abbrev.*, pp. 221, 234; KB 27/124 m.12d (IMG 7660) and m. 14 (IMG 7475); KB 27/142 m. 26 (IMG 3008), m. 26d (IMG 3137); 58 SS 33, p. 29.

118 JUST 3/164 m. 42 (IMG 86).

119 9 *SS* p. 14.

120 F.C. Hamil, 'Presentment of Englishry and the Murder Fine', *Speculum* 12 (1937), 285–98; Paul Brand, *Kings, Barons and Justices: The Making and Enforcement of Legislation in Thirteenth Century England* (Cambridge, 2003); Hudson *OHLE* II, pp. 405–9; Bruce O'Brien, 'From Mordor to Murdrum: the Preconquest Origin and Norman Revival of the Murder Fine', *Speculum* 71 (1996), 321–57. *Britton*, book I c. 2 no 15; *Fleta* book 1 c. 30; *Bracton*, II, pp. 391, 393.

121 *Bracton* II, p. 376; *Fleta* book 1 c. 30; *Somersetshire Pleas*, App. B.

male corpses.[122] The impression which is given is of a variety of local rules with different perspectives on the role of sex and family within this area: women were not necessarily incapable or untrustworthy, but some opted to exclude them. The common law thus had notice of and accommodated opposing views and practice concerning women's involvement as non-party actors in legal proceedings.

Another partly 'witness-like' function was that of 'first finder' in relation to homicide. *Bracton* made it clear that women (and minors) were potentially responsible in relation to violent deaths and must be examined by coroners.[123] Women as well as men, if present at such a death or finding a corpse, were to be identified and examined. It was to be pronounced whether they had discretion and could speak. In a sense, they were suspects, and would be held until it was decided they were not suspected.[124] There are numerous records of them acting or being treated as first finders in this way.[125] Women were also expected to raise the hue and cry – at least in cases which they would make the subject of an appeal, and might do so at other times, for offences to themselves or to others.[126] The position of 'oath-helper' or compurgator was also somewhat witness-like, and essentially involved supporting the credibility of a party rather than giving testimony as to particular facts. In common law sources, there is little information with regard whether women could act as oath helpers, as opposed to using them, and no positive evidence that they did so.[127] Local law did in some cases allow women to act as compurgators,[128] though elsewhere women might be barred from such roles.[129]

A different sort of witnessing, also relevant to the common law, was adding one's seal to a charter. There was no overt exclusion of women from this activity. Noblewomen in particular might be asked to seal and confirm a land transaction, and an increase in female attestations over the course

122 For the idea that women should be used to prove matters in relation to women and men for men, see Helmholz, *OHLE* 1, p. 15.

123 *Bracton* II, pp. 243, 342.

124 *SR* I, p. 40. *Britton* book 1 c. 2 no 5; book 1 c. 10.

125 E.g. JUST 1/569A mm. 25, 28 (IMG 8166, 8172); Butler, *Forensic Medicine*, p. 161; Hanawalt, 'Voices and Audiences', p. 162.

126 (Wife of deceased): JUST 1/804 m. 49 (IMG 2385); *Wilts GD and T* no. 141, 795 (burglary). Deceased's female servant raises hue: KB 27/282 m. 5 (IMG 306). See also Samantha Sagui, 'The Hue and Cry in Medieval Towns', *HR* 87 (2014), 179–93; Janka Rodziewicz, 'Women and the Hue and Cry in Late Fourteenth Century Great Yarmouth', in *Women, Agency and the Law*, ed. by Kane and Williamson (London: Pickering & Chatto Publishers, 2013), pp. 87–97.

127 Using them: see, e.g., Seipp 1283.012ss; 1304.008rs; 1310.039ss; 1313.456ss; 1469.074.

128 18 *SS* 1 pp. 183, 186; 21 SS p. xxx.

129 21 SS p. xxx. Women could take oaths: 132 *SS*, p. 60. They could perform the ordeal, generally that of hot iron, rather than water, see further below, p. 145 note 136. They could do homage, with adjustments: *Britton* book III, c. 4, 17.

of the twelfth century has been noted.[130] Even so, women charter witnesses remained a distinct minority, and they might not have been performing quite the same function as male charter witnesses. It is possible that married women, named in charters relating to their husbands' transactions, or widows, named in the context of their sons' transactions, were often noted less because of their inherent creditworthiness and more in order to tie them into the transaction and make it more difficult for them to challenge it later.[131] This would explain why, despite appearing on the witness lists of 'private' transactions, women do not seem to have been produced in court to confirm transactions: they were not seen as witnesses of the same type.[132] This appears to be in line with the idea, seen above in relation to curtesy and proof of age, that the main inhibition was against women performing the witness-in-court function. There is no sign that women were thought incapable of taking an oath, but, as well as a general feeling against women speaking authoritatively in court, there may perhaps have been an issue with regard to the theoretical requirement for a charter witness to fight a duel, as suggested in *Glanvill*, there being a strong assumption that this was inappropriate for a woman.[133]

Overall, the picture with regard to women's witnessing roles is far from clear. Perhaps the safest conclusion is that there were not absolute rules here. There were different ideas at play in this field, some which pushed towards women's inclusion in circumstances regarded as particularly female, perhaps especially in the dangerous and mysterious area of women's reproductive systems, and others which pushed towards exclusion or at least lesser credibility and value of women's testimony.[134] By the time the

130 Susan M. Johns, *Noblewomen, Aristocracy and Power in the Twelfth Century Anglo-Norman Realm* (Manchester, 2003), c. 5. On whether inclusion in a witness list indicates presence, see D. Broun, 'The Presence of Witnesses and the Writing of Charters', in *The Reality behind Charter Diplomatic in Anglo-Norman Britain*, ed. by Dauvit Broun (Glasgow, 2011), pp. 235–90; F.W. Maitland, 'History from the Charter Roll', *EHR* 8 (1893), 726–8, 727; Paul R. Hyams, 'The Charter as a Source for the Early Common Law', *JLH* 12 (1991), 173–89, 188–9, 182–3.

131 Note variation as to whether or not W included in H's charters, Johns *Noblewomen*, 89. 90: See also, e.g., David Postles, 'Choosing Witnesses in Twelfth-Century England', *Irish Jurist* 23 (1988), 330–46, 335.

132 Johns, *Noblewomen*, pp. 81, 86, 92–4; *P & M* 1, pp. 484–5; John Hudson, *Land, Law and Lordship in Anglo-Norman England* (Oxford, 1997), p. 142, c. 5 and c. 6; JUST 1/111 m. 2d (IMG 3772); JUST 1/183 m. 5 (IMG 1754). Debt case, male witnesses listed, e.g., CP 40/317 m. 308 (IMG 626). Note, however, the expectation that a woman might have to bear witness to the terms of a transaction: Philippa C. Maddern, 'Widows and Their Lands and Texts in Fifteenth Century Norfolk', *Parergon* 19 (2002), 123–50, 129; *TNA* E 210/4949.

133 *LHP* 5, 35; Broun, 'Presence of Witnesses', p. 273; *Glanvill*, X.12. The fact of having property in the relevant area was also important for the credit of a witness: JUST 1/418 m. 13 (IMG 2567).

134 See, e.g., M. Madero, 'Savoirs féminins et construction de la vérité: les femmes dans la preuve testimoniale en Castille au XIIIe siècle', *Crime, Histoire et Sociétés* 3 (1999), 5–21.

common law sources came to discuss witnessing and proof in a more systematic way, women were not seen to be a problem worthy of particular attention. The discussion is in terms of the need for 'credible' witnesses. Whether this means that it was settled that women could not generally be witnesses, or that they could, is not clear.[135] Concern seems to have turned to the narrower question of whether married women could give evidence against their husbands.[136] Women were, however, specifically rejected as jurors until the twentieth century.[137]

Conclusion

Women's participation in the common law as non-party actors was severely limited. The nature of this limitation, and contemporary thought around it, is, however, of far greater interest than Maitland and his followers have supposed. It is best seen not as an obvious rule with some curious but ultimately trivial exceptions, but as a highly contingent preference, based on a shifting set of justifications. Just as a woman might be excluded from parliament 'because she is a woman', exclusion of women from participation in legal processes was sometimes made explicit, a direct disapproval or barring of their participation, based on misogynist views of women's capacities and character.[138] Often, however, their exclusion was passed over in silence or was the indirect result of other, gendered, legal or social factors, such as their perceived inability to fight in trial by battle or the inferior position, in which the common law placed them with regard to property or a disinclination to allow them to speak in public with authority.[139] When there was seen to be a need to allow women's participation, medieval common lawyers, like other educated medieval men, seem to have been relaxed about criticising women's nature and competence while in fact relying upon their knowledge and information.[140] Such need was perceived in particular in

135 *Butler and Baker's Case* 3 Co. Rep. 25a, 36a–b; Statute of Frauds 2 Car. II, c. 3. Co. Litt 6b has little more to say, though logically its citing of occasions when female witnesses are not allowed suggests no general rule against female testimony. William Nelson, *Lex Testamentaria* (London, 1714), p. 578; Baker *OHLE VI* 515. Some early modern jurisdictions used women in relation to the discovery of 'witches' and rape of children: Malcolm. Gaskill, Witchcraft and Evidence in Early Modern England', *P & P* 198 (2008), 33–70, 39, 48; C. Holmes, 'Women: Witnesses and Witches', *P&P* 140 (1993), 45–78, 47, 65; Bellamy, *Criminal Trial*, p. 173; Hale, *HPC*, I, p. 633.

136 Co. Litt. 6; Anon., *A Treatise of Femes Coverts or the Lady's Law* (London, 1732), p. 109.

137 *Bl. Comm.*, Book III, c. 23.

138 *P & M* I, p. 466, *RP* IV, p. 270 (1425).

139 For disquiet about 'scolding' (particularly associated with women), see Sandy. Bardsley, *Venomous Tongues: Speech and Gender in Late Medieval England* (Philadelphia, 2006). Note, however, the need for women's personal appearance and speech in appeals: Klerman, 'Women Prosecutors', p. 307.

140 Bronach Kane, 'Women, Memory and Agency in the Medieval English Church Courts', in *Women, Agency and the Law*, ed. by Kane and Williamson, c. 3, pp. 43–62.

cases regarding other women and their bodies, and those in which choices made by the system to allow some women some rights in land meant that it was necessary to involve them. Women did perform important 'law-related' functions, from acting on a 'jury of matrons' to witnessing charters, to giving and taking homage, and their regular appearances as executors for their husbands or male relations suggests some confidence in their competence.[141]

Women's more general absence is also worthy of comment rather than dismissal. It had, no doubt, a reflective relationship with the power and authority of women, shutting them out from possibilities of influence in a social sense.[142] Legal historians should keep in mind the likelihood that this absence will have had an impact on the development and administration of the law itself as well as upon those women who found themselves before a court in a distinct minority. The nature of this impact upon the law is naturally impossible to prove, but we may see its probable influence, for example, in some of the failures to mention or choices not to mention women in prescriptive sources, as described in Chapter 1, in the more impractical metaphorical constructions of women seen in Chapter 2, and in some of the legal formulae and exculpatory or mitigating doctrines formed with a masculine paradigm in mind, which will be discussed in Chapters 5 and 6. The absence of women must be allowed its weight and importance, and neither be dismissed with a glib summary nor allowed to be overlooked in favour of occasional and attractive examples of female influence.

141 On homage, see *Glanvill* IX 1, 2 (a woman could receive but not do homage); *Bracton* II, 228 ff (she could do both); P & M II 286 (no further discussion); P & M II 338; Wilkinson, *Women*, p. 110; 100 *SS* p. 49 case 4.10; CP 40/416 m. 430, 1363M. H. Maurer *Margaret of Anjou*, 9. *PCCG*, 40: woman appears to be head of a mainpast. See also 10 *SS* p. 113 no. 116.

142 Everard, 'Power and Authority', p. 123.

Part III

Women's complaints and complaints of women

One of the band of distinguished early twentieth-century women historians engaged in transcribing and editing legal records, to the enduring benefit of all legal historians, remarked that '[t]he medieval Englishman was incurably litigious'.[1] In terms of numbers populating the plea rolls, it was indeed English*men* who predominated; though there is no exhaustive study of women as a proportion of complainants or defendants, it is clear that women are a less frequent presence in common law records than men, both as plaintiffs or accusers and as defendants. Looking at a period before the relatively standardised records of the central courts began, Van Caenegem noted the 'predictable underrepresentation' of women in twelfth-century sources referring to litigation, with less than 5% in 1161–80 and no more than 8% at other points in the century.[2] From the thirteenth century to the end of the medieval period, records are more copious, but the nature of the material, with alterations in jurisdiction and procedure, does not make it easy to draw detailed conclusions about trends in gender ratio or the reasons lying behind them. We can, however, be confident that women were always a minority presence in legal proceedings, 'civil' and 'criminal', bringing and defending actions and accusations. Some figures will suffice to show the consistently lower level of women's participation, in comparison to men, as prosecutors, claimants and defendants. Hanawalt's survey of 'crimes' in the rolls of the Lincolnshire eyre of 1202 shows women brought roughly 20% of the appeals and 17% of criminal complaints overall (the latter including all-male presentments).[3] Klerman's study of women's appeals in the thirteenth century has shown that 'more than a third of all thirteenth-century private prosecutors were

1 *The Earliest Lincolnshir Assize Rolls, AD 1202–1209*, ed. by Doris Mary Stenton, Lincolnshire Record Society vol 22 (1926), p. xvii. For attitudes to women researchers in legal history, see, e.g., Maitland's enquiry as to whether a fellow male scholar is 'opposed to female labour', in the shape of Mary Bateson, proposed as a possible editor of 'Jew rolls': *Letters of F. W. Maitland* vol 1, p. 213, Letter 212 (1898).

2 106 *SS*, p. xxiv.

3 Barbara Hanawalt, 'Justice without Judgment: Criminal Prosecution before *Magna Carta*', in *Magna Carta and the England of King John*, ed. by Janet Loengard (Woodbridge, 2010), pp. 120–33, using Stenton's *Lincolnshire Assize Rolls 1202–1209*.

women', but that all appeals declined as a proportion of prosecutions over the course of the thirteenth century, and did not recover, the gap being filled by all-male modes of commencing a 'criminal' case. Prosecutions brought by women therefore declined considerably as a proportion of all complaints.[4] A substantial minority of cases including women as 'civil litigants' can be seen in some thirteenth-century rolls, particularly in relation to cases involving land and with dower to the fore. Walker has noted the particular frequency of women's dower actions in the thirteenth century.[5] As many as 39% of entries relating to new cases in the Curia Regis Roll for Michaelmas 1250 included a female claimant, alone or with a man, with dower featuring as a leading cause of action amongst these.[6] The decline in actions of dower, in particular, has, however, been charted in detailed studies,[7] and it has been suggested that the overall pattern is one of a decline in women's participation as claimants at common law, over the course of the later fourteenth and fifteenth centuries. A sample from the 1320s in a study by Stevens, looking at Common Pleas cases involving Londoners, showed around 26% as a minimum of cases brought by a woman, with the sample from the 1420s indicating a decline to 15%.[8] The Michaelmas 1349 Common Pleas roll contains 17% cases involving women claimants (alone or with a man).[9] For the Trinity 1377 Common Pleas roll, this proportion is 11%,[10] and for the Easter 1440 Common Pleas roll, 8%.[11] Research on the late fifteenth-century Common Pleas and King's Bench suggests a decline to around 5% of litigants in the King's Bench and Common Pleas.[12] There is also some evidence that women were a more substantial minority in other, non-common law courts, including those developing in the later part of the period covered here.[13]

4 Daniel Klerman, 'Women Prosecutors in Thirteenth-Century England', *Yale Journal of Law & the Humanities* 14 (2002), 271–320, 271, 287, 289, 317.

5 Walker, 'Introduction', in *Wife and Widow* ed. by Walker (Ann Arbor: University of Michigan Press, 1993), 1–16.

6 *CRR* vol 20, Michaelmas 1250, KB 26/143.

7 See Phifer, 'Property, Power and Patriarchy', especially at pp. 167, 256.

8 KB 27/239–KB 27/278; KB 27/635–KB 27/638; M.F. Stevens, 'London Women, the Courts and the 'Golden Age': A Quantitative Analysis of Female Litigants in the Fourteenth and Fifteenth Centuries', *London Journal* 37 (2012), 67–88. For the rate of women's litigation in the common law courts in the fifteenth century, see also Loengard, 'What is a Nice Englishwoman', pp. 55–6; Emma Hawkes 'She Will Protect and Defend Her Right…' Women's Knowledge of Common Law and Equity in Late Medieval England', in *Medieval Women and the Law*, ed. by Menuge, pp. 145–62, 148–51.

9 CP 40/359.

10 CP 40/466.

11 http://aalt.law.uh.edu/Indices/CP40Indices/CP40no717/CP40no717Pl.htm.

12 Hawkes, 'She Will Protect'.

13 Hawkes, 'She Will Protect', pp. 148–51; Bardsley, *Venemous Tongues*, p. 71. Jeremy Goldberg, 'Echoes, Whispers, Ventriloquisms: On Recovering Women's Voices from the Court of York in the later Middle Ages', in *Women*, ed. by Kane and Williamson (London, 2013), 31–41, p. 31.

Women were also much less frequently accused or sued in common law courts than were men. For example, the Curia Regis rolls from Hillary term 1201 show a rounded up 'male only: female included' ratio of 88:12.[14] The crown pleas roll of the eyre of London 1276 including accusations from 1251–2 to 1275–6 had a presentment rate of roughly 89:11.[15] A ratio of 9:1 or lower for felony charges is noted in Hanawalt's surveys of indictments in the first half of the fourteenth century, her survey of coroners' rolls from Northamptonshire 1300–420, Oxford 1296–393 and London 1300–40 notes even lower proportions of female homicide suspects, 3% or less, and her study of mid-fifteenth-century Yorkshire gaol delivery rolls showed an estimated 4% of recorded felony prosecutions being brought against women.[16] Other studies focused on records of homicide cases have also shown that accusations against men predominated in the thirteenth and fourteenth centuries.[17] The Rex section of a King's Bench roll of 1384 shows a ratio of entries relating to male defendant only: female defendant included of roughly 92:8.[18] More specialised studies confirm varying but always lower proportion of women accused of other 'criminal' offences and as defendants in 'civil' cases.[19]

14 *CRR* vol. 1, p. 374 ff; from KB 26/21 and KB 26/24.

15 *The Eyre of London 1276*, ed. by Martin Weinbaum (London, 1976). The calculation is mine. The proportion of males would be higher if confession and abjuration were included, individual accused offenders (in multiple offender entries) counted or offences against the assizes of wine and cloth included.

16 Barbara A. Hanawalt, 'The Female Felon in Fourteenth Century England', *Viator* 5 (1974), 253–68; Barbara A. Hanawalt, 'Violent Death in Fourteenth and Early Fifteenth Century England', *Comparative Studies in Society and History* 18 (1976), 297–320, 305–8; Barbara A. Hanawalt, 'Women before the Law: Females as Felons and Prey in Fourteenth-Century England', in *Women and the Law*, ed. by D. Kelly Weisberg (Cambridge, MA, 1982), vol. I, pp. 165–95, 171.

17 Wilkinson, *Women*, pp. 142, 153–4, 156–7; James B. Given, *Society and Homicide in Thirteenth Century England* (Stanford, CA, 1977) c. vii; Sara M. Butler 'Violence and Murder in Medieval Europe', in *Cambridge World History of Violence, Volume 2: AD 500–AD 1500*, ed. by Matthew Gordon, Richard Kaeuper, Harriet Zurndorfer, (Cambridge, 2020), c. 16, p. 338; Carl I. Hammer, Jr., 'Patterns of Homicide in a Medieval University Town: Fourteenth-Century Oxford', *Past & Present* 78 (1978), 3–23, 13. A rate of accusation or confession of homicide by women of c. 3% and 6 % for theft offences can be seen in *Eyre of London 1244*.

18 KB 27/491.

19 Rose, *Maintenance*, p. 324, shows women as 1% of maintenance defendants. Alice Seabourne and Gwen Seabourne, 'Suicide or Accident? A Series of 198 Cases from the Eyre Records', *British Journal of Psychiatry* 178 (2001), 42–7, noted a male: female proportion of 68:32 in felonious suicides in thirteenth- and fourteenth-century eyre and coroners' rolls. *CRR* vol 20. Michaelmas 1250, roll KB 26/143 has 19% of cases, including a female defendant. A sample roll of 1282 showed 91% of entries relating to civil cases involved male defendants alone, one from Hillary 1295 has male only, including a woman defendant proportions of 88:12 and a sample from a roll of 1306 gives the male-only proportion as 85%: KB 27/66; KB 27/143; KB 27/183. The common pleas section of a King's Bench roll of 1384 showed defendants in entries in the male alone: female included proportions 92:8: KB

It is not claimed that these figures give anything more than a very approximate picture. There is clearly a need for more intensive quantitative study, to give a more detailed idea of rates of change, a task which may be made easier for future scholars with improvements in manuscript-reading software. For the purposes of this inquiry, however, these rough figures give a sufficient indication of the probably unsurprising fact that far more cases were brought by men than women and against male than against female defendants. This general disproportion is well known to historians, even if it does not usually impinge upon legal historians' narrative of the expansion of the scope of the common law over these centuries. Nevertheless, their lower level of participation should not efface the fact that women were present as claimants, defendants, accused in the courts of common law: there is much to consider with regard to this presence, and that is the task of this part of the book. The outline of records of three rather different cases will serve to introduce some of the themes emerging from the records of women's involvement in court and in legal proceedings which will be explored here.

The first is in a Somerset roll of Henry III's reign, and records the Hundred of Houndsborough reporting that one Nicholas the gardener killed Gunnilda de Norton 'because she would not permit him to rape her daughter', and he then fled. Gunnilda's daughter had proceeded against him in three county courts. She was told to prosecute her suit and it was ordered that Nicholas was to be exacted and outlawed, and that there should be an inquiry into his chattels.[20]

The second is to be found in a King's Bench roll record and Year Book entry of 1369. *Tyryngton v Beauchamp* (1369) shows a dispute centred on two women, one claiming dower and one resisting that claim.[21] Joan Tyryngton and her new husband, William Tyryngton, claimed dower from the property of her former husband, Robert Fitzwyth. The claim was opposed by John Beauchamp and his wife, Joan, Fitzwyth's daughter and heiress. The disputed point was whether Joan Tyryngton was disqualified from bringing her action because she fell within c. 34 of the Statute of Westminster II (1285), having eloped with an adulterer and not having been reconciled with her husband,[22] and more specifically, whether it was enough for Joan Tyryngton simply to deny that she had left Robert of her free will rather than formally denying the whole allegation. John Beauchamp did not take

27/491. A sample of entries in one Commom Pleas roll for 1495 (CP 40/931) shows a 'male alone v. female included' ratio of roughly 94:6.

20 JUST 1/755 m. 3 (IMG 2771) 1225; *Somersetshire Pleas*, no 212.

21 *William de Tyryngton and Johanna his wife* v. *John Beauchamp del Holte and Joan his wife* (1369). CP 40/435 m. 387 and m. 387d (IMG 773 and 1857); *Seipp* 1369.059; YB 43 Edw. III Trin. pl. 5. See Gwen Seabourne, 'Coke, the Statute, Wives and Lovers: Routes to a Harsher Interpretation of the Statute of Westminster II c. 34 on Dower and Adultery', *Legal Studies* 34 (2014), 123–42.

22 *SR* I, p. 87.

an active role, but Joan Beauchamp was allowed to 'defend her right'. The Tyryngton side managed to convince the court that what was portrayed by Joan Beauchamp's side as an elopement had in fact been a violent abduction, during an attack in which Robert Fitzwyth had been mortally wounded, and that Joan Tyryngton's pleading sufficed to nullify Joan Beauchamp's allegation. The Tyryngtons triumphed and there were amercements for John and Joan Beauchamp, and Joan Beauchamp separately.[23]

The last of the three illustrative cases is in a gaol delivery roll for a session at Lincoln castle in 1383, which includes the record of two people, Walter Skryvenere and Alice Cosyn, accused of receiving murderous thieves. Although both pleaded not guilty, the jury pronounced them guilty of this offence. There was a difference in their ordained fate: Alice was to be hanged, whilst Walter made a successful claim of clerical status and lived.[24]

These three cases show something of the range of medieval women's participation in common law cases, in both 'criminal' and 'civil' actions, accusing and being accused of wrongdoing, claiming and defending rights, alone or with a husband, having a case brought by another with regard to a wrong to them and experiencing a variety of different outcomes. The last case in particular brings home some clear and stark differences made by common lawyers and the common law between men and women. These cases also show some of the interest and complexity of researching women's participation in common law courts through the documents which were made and which have survived. In the first and third cases, there is a solitary, brief record on a plea roll or gaol delivery roll. In the second case, the dispute attracted the attention of law reporters as well as appearing on the plea roll. Such additional perspectives, where they occur, can be particularly valuable in illuminating the partial nature of the information which we must use. This should be accommodated – by circumspection in making claims about women and medieval law – but the imperfection of the remaining evidence is no excuse not to try to investigate and understand a crucial area of women's interaction with law and law's treatment of women.

23 *TNA* E 42/227.

24 JUST 3/167 m. 44 (IMG 96).

4 Voice, agency and 'playing the victim'

Several records, dating from 1318 to 1322, note proceedings relating to the allegation of Agnes de Haldenby that, in 1317, she had been subjected to a break-in, robbery and extreme personal violence. As the complaint was summarised in a commission of *oyer and terminer* to Henry le Scrope and his colleagues, she claimed that Simon de Drayton and 23 others had broken into her house at Thrapston in Northamptonshire, taken her to Northampton, where they confined her, and had then taken her to Shuckburgh in Warwickshire, where they ripped out her eyes and cut out her tongue.[25] There is elaboration of the allegation elsewhere, to include the claim that Agnes had been taken away and confined without food and drink, before the ripping out of her eyes and cutting out of her tongue, and at times further condemnation is provided by the use of *inhumaniter* to describe the manner of the offenders' attack.[26] The records also tell a story of royal and common law responses to the allegations, and to further claims that she was subjected to a malicious and false accusation of trespass, in order to divert her from her dogged legal pursuit of those she considered responsible for the wrongs she had suffered.[27]

Agnes's case is one of allegedly spectacular brutality. It is certainly not typical of medieval court rolls. Nevertheless, it provides a useful prompt for consideration of two important issues for those investigating women's litigation. First, it brings up the question of 'voice'. This has a literal and a metaphorical sense: obviously, one of the atrocities allegedly visited upon Agnes was deeply connected with removing her ability to speak and

25 *CPR 1317–21*, p. 292.

26 KB 27/239 Rex m. 10 (IMG 203).

27 See also: SC 8/83/4108B; *CPR 1317–21*, pp. 402–3, *CCR 1318–23*, pp. 71, 84, 402–3; KB 27/239 Rex m. 10 (IMG 203); KB 27/241 Rex mm. 2, 8, 14, 16 (IMG 225, 237, 250, 346); and Rex mm.1 d, 15d (IMG 213) (IMG 242); KB 27/243 Rex m. 13d (IMG 263) and m. 15d (IMG 267); KB 27/244 Rex m. 1 (IMG 261) and m. 5d (IMG 260); KB 27/245 Rex mm. 7 and 14 (IMG 219, 233) and mm. 1d and 7d (IMG 194 and 207); KB 27/246 Rex m. 16 (IMG 324); KB 247 Rex m.11d (IMG 180), KB 27/250 Rex m. 12 (IMG 226) and m. 6d R (IMG 211). See also *CPR 1317–21*, 591. Agnes seems to have obtained at least some financial recompense: *CCR 1318–23*, p. 377 (1321). See also *RP*, I, p. 375.

communicate, but we also always need to consider the more attenuated ideas of 'voice' as the possession of standing to speak in legal proceedings on one's own behalf (a usage with contemporary support, as may be seen in statements that a woman did not have a voice in litigation without her husband: *vocem agendi non habet per se sine viro*)[28] and the production and mediation of the words which appear in surviving documents. Finding the subjective views of women – hearing their actual words and their intended meaning – is, clearly, generally beyond us. A second matter raised by this case, which is worth considering at this point, concerns whether or not it is appropriate to regard somebody like Agnes or, indeed, any of the many other female complainants to be encountered in medieval plea rolls as a 'victim' or an 'agent'.

Voice

Although women are frequently mentioned in records and reports, there are profound difficulties in knowing the extent to which we can 'hear' their actual words or sentiments. The issue of women's 'voice' in such documents is complex, showing traces of the accents of both general social attitude and also specific legal frameworks. As well as the usual issues of authorship and scribal mediation, 'voices' are affected by the specific distortions of common law forms and practice. It is clear that all legal material was mediated in some way, affected by the need to play by the 'rules of the game' in order to achieve the desired result, and that its formulation might also be affected by ideas of acceptable and effective gender roles.[29] Common law records for some cases give us a valuable opportunity to detect and consider this mediation, since, if we have both a plea roll and a Year Book report, we are in a position to compare their accounts of a case, and may see that the different species of record have different things to say about the participation and conduct of the women involved.[30] We still cannot, of course, know 'what actually happened', but having two points of reference can be very informative and help us draw conclusions for the larger body of cases for which only one source remains.

That surviving common law documentation may give a misleading picture of the level of women's participation in litigation is apparent from a study of the Year Book report and plea roll record in *Tyryngton*, for example.[31]

28 87 *SS*, p. 85 no 170b.

29 See Tim Stretton, 'Women, Legal Records, and the Problem of the Lawyer's Hand', *JBS* 58 (2019), 684–700.

30 Paul Brand, *Observing and Reporting the Medieval Bar and Bench at Work; the Origins of Law Reporting in England* (London, 1999), pp. 3–4.

31 See above p. 98 and Gwen Seabourne, 'Copulative Complexities: The Exception of Adultery in Medieval Dower Actions', in *Law and Legal Process: Substantive Law and Procedure in English Legal History*, ed. by Matthew Dyson and David Ibbetson (Cambridge,

Aspects of female activity and participation are played down in the report, which focuses on the arguments of (male) legal professionals at the expense of others involved, while the record may over-emphasise women's role in proceedings, diminishing the participation of some of the legal professionals.[32] There are also differences in terms of personal and factual details: the plea roll gives the names of the parties, the plaintiffs' attorney and the abductor, landholding and geographical locations, dates of events, stages of legal process, including the fact that Joan Beauchamp defended the action herself after her husband had defaulted. It also includes more details on the consequences of the litigation. The Year Book reporter apparently regarded William Tyryngton as unworthy of note and glossed over the independent role played by Joan Beauchamp, but gave additional information which is not on the plea roll: information of a sort calculated to interest legal professionals, concerning fellow lawyers, the serjeant and judge and the key points of pleading.[33] The Plea Roll sets out proceedings and arguments as if it was only the parties who were present in court, though the Tyryngtons at least had an attorney and there seem to have been serjeants on both sides. Fortescue, in his *De Natura Legis Naturae*, may have imagined a court dispute including a woman arguing her own case, but this was unlikely to have been the situation in the central courts of common law, either in his day or in the fourteenth century. Even portrayals of litigation which state that a woman 'comes in person and says …' are likely to be masking the involvement of a serjeant.[34] There are occasional reports which suggest that a woman did speak in court, and this cannot be ruled out, but given the increasing technicality of the law and its language, requiring expertise which could only be obtained in institutions which excluded women, it is very unlikely to have been usual.[35]

Distortions of the levels of participation and initiative by those involved in a case can also be affected by common law conventions and rules relating to married women, who could not generally take legal action without the participation of their husbands. This means that it is not usually possible to distinguish the woman's and the man's role in bringing such an action. Also worthy of note as, in a sense, effacing the involvement of women are the instances in Year Book reports of serjeants identifying themselves with their

2013), pp. 34–55; and, e.g., Walker, '"Litigant Agency" in Dower Pleas in Royal Common Law Courts in Thirteenth and Early Fourteenth Century England', *JLH* 24 (2003), 1–22 'Litigant Agency'; Hanawalt, 'Whose Story Was This? Rape Narratives in Medieval English Courts', in *Of Good and Ill Repute: Gender and Social Control in Medieval England*, ed. by Barbara A. Hanawalt (Oxford: Oxford University Press, 1998), pp. 124–41.

32 Brand, *Observing and* Reporting, pp. 3–4. *Bracton* III, p. 358, envisages woman setting out dower claim in person or by attorney.

33 Walker, 'Wager of law'; st. Westminster II, c. 3.

34 See, e.g., CP 40/317 m. (IMG 668).

35 See Walker, 'Litigant Agency', p. 13; YB Trin. 20 Edw I pl. 85; *Seipp* 1292.134rs, which appears to be JUST 1/302 m.33d; JUST 1/303 m. 21; Brand, *Origins*, p. 47.

clients, to the extent of taking on the persona of a party. If their client was a woman, they do not appear to have felt any inhibition from speaking 'as' her, even when this involved them asserting a relationship with a man. For example, Serjeant Passeley's assertion that a presentment 'should not hurt us, for at that time we were covert by a husband and within age' puts him in the place of his female client in a way which might seem surprising if we assume either rigidity of gender ideas or unmitigated misogyny in medieval men.[36]

Of the interaction between women and their lawyers, we know little, though Walker has drawn attention to one example of a woman being harried by attorneys desperate to represent her.[37] Year Books may give additional clues to attitudes in the courtroom, when women were involved. In *Tyryngton*, for example, the Year Book includes a digression about what would have happened if a baby had been produced as a result of the adultery which was alleged against Joan Tyryngton: would it have been presumed the legitimate offspring of her husband? This appears to illustrate the idea of women and gender relations as legally interesting, and problematic. Recording of such material gives glimpses into the mental world of the common lawyers, and the attitudes women faced when their cases were litigated in common law courts, as well as highlighting the unmappable distance between what happened in court and much of the remaining documentation.[38] Other reports give occasional clues to the courtroom experiences of women (and girls): for example the cases cited in Brand's article about young widows' qualification for dower include references to intimate questioning of young girls as to what they had done in bed with a husband before his demise, and to physical inspection, apparently by male lawyers, to ascertain whether the young widow was of an age to be capable of 'supporting a husband' (i.e. coping with being penetrated by him).[39]

The voice of all litigants was constrained by the man-made forms of the common law, the formulaic writs, the rules of pleading and of proof.[40] Constraints – both external and internal – can also be seen to some extent even in the less regulated common law bills and plaints and in petitions. Portrayals of women in petitions, for example, adopted what were considered appropriate and effective language and emphasis.[41] These include portrayals of the petitioner as having been wronged, perhaps repeatedly, or fearing

36 17 *SS*, p. 31, *Knyveton v. Abbot of Newboth* (1308).

37 Walker 'Litigant Agency', p. 13; CP 40/180 m. 18d (IMG 36).

38 For chronicle and literary examples of women speaking in court before the king, see the case of Isabel of Arundel, above XXX; Cannon, 'The Rights of Medieval Englishwomen', p. 157.

39 Brand, 'Deserving and Undeserving', pp. 5–6; 20 SS, pp. 189–91; *Seipp* 1310.108ss.

40 See, e.g., Baker, *Introduction*, cc. 4 and 5.

41 Gwilym Dodd, *Justice and Grace: Private Petitioning and the English Parliament in the Late Middle Ages* (Oxford, 2007), pp. 214, 283; SC 8/1/31; SC 8/6/292; SC8/7/336; 41/2011. SC8/43/2103.

being wronged, suffering and highlighting the influence, power of others and the lack of power, influence and assistance of the petitioner.[42] This is not the only representation, however; there are also instances of women shown in more active roles, coming together to petition in groups, or portrayals of them taking their own steps to resist injustice or crime, including protecting or rescuing their husbands and protecting other women from spousal abuse.[43]

Victims, agents, both and neither

It has become common in discussions of medieval women to deploy the terms 'agent' (or 'agency') and, separately or by way of contrast, 'victim'. These terms, 'victim' and 'agent', however, raise some particular problems in the area of wrongs to women and women's complaints, which must be considered. They encourage a strong distinction between roles or perspectives which cannot easily be separated, and they may have other, more general distorting effects, for example by encouraging focus on those able to take action rather than those rendered less able to do so by a variety of factors and structures, including the legal.[44]

There is a tendency, in recent histories of women and gender, to claim that other historians portray women as victims, and that this must be corrected. Thus, for example, a statement in a recent study of women's intellectual leadership claimed that '... modern scholars have ... tended to study ... women, generally, as victims'.[45] In such statements, 'victim' tends to be coloured, explicitly or implicitly, with disapproval; thus we see the construction of the 'passive victim', the 'cowering victim', the 'helpless victim', the 'willing victim', the victim set in opposition to the saint or *virago* or to the 'agent'.[46] I would like to suggest that there is a need to reconsider some of this species of 'victim talk'. In such commentary, 'victim' seems, at times, to have unstable or overlapping meanings, covering both one who has been wronged on a particular occasion and also importing a larger-scale judgement on an individual or group, generally oppressed by some situation or structure.[47] The latter 'holistic' usage alienates many modern commentators on women's

42 See, e.g., SC8/49/2410; SC 8/41/2026; SC 8/17/850; SC8/7/336; SC 8/6/292 and Rose, *Maintenance*, p. 58, SC 8/33/1623.

43 See, e.g., SC8/120/5983 120/5985; 346/E1388; SC8/57/2833; SC8 307/15333; 280/13994. JUST 1/739 m. 55d (IMG 1739).

44 See Karras, *Common Women*, p. 7.

45 Kerby-Fulton, 'Introduction'; in *Women Intellectuals and Leaders*, ed. by Kerby-Fulton and others, (Woodbridge, 2020), p. 1.

46 J.R.S. Phillips, *Edward II* (New Haven, CT and London, 2010), p. 291; Skoda, *Medieval Violence*, p. 61; Karras, *Common Women*, p. 7; Carole Weinberg, 'Victim or Virago: the Construction of Guinevere in Laȝamon's *Brut*', *Reading Medieval Studies* 35 (2009), 27–43; *Victims or Viragos*, ed. by Catherine Lawless and Christine. Meek (Dublin, 2005).

47 Hanawalt, *Wealth of Wives*, p. vii.

history or gender history, who do not see or do not wish to tell a story of general disadvantage or victimisation of medieval women.[48] It is interesting to note that, despite such frequent usage in modern works, 'victim' is not a word generally encountered in classical medieval common law sources, and its use in other writings of the medieval period might be very different, with one prevalent image – that of Jesus as victim – likely to have lent it a much less negative resonance to contemporaries.[49] We should also note that the word 'victim' is sometimes brought in in later translation, when the original source describes one who is wronged in much more mundane, neutral terms.[50] Although none of this should be a bar to its use in modern commentary, it should serve to raise questions as to whether considering wrongs to medieval women or reaching a negative conclusion as to their situation is appropriately summarised in this way, with the word 'victim'. Some clarification and improvement in this area of discussion may be introduced by appealing to the considerable modern legal scholarship interrogating the usage of 'victim', especially that by scholars of criminal justice.[51] It would, for example, be useful to bear in mind distinctions between the 'bilateral individualist construction of victimhood' (relating to a person affected by an identifiable action) and broader constructions of a person's or a group's entire existence as partaking of the nature of victimhood.[52] This general status idea has sometimes been unpopular within modern feminism or 'gender and law' worlds, especially in the study of sexual violence. Here, we often see the replacement of the label rape or abuse 'victim' with that of rape or abuse 'survivor' and the questioning of 'victim feminism'.[53] Nevertheless, other parts of feminist study of rape, more focused on particular events, accept the word and some degree of generalisation: thus we have the idea and term 'victim-blaming'. There has been some attempt to rehabilitate 'victim' in both of its meanings, arguing for the acknowledgement of victimisation and the possibility of learning from it, without condemning or writing off

48 See, e.g., Caroline Dunn, *Stolen Women in Medieval England: Rape, Abduction and Adultery 1100–1500* (Cambridge, 2012), p. 95.

49 See, e.g., Helmut Koester, 'Jesus the Victim', *Journal of Biblical Literature* 111 (1992), 3–15; Skinner, *Studying Gender,* p. 134.

50 Note its use to translate *home* in 97 *SS*, p. 203 no. 1.

51 Tyrone Kirchengast, 'Victim Lawyers, Victim Advocates, and the Adversarial Criminal Trial', *New Criminal Law Review* 16 (2013), 568–94; Jessie K. Liu, 'Victimhood', *Missouri Law Review* 71 (2006), 115–77; Laura Jeffery and Matei Candea, 'The Politics of Victimhood', *History and Anthropology* 17 (2006), 287–96; A. Leisenring, 'Confronting "Victim" Discourses: The Identity Work of Battered Women', *Symbolic Interaction* 29 (2006), 307–30.

52 Stephen L. Carter, 'When Victims Happen To Be Black', *Yale Law Journal* 97 (1988), 420–47, 435.

53 Rebecca Stringer, *Knowing Victim: Feminism, Agency and Victim Politics in Neoliberal Times* (London and New York, 2014), p. 12.

those who are (at least sometimes) victims.[54] This seems to be an appropriate model for examination of women raising complaints and accusations of wrongdoing in the medieval courts of common law: those who suffered – or say that they suffered – wrongs are worthy of our interest and attention, and are an important part of the picture of women's relationship with the common law.

Agency, the concept sometimes placed in opposition to victimhood,[55] has many useful qualities as a perspective from which to view medieval women and their relationship with the common law, but also some difficulties. First, and least importantly, it is a confusing word for those trained in common law, who understand this word in a very different way. Agency in the legal sense is a long-established term, rooted in the positioning of the agent in relation to, on the one hand, a 'principal' for whom the agent acts, and, on the other, a third party or third parties.[56] In contrast, 'agency', as used in historical writing, may be used without much or any definition, and where definitions are given or can be deduced from context, they vary from that which may formerly have been described as 'power', to the range and scope of things a person 'actually could or could not do', to capacity for independent action.[57] Agency in this sense can be private, individual, collective, conscious or unconscious; it may or may not be tied to the effecting of change.[58] It seems to operate at several different levels of abstraction or generality. It may be a state of things, or something which can be exercised or enjoyed.[59] At its most extreme, agency is assigned even to spaces and

54 See, e.g., R.M. Hayes, K. Lorenz and K.A. Bell, 'Victim Blaming Others: Rape Myth Acceptance and the Just World Belief', *Feminist Criminology* 8 (2013), 202–20; T.C. Kulig and F.T. Cullen, 'Where is Latisha's Law? Black Invisibility in the Social Construction of Victimhood', *Justice Quarterly* 34 (2017), 978–1013; Stringer, *Knowing Victim*, p. 2. The term is acceptable to government. http://esrcvictims.org/. Accessed 29th July, 2020.

55 See, e.g., Emma Hawkes, '"She Was Ravished against Her Will, What So Ever She Say": Female Consent in Rape and Ravishment in Late-Medieval England', *Limina* 1 (1995), 47–54, 51–2.

56 See, e.g., R.J.C. Munday, *Agency: Law and Principles*, 3rd edn (Oxford, 2016); Baker, *Introduction*, pp. 526–7.

57 Kane and Williamson, 'Introduction', in *Women, Agency and the Law*, ed. by Kane and Williamson (London, 2013); Kim M. Phillips, 'Masculinities and the Medieval English Sumptuary Laws', *Gender and History* 19 (2007), 22–42, 32; Elizabeth Fowler, 'Civil Death and the Maiden: Agency and the Conditions of Contract in Piers Plowman', *Speculum* 70 (1995), 760–92; Lisa Benz St John, *Three Medieval Queens: Queenship and the Crown in Fourteenth Century England* (New York, 2012), pp. 9, 17.

58 See, e.g., Garthine Walker, *Crime, Gender and Social Order*, p. 212; Anthony Giddens, *Social Theory and Modern Sociology* (Oxford, 1987), pp. 219–23; Anthony Giddens and Philip W. Sutton, *Essential Concepts in Sociology* (Cambridge, 2014), p. 23; Skinner, *Studying Gender*, p. 46; Kane, *Popular Memory*, p. 22.

59 Bronach Kane, 'Women, Memory and Testimony in the Medieval Ecclesiastical Courts of Canterbury and York', in *Women, Agency and the Law*, ed. by Kane and Williamson, (London, 2013), pp. 43–62, 44; S.H. Rigby, 'Introduction', in *A Social History of England 1200–1500*, ed. by Rosemary Horrox and W. Mark Ormrod (Cambridge, 2006), p. 9.

inanimate objects.[60] It does not seem to be too ignorant a claim that there is some vagueness about this term, nor that it may seem to skate over the problem of volition, and have the tendency to treat willed and coerced action as virtually equal, a serious difficulty for considerations of offences against the medieval common law, in which there is considerable evidence that a 'guilty mind' as well as particular action was relevant to the application of penalties.[61]

More importantly, an emphasis on women's agency in the sense of action pushes into the background those women who cannot be described in more or less active terms. 'Litigants, witnesses and suspects' fit into a narrative of active women, those sustaining injuries but not taking legal action themselves, those accepting or enduring, or never being in a position to consider taking action, less so. Even a recent avowedly 'subversive' account of legal history emphasises agency, thus shoring up the law's traditional interest in the active over the passive, and certainly over those on the receiving end of overwhelming exertion of power.[62] It would be wrong to see an equation of active with male and passive with female (though there are some medieval texts make just this link),[63] but it is worth at least considering whether the very strong emphasis on 'agency' may be particularly unhelpful in the study of medieval women and the law.

Strongly emphasising the active as positive may also mask the fact that participation in litigation is not necessarily a wholly positive sign either for an individual woman or for women overall. For example, the frequency of widows' pursuit of their dower through the courts is well known, but rather than emphasising the 'agentic' aspect of such litigation, it may be more appropriate to be open to seeing it as a sign of the ease with which a woman's right could be denied and delayed, obliging her to take expensive and inconvenient legal action.[64]

Too close a focus on agency may also be associated with a tendency to look only at 'upward exceptions' to limitations – stressing those who overcame apparently clear limitations – rather than also considering 'downward exceptions' – examining instances of apparent oppression involving stretching, or going beyond the limiting rules or, indeed, questioning the clear nature of the rules themselves. In addition, a wish to downplay 'victimhood' risks exaggeration of the possibility of evading, negotiating or manipulating patriarchal structures, including legal processes, which was

60 Joanne Begiato, 'Beyond the Rule of Thumb: The Materiality of Marital Violence in England c. 1700–1857', *Cultural and Social History* 1 (2018), 39–59.

61 Note the infrequency of 'agency' in Kamali, *Felony*, a legal historical account of intention.

62 Sandberg, 'The Time for Legal History', p. 31.

63 See Ruth Mazo Karras, *Sexuality in Medieval Europe: Doing unto Others* (New York, 2012).

64 Walker, *Wife and Widow*, Introduction, pp. 1, 6.

realistic for medieval women.[65] Giving victimhood its due does not mean rejecting examples of women who transcended limitations, nor belittling efforts of women to do so; it does mean balancing these with indicators of women who did not transcend limitations, or who encountered additional and illicit obstacles.[66] This is as true for historical study as it is for present day law and policy.

A final matter which casts some doubt on the advisability of focusing too exclusively on women's agency in relation to law is that doing so may tend to lead to the passing over of instances in which women's complaints, and wrongs to women, were initiated by men: women's kin or their neighbours. From a modern viewpoint, this appears problematic, patriarchal and antithetical to women's agency. Nevertheless, numerically speaking, cases in which the complaint is made by a man or by men, with regard to a wrong to a woman, are very significant. Given our general lack of knowledge as to the process which lay behind instances of accusation such as presentments and indictments, we should entertain the possibilities (a) that women's complaints may have lain behind the formal initiation of process by men, and (b) that women saw some value in having wrongs done to them brought to the common law, even in an indirect, male-led fashion. These instances of action by men, in relation to women, must form part of the story of women and the medieval common law, and will be mentioned in the next chapter.

Conclusion

Agnes de Haldenby – according to the claim recorded in surviving documents – was the victim of an appalling attack. She was also sufficiently active in pursuing the wrongdoers to qualify as having exercised 'agency' on most definitions of that concept. Clearly, there is no need to set these ideas up in opposition to one another, nor to see her case from only one perspective. Equally clearly, we must know that there are at least gaps, and possibly distortions, in the account left to us in the records. There are discrepancies with regard to her injuries, and there is silence on who was helping her to present her case, since, in the circumstances, unless her allegation was a complete and particularly bold lie, she cannot possibly have done this herself. Hers is an extreme case, but it has lessons which are more general for those of us examining women and their participation as litigants in cases at common law.

65 Bellamy, *Criminal Trial*, p. 164; Caroline Dunn, 'Damsels in Distress', p. 33.

66 See, e.g., Klerman, 'Women Prosecutors', p. 272 (women pressured to marry despite the formal requirement of consent); Rowena Archer, 'How Ladies ... Who Live on Their Manors ought to Manage Their Estates' Women as Landholders and Administrators in the Later Middle Ages', in *Woman is a Worthy Wight*, ed. by P.J.P. Goldberg (Stroud, 1997), p. 199; Hawkes, 'She Will Protect', pp. 148–51.

5 Limits and accommodation

A record from the Easter term 1321 plea roll of the King's Bench gives details of the case of *Isabella, widow of William de Bernard v. Walter de Manston and Agnes daughter of John Herdeman*.[1] This case was an appeal of rape – an individual prosecution – brought by Isabella, who alleged that on 5th August, 1320, at the hour of vespers, in the vill of Bandon, Walter grabbed her, slung her across his horse, took her to Southwark, put her in one Thomas Dod's cellar, threw her to the ground and then and there lay with her (*secum concubuit*) against her will, and against the king's peace, then fled. She said that she was ready to prove this.

Walter denied the accusation, and argued that there was a reason that the case should not even be put to proof. He said that Isabella should not be answered in relation to this appeal, because she was his wife. In support of this claim, he stated that she had previously appealed him of robbery, and on that occasion, he had made a successful defence on the basis that the pair had been married at St George's church in Southwark and that this had been certified by the bishop of Winchester. The rolls were ordered to be searched, and the bishop's certificate was produced.[2] The bishop's certificate noted that the marriage had taken place on 25th August, 1320, predating the alleged rape, and the appeal of rape therefore failed. A husband could not be found to have raped his wife.

This record shows a woman bringing accusations against a man (and also against another woman, the nature of whose alleged participation is unclear) with regard to wrongs she alleged he had done her, and this accusation being entertained by a court of common law. It also shows some of the limitations placed upon her by that law: her ability to act and the alleged perpetrator's liability were both affected by the substantiated claim that they had gone through a marriage ceremony. The facts behind the

1 KB 27/244 Rex m. 5d (IMG 262).

2 Record of the appeal of robbery, with certification of the marriage: JUST 3/ 41/1 m. 31 (IMG 69). This provides the additional information that Walter was a tailor, and that Isabella probably had some assets, since she alleged that goods worth £20 had been stolen from her.

case are beyond reach: was this a woman who had married a man then swiftly regretted her choice, or was it a case of rape and forced marriage which barred her from any effective action at common law? The allegations in the appeals put the robbery three days after the rape. One speculative construction is, therefore, that Walter forced Isabella to go through a marriage ceremony, then took her goods. Having failed in her appeal of robbery, because of the certification of marriage, Isabella may have brought the rape appeal in an attempt to show that the marriage was forced, but the bishop's certificate blocked off this route. What is clearly shown, however, is that the common law both facilitated and also obstructed women's litigation. Women were allowed within the system, but only up to a point. This might serve as a summary to more than 'criminal' appeals, and this chapter will also bring in other species of legal action which might be brought by women, or in relation to their claims and complaints. Despite the fact that there is little explicit discussion by medieval common lawyers of their overall view of women's role as litigants,[3] existing evidence of practice, showing the ways in which the common law accommodated and did not accommodate their claims and grievances, can go some way towards elucidating their ideas, and thus the world in which women had to operate, in their relations with the common law.

Appeals

Isabella's actions of robbery and rape were appeals: individual prosecutions, used for allegations of serious offences. Bringing appeals was one of the most visible roles of women within the medieval common law system. They had no direct access to other forms of 'criminal' prosecution: the inclusion of wrongs against women in presentment or indictment, or special commissions, depended on securing the support of male jurors, coroners and officials. Although all appeals were in relative decline from the thirteenth century onwards, women's appeals appeared in records and reports throughout the medieval period.[4] Furthermore, they retained more of a presence in legal consciousness throughout and beyond the period than numbers alone would have suggested, as they continued to be a matter of

3 For an unusual example of wider-ranging discussion of the rights of women in law suits, ranging through implications of marital status in dower, *cui in vita* and appeals, see *Seipp* 1376.028.

4 Klerman, 'Women Prosecutors', p. 271; Kerr, 'Husband and Wife', pp. 226, 232; Daniel R. Ernst, 'The Moribund Appeal of Death: Compensating Survivors and Controlling Jurors in Early Modern England', *AJLH* 28 (1984), 164–88, 164. Hyams, 'Maitland', p. 230; Daniel Klerman, 'Settlement and the Decline of Private Prosecution in Thirteenth-Century England', *LHR* 19 (2001), 1–65, 3; Whittick, 'The Role of the Criminal Appeal in the Fifteenth Century', p. 55; *Seipp* 1302.189rs; 1320.006; 1351.075; 1399.011; 1405.080; 1457.022; 1468.044; 1481.042; 1497.018; 105 *SS*, cxlvii p. 180; lxv; 132 *SS*, p. 184.

interest for legal scholars and writers well beyond the medieval period.[5] The picture which is emerging from considerations of the extent to which women's appeals were limited, formally, practically, and in terms of the chances of success (however that is defined) is one of complexity and interest, which challenges legal historians to examine their understanding of the nature of the common law in medieval England.

Subject matter

Statements from the twelfth century onwards assert limitations on the circumstances in which a woman could bring an appeal. These are present in *Glanvill*, in later treatises, in the *Magna Carta* of 1215 and its descendants and in some records of practice. It should be noted however that these sources set out somewhat varying versions of the limitations. All accounts agree that a woman might appeal alleged killers of her husband (although, as will be discussed below, the basis for permitting her to do so is not clear). This alone is mentioned in Magna Carta 1215 c. 54, but not in such a way as to exclude the possibility of appeals for other offences.[6] There is less apparent consensus as to the other circumstances in which she might appeal. The offence which is mentioned next most frequently as one which could form the subject matter of a woman's legitimate appeal is rape, which may be specified or may be presented as an example of the wider category of harm to the woman's body.[7] Some statements include the possibility of a woman's appeal for the killing of a foetus with which she was pregnant, following assault or other misconduct.[8] This, too, might be regarded as a development of the idea of harm to the woman's body, though this is never made clear. There were appeals (and other prosecutions) based on the death of a foetus, but there was variation in terms of who brought these – the woman, the father/husband or both.[9] The absence of consensus on whether the death of a foetus was something which should found an appeal, and if so,

5 See, e.g., F. Pulton, *De Pace Regis et Regni* (London, 1609), f. 156 ff; W. Hawkins, *A Treatise of the Pleas of the Crown,* 2nd edn (2 vols, London, 1724–6) II, pp. 162, 17; *Bl. Comm.*, book IV c. 23.

6 See *Placita Corone*, p. xxviii; Carpenter, *Magna Carta*, p. 106; JUST 1/1098 m. 72 (IMG 7352).

7 Hudson *OHLE* II, p. 722; *Glanvill* XIV, pp. 1, 3–4, 6; *Bracton* II, pp. 416, 419. Statements that women have appeals only for death of husband or rape: (1202) 1 *SS* p. 13 no. 32; *Somersetshire Pleas*, p. 263 no 929, JUST 1/756 m. 17d, (1243); death of husband and injury to her body only (1290) KB 27/125 m. 22d (IMG 8048).

8 *Bracton* II, 341; *Fleta* book 1 c. 23, 33; *Placita Corone*, xxviii; *Britton* book 1, c. 24, s.7. (1261); death of H, rape of virginity (and abortion). JUST1/82 m. 23 (IMG 484). No appeal for women for death of a foetus: *Mirror*, book IV, c. 16, p. 139. 132 *SS*, p. lxxix: readers disagree on whether killing a foetus amounted to felony.

9 Women's appeals for killing a foetus: 1 *SS* p. 39, no 82 (1200); 1202 JUST 1/479 m. 3d (IMG 1280); *Lincs RS 22*, no 690 (though note those in no 629 and 638 are brought by H); JUST I/996 m. 40 (IMG 94) (1249); JUST 1/ 778 m. 50 (1256); JUST 82 m. 23 (IMG 484)

whether such an appeal (or, indeed, some other action) should be brought by the woman, by the father/husband, by both or by neither, is not surprising, given that ideas about the nature and value of the foetus were in flux amongst common lawyers in the thirteenth and fourteenth centuries, at the same time that there were changes in the range of possible legal actions for personal injury.[10]

Women did bring appeals of wounding and mayhem, from at least the mid-thirteenth century, without regular, obvious, objection.[11] These fall within the scope of those statements of their legitimate appeals, which include a general reference to bodily injury, rather than specifying rape.[12] There was clearly a threshold of severity test for appeals of wounding, since a case of 1292 showed a woman's head wound to be considered insufficiently serious to found the action, though it was thought she could recover damages by plaint.[13] Appeals of mayhem, unlike other appeals, were understood to focus on the obtaining of compensation rather than the corporal or capital punishment of the offender.[14] An interesting matter with regard to women's appeals of mayhem is that treatises generally defined mayhem in terms of damage to a man who might otherwise fight for the king, its masculine character being emphasised by references to damage to the testicles.[15] Nevertheless, the appeal of mayhem became a more general route for those,

(1261) 1268–9, JUST 1/569A m. 28d (IMG 8247); JUST 1/486 m. 8 (IMG 2735) (1281–4); JUST 1/1006 m. 61 (IMG 9977) (1289); JUST 1/739 m. 81 (IMG 1594) (1292).

10 Butler, 'Abortion by Assault', p. 16. Husband's/male's appeal, e.g., *PCCG* 16 p. 140; 1 *SS* 1 p. 11; JUST 1/111 m. 28d (IMG 3822) 1284. Married woman's appeal, e.g., 1 *SS* p. 32 no 73 (1203). Presentment or indictment, e.g., *Somersetshire Pleas*, 321 no 1243 (1242–3); JUST 1/302 m. 85 (IMG 8370); JUST 1/1015 m. 13 (IMG 1231); JUST 1/547A,/ 20d (IMG 5833); KB 9/167 m. 19 (IMG 36); 1350 KB 27/365 m. 15 (IMG 7174); JUST 3/20/4 m. 44 (IMG 105) 1411–12. On the legal status and value of the foetus, see Wolfgang Mueller, *Criminalization of Abortion in the Medieval West* (Ithaca, NY, 2012), p. 12; *Seipp* 1348.302ass. Killing a foetus arose in indictments and coroners' rolls thereafter, where the woman, too, was killed or where she was raped: see, e.g., 9 *SS* 114 (1361–2); KB 9/219/2 mm 12 and 13 (IMG 24 and 26); KB9/269 m. 37 (IMG 70).

11 Wounding/mayhem; see, e.g., *CRR XX (1250)* no. 1034 p. 186; KB 27/497 m. 14 (IMG 29). KB 27/582 m. 56 (IMG 139); *Wilts GD and* T, p. 33; (assault on female servant, trespass) KB 27/584 m. 93d (IMG 191); KB 27/420 m. 16d (IMG 295). Presentment/indictment, see, e.g., KB 27/313 Rex m. 14 d (IMG 236).

12 See, e.g., JUST 1/1098 m. 14 (IMG 6774); JUST 1/569 m. 33 (IMG 8183); JUST 1/135 m. 16d (IMG 7066); JUST 1/568 m. 26 (IMG 8003); JUST 1/111 m. 30 (IMG 3744): see also P.R. Orr, '*Non potest appellum facere*: Criminal Charges Women Could Not, but Did, Bring in Thirteenth Century English Royal Courts of Justice', in *The Final Argument: The Imprint of Violence on Society in Medieval and Early Modern Europe*, ed. by D.J. Kagay and L.J.A. Villalon (Woodbridge, 1998), pp. 141–62, 145, 147.

13 JUST 1/409 m. 7 (IMG 17).

14 See, e.g. a 1284 case JUST 1/111 m. 30 (IMG 3744).

15 *Bracton* II, p. 409; *Fleta* book 1 c. 38; *Mirror* book 1 c. 9. Baker, *OHLE VI* pp. 513, 553. On wounding and mayhem: *Bracton* II, pp. 408, 411; *Fleta* book 1 c. 25; Seipp 1407.011 1484.038; 1498.005. On castration: *Bracton* II, p. 408, borrowing from *D.* 48.8.3.4–5.

including women, who suffered injury, to seek redress. This may well not be a matter of contradiction between 'law' and 'practice', but between gendered expression in legal treatises and a legal practice which did not recognise or did not concern itself with the explanation of mayhem as connected to fighting capability.

Beyond homicide, rape and mayhem, the overall position is one of some uncertainty. A tension has been identified in this area between apparent rules and actual practice, with women observed to have been allowed to bring appeals where this should not have been allowed. The presence of what have been classed as 'unconventional appeals' has been taken to indicate that 'the rules' were 'feebly enforced'.[16] This might be due some reconsideration. One of the main 'transgressions' was women's relatively frequent appeals for robbery. We have seen that Isabella de Bernard had brought such an appeal, before her appeal of rape. Clearly this offence was not listed in the treatises amongst the legitimate subject matter for their appeals, but while the more usual view was that women should not, strictly speaking, be allowed to bring appeals of robbery, this was not so unquestioned that we can label all examples of such appeals as clear exceptions to a definite rule.[17] Some robberies involved assault to the person and might, therefore, be associated with the 'damage to the body' category of legitimate appeal.[18] A record of a case of 1212 shows a woman's apparent uncertainty as to whether she could in fact bring an appeal of mayhem and robbery,[19] suggesting that it was not out of the question at that point that she could bring an appeal of robbery, at least in combination with another perhaps more securely legitimate, matter. Isabella de Bernard's allegation of robbery also seems to have been based upon a scenario which involved physical force. Numerous women did bring appeals of robbery alone without objection based on sex,[20] and some later opinions did in fact include robbery as a legitimate female appeal.[21] The exclusionary rule here is not as clear as has been assumed. Other sorts of appeal seem to be clearer 'exceptions', especially those for killings of those other than a husband or for harm to a husband which had not (yet) resulted in death,[22] and outlying female appeals of arson, (possibly)

16 Kerr, 'Husband and Wife', p. 245; *Placita Corone*, p. xxviii.

17 *Seipp* 1313.305ss. 24 *SS*, p. lxxx.

18 Green, *Verdict*, p. 60. Note a prioress appealing for robbery: JUST 1/956 m. 38 (IMG 7841). The example appeal of robbery in *Placita Corone*, at p. 10, is certainly violent.

19 *Alice v Coventry* (1212), 1 *SS*, p. 38 pl.105; *Plac. Abbrev.*, 84. For uncertainty, see also 24 *SS*, p. lxxx.

20 See Orr, 'Non potest', and, e.g., 24 *SS*, p. xxx; *Seipp* 1302.212rs; 1313.288ss; 1344.162rs; JUST 1/996 m. 23d (IMG 145); JUST 1/804 m. 48d (IMG 2550); 1 *SS*, p. 6; KB 27/596 m. 49 (IMG 115); KB 27/839 m. 58 (IMG 136).

21 105 *SS*, p. cxlvii on c. 34. no. 66 p. 87; pp. 180, 184; Pulton, *De Pace*, p. 159.

22 See, e.g., KB 27/125 m. 22d; KB 27/181 m. 55; Stenton *LRS* vol 22 no 630; JUST 1/804 m. 57d (IMG 2567); JUST 1/996 m. 27d (IMG 152); JUST 1/996 m. 33 (IMG 81); *Somersetshire Pleas*, pp. 18–19; p. 232 no. 764. 1242–3, JUST 1/756 m. 13d (IMG 2888). Appeals by

sorcery and ejection from a home.[23] There are instances of objection that particular appeals are not allowed to women, but these are comparatively few. The presence in Year Books of 'unconventional appeals' shows that they did not horrify common lawyers or judges. Perhaps the overall picture can be framed as one of loose or evolving rules as much as strict law *v.* looser practice. Statements of the law are not consistent, not reasoned and do not provide a complete code; the records also suggest inconsistency.[24]

In a sense, it is hardly surprising that there might be uncertainty or disagreements about exclusion, since the reasons for including women at all were never clearly articulated. Allowing women the initiative in some 'criminal' proceedings was not the product of a single, clear, rationale: reasons for allowing women's appeals may have ranged from the desire to ensure prosecution in situations with a likely lack of other witnesses, through the location of damage (physical or economic) in the woman personally, to an idea of a woman's right or duty to seek revenge in certain circumstances. *Glanvill* appears to take into account ideas of witnessing, kinship and the 'one flesh' metaphor, under which violence against the husband might be deemed violence against the wife herself.[25] This is extended in some later sources to call the death of the husband a 'dismemberment' of the wife.[26] Revenge and interest based on the woman's economic loss are noted by later common lawyers as reasons for a widow to be allowed to bring an appeal,[27] and her role as a likely witness seems important elsewhere.[28] Opinions might differ as to whether the right to bring an appeal resided in only one individual (so that if the 'wrong' person appealed, the appeal would fail) or whether more than one person might be entitled to bring an appeal, and, further, if there was a 'pecking order', how a woman's claim would rate against those of others. This debate or uncertainty, too, reveals a lack of consensus on the foundation of a right to appeal. *Britton* insisted that the male was to be received before the female, but also that the 'next of blood' was to be received before the more remote, setting up the possibility of competing principles.[29] A case of 1353 showed a degree of disagreement with regard to the relative importance of sex and closeness of relationship or inheritance rights,

---

W for not (yet) fatal assault on H: 1 *SS*, pp. 10, 24, 25; *Somersetshire Pleas* p. 347. JUST 1/756 m. 17d p. 260 no 962.

23 *P & M* II, p. 552: *Placit. Abbrev.* 62; arson: JUST 1/1256 m. 55 (IMG 210). JUST 1/996 m. 39 (IMG 94).

24 Hudson, *OHLE* II, p. 723.

25 Hudson *OHLE* II, p. 722; *Glanvill* XIV, 3. *Placita Corone*, p. xxviii.

26 132 *SS* lxix, p. 265.

27 *Seipp* 1407.029; 1442.085; 132 *SS*, p. 385.

28 *P & M* II, p. 485; *Britton*, book I, c. 24, note q.; Whittick, 'Role of the Criminal Appeal', pp. 57, 65.

29 *Britton* book 1, c. 2 no 7.

in relation to who should bring an appeal.[30] There are examples of objections to a male relative's appeal, on the grounds that the slain man has left a living widow,[31] suggesting that there is a 'pecking order', with the widow ranked first, and it seems unlikely that the many husbands whose wives appealed in relation to their death had no male kin. There are even suggestions by a fifteenth-century judge – supported to some extent by a reading from the end of the fifteenth century or very beginning of the sixteenth century – that the widow's right is so strong that a wife who has taken part in her husband's killing can appeal her own partners in crime.[32] Given ideas as to 'petty treason', to be discussed below, this seems odd, and no cases supporting such a view have been found. Nevertheless, it is interesting that the suggestion could be made, showing strong support for the widow taking the lead in the search for justice or vengeance. There are also examples of what may be a more permissive regime, less insistent on the widow's pre-eminent right and with more than one person having the right to appeal.[33] A fifteenth-century reading, which Baker dates c. 1455/60, admits that there is some disagreement as to the relationship between the right of the widow and the heir of a slain man to bring an appeal, and, in particular, the right of the heir to bring an appeal if the widow does not do so at all or in a timely manner.[34]

Where there is some indication of motivation or policy, limitation of women's right to appeal might be based more or less squarely on low estimations of women's capacities and ideas as to their appropriate role.[35] Extreme ideas of the relevance of sex can be seen in the argument that the contamination of womanhood travelled down the generations, and a right to appeal could not even be passed on to a man through a female ancestor.[36] Incapacities imposed upon women by the common law might also lead to their exclusion. Legislation of 1285 concerning appeals expressed a concern that somebody might bring a false appeal, but then not have the resources to compensate the disgruntled accused, leaving him without a satisfactory means of redress. This was not stated to be about appeals by women, but their lower economic position might mean that they could have

30 Debate on the relative claims of a female cousin and heir and a male rival: *Seipp* 1353.150ass.

31 *Seipp* 1314.017ss; Klerman, 'Women Prosecutors', p. 293; Susanne Jenks, '*Occidit ... inter brachia sua*: change in a woman's appeal of murder of her husband', *JLH* (2000), 119–22, 120.

32 Seipp 1421.092rog; 132 SS, p. 271. Compare *Seipp* 1449.070abr. st. 3 Hen. VII c. 2. For a 'pecking order' between brothers, see KB27/218 m. 10 (IMG 24); *Seipp* 1412.047abr.

33 *SR* II, 511, expects the widow of a murdered man or the heir to bring an appeal. Whether there is a 'pecking order' between them is unclear.

34 132 *SS*, 268.

35 R.H. Helmholz, 'Magna Carta and the ius commune', *University of Chicago Law Review* lxvi (1999), 297–371, 350–2.

36 *Seipp* 1322.020; 1442.085; 1477.012; 51 *SS* p. 95 case 24.

been used by others to bring appeals in this way, before the statute put 'abettors' of such an appeal at risk of being held financially responsible for the damage caused to the defendant.[37] Another limitation imposed upon women which might affect their perceived suitability to bring appeals was the convention that women did not take part in trial by battle, the traditional mode of proof for the appeal. *Bracton* stated that a woman could not do battle 'because of her sex'.[38] The *Mirror* gave a partial elaboration upon this, to the effect that the sex disqualification was based upon the fact that men and women were not peers or equals (the assumption being made that the defendant would be male). For good measure, but without explanation, it was said that women could not do battle with other women either.[39] It was true that women did not participate in trial by battle in appeals, though there is a chronicle report of a battle supposedly ordered, albeit not fought, in 1402 between a woman and an elderly Franciscan friar.[40] A reported case of 1313 supports the view that the fact that women could not engage in these judicial duels contributed to the limitation of their right to appeal.[41] By this time, trial by battle was in decline, but clearly the connection persisted in the minds of common lawyers.[42] The fifteenth-century 'ordinary gloss' of the common lawyers on *Magna Carta* c. 34 (1225; c. 54 of 1215) also used the explanation for the restriction of women the fact that women's appeals involved removing from (male) defendants the possibility of trial by battle. As Baker notes, there are some logical flaws in such an explanation (at least as a whole explanation for a reduction of women's possibility of appealing), in that it did not rule out other instances in which a defendant would not have been able to wage battle (e.g. actions brought by those too young or old to fight).[43]

Building on the fact that women were neither allowed nor required to fight battles, and that this might form a link with their limited role in appeals, modern commentators have added the idea of a fear that women, because they would not have to risk themselves in battle, would be put up to bringing malicious and ill-founded appeals. While there are allegations of false accusation, however, there is a need for care in evaluating them and in drawing conclusions. Some 'false appeals' may have been exaggerations of actual wrongs rather than complete fabrications, and some may not have been false

37 st. Westminster II (1285) c. 12.
38 *Bracton* II, pp. 402, 403; *Fleta* book 1, c. 32.
39 *Mirror*, book III, c. 23. See also *CRR XV* 1233–7, pp. 191–2 no 905.
40 *Mirror* book III, c. 23; Orr, 'English Women', p. 27; *Seipp* 1356.077. Bellamy, *Law of* Treason, p. 145; F. S. Haydon (ed.), *Eulogium historiarum sive temporis*, Rolls Series, 9 (3 vols, London, 1858–63), vol. 3, p. 389.
41 *Seipp* 1313.305ss.
42 Baker, *Introduction*, p. 544; M.J. Russel, 'Trial by Battle and the Appeals of Felony', *JLH* 1 (1980), 135–64.
43 132 *SS*, lxxix, pp. 266, 269, 279.

at all.[44] While we should not take at face value accusations in legal records, our doubt should not be selective: the recording of an appeal as 'false' is not any more trustworthy than the allegation in the initial appeal, and allegations of conspiracy to concoct and bring a false appeal may be untrue.[45] The best evidence of false appeals by women may be their own allegations that they were forced to bring appeals (though even here we cannot be sure of veracity).[46] It should be noted that allegations of the bringing of false accusations are by no means confined to appeals by women, and that women are not singled out by contemporaries as particularly likely to bring a false appeal.[47] Statements of fear of the number of false appeals of homicide in a late thirteenth-century statute, for example, do not cite women as the concern, and it is minors and (male) approvers who are noted in enactments as posing a specific problem in this area, not women.[48] The existence of 'false appeal' allegations or findings against women is not a strong argument for their particular likelihood of bringing dishonest proceedings, nor for the fear that they would do so. In addition, if the manipulation of women into bringing false appeals was feared, that would seem to be a reason to bar all appeals by women against men, giving the right to male kin in the event of homicide of a married man, for example, rather than allowing some female appeals, but the common law did not go down that path.

The 'conventional' categories for women's appeal were themselves neither straightforward nor free from restriction. The appeal for death of a husband was not without difficulty. A remarried widow might lose her right to appeal, for example, on the basis that when she married a new man, 'her grief is thus at an end'.[49] Another limitation might be caused by the requirement,

44 Apparent exaggeration of an attack, brought as appeal of wounding: JUST 1/756 m. 17d (IMG 2897).

45 Coss, *Lady*, p. 140. Alleged conspiracies to have a woman bring a false appeal: KB 27/160 m. 44 (IMG 2156); SC8 77/3832; Rose, *Maintenance*, p. 115; KB 27/369, Rex m. 55d (1352), (IMG 9775). See also Rose, *Maintenance*, p. 125; JUST 1/166, m. 49d, (IMG 9781 and 127); JUST 1/24, m. 47 and 47d (IMG 110, 231).

46 See, e.g., SC8/50/2493; Coss, *Lady*, p. 140; 96 *SS* no 672 (1256).

47 Alleged baseless appeals: Whittick, 'Role of the Criminal Appeal', p. 68; SC 8/77/3832; 221/11030; 41/2028. KB 27/514 m. 26; SC 8/50/2493; *Seipp* 1345.053rs; KB 27/134 m. 27d (IMG 1770). *Odio et atia*: e.g., two women ordered to gaol: JUST 1/778 m. 50 (IMG 7903); see Kamali, *Felony*, p. 291, Susanne Jenks, 'The Writ and Exception *de odio et atia*', *JLH* 23 (2002), 1–22. For consequences of maliciously brought accusations, see, e.g., (1340) KB 27/322 Rex m. 11 (IMG 371).

48 st. Westminster II c. 12, *SR* I, p. 81. Statute of Conspirators, *SR* I, p. 145; Anthony. Musson and Edward Powell, *Crime, Law and Society in the Later Middle Ages* (Manchester, 2009), p. 119; *SR* I, p. 165, c. 34. For a complaint about women's litigation, particularly that of Alice Perrers, see *RP* II, p. 329 and note XXX, though this does not concern false appeals.

49 Richard Littleton, 1493, CUL MS Hh 3.6 f.5, cited in Whittick, 'Role of the Criminal Appeal', p. 65. Disputes as to marriage, divorce: *Seipp* 1376.028; 1410.023; 1425.145abr; KB 27/516 m. 32 (IMG 67), Jenks, '*Occidit*'.

seen in some prescriptive sources, that the woman's husband was killed, or died, 'in her arms'.[50] Sometimes, it appears that the allegation was that he actually did die in her arms (not a particularly far-fetched scenario, if she was present when he was attacked), but often this formula was no more than a justification of her action by an indication of her presence at his death, whether factually true or not, casting her in a witness-like role.[51] The importance of the 'in her arms' formula has been shown to have changed over time: crucial in the reign of Edward I, it dropped out of use by the reign of Richard II, having come to mean only that the couple had been lawfully married. Because an exception could be raised to an appeal brought by a woman for the death of her husband on the grounds that she was not his wife, even without this phrase, its inclusion now appeared redundant.[52]

While widows were understood to be the only women able to bring appeals of homicide, appeals of rape were not explicitly limited to a particular subset of women, and *Bracton* expressed the view that they could be brought by female children, by virgins and by sexually experienced women.[53] Nevertheless, the treatise sees the virgin as the paradigm complainant, with men who rape other women subject to lesser penalties at most.[54] A large proportion of cases allege 'defloration', supporting the idea that rape of virgins was the central concern, and documents of practice suggest that thirteenth-century rape appeals were almost always brought by unmarried women (and some by girls as young as seven had to appeal in the same way as adults).[55] Married women were certainly restricted in that they could not bring appeals of rape against their own husbands – the problem faced by Isabella de Bernard, the woman found to have married Walter Manston, in the case at the beginning of this chapter.[56] The shielding of rapists and abductors who managed to force women into a form of marriage led to legislation in the fifteenth century, but remained a conundrum.[57] A married

50 For this formulation in appeals, e.g., JUST 1/643 m. 4 (IMG 542); KB 27/313 Rex m. 22d (IMG 252). See *Placita Corone* p. xxviii; Jenks, '*Occidit*', p. 120, *Mirror*, book II, c. 7; *BNB* no 1600; *Glanvill*, XIV c. 3; *Bracton*, II, pp. 388, 397.

51 KB 27/114 m. 50d (IMG 6155). Jenks, '*Occidit*'; *Placita Corone*, p. 5; *Fleta* book 1 c. 33.

52 Jenks, '*Occidit*', p. 120; Coke, Inst. II, 68. For the phrase used for holding somebody to facilitate a third person's attack: e.g., JUST 1/934 m. 4 (IMG 5656). See also 1 *SS*, p. 59.

53 JUST 1/1256 m.64 (IMG 0228), SC 8/199/9943. Objections to execution, use for non-virgins: *Mirror*, book V, c. 1.

54 *Bracton* II, p. 415. *Mirror* book II, c. 31; J. Carter, 'Rape and Medieval English Society: The Evidence of Yorkshire, Wiltshire and London, 1218–76', *Comitatus* 13 (1982), 33–63, 50. *Britton*, book 1 c. 15, defines rape as a felony, whether or not the woman is a virgin.

55 Kerr, 'Husband and Wife', pp. 226, 243, Roger D. Groot, 'The Crime of Rape Temp. Richard I and John', *JLH* 9 (1988), 324–34, 324–5. For an appeal by a seven-year-old, see JUST 1/1256 m. 64 (IMG 228); SC8/199/943.

56 See also KB 27/365 Rex m. 1 (IMG 7144) (jury presentment, pardon because the defendant married the girl or woman in question), and 115 *SS* pp. 98–101, KB 27/925 m. 87d, KB 27/923 m. 54d.

57 Seabourne, *IMW*, pp. 100–3; SC8 336/15869; SC8 27/1316; *RP* IV, 498; *RP* V, 14b–15b.

woman also required the co-operation of her husband to bring appeals of rape by another man.[58] A more shadowy area of possible restriction related to female villeins, especially with regard to rape by their lord. At the end of the period, Littleton thought it worth emphasising that they did have a right to an appeal of rape, suggesting that there had been some doubt about the matter (that is to say, doubt as to the right to bring an appeal, not whether a lord could force sex upon his villeins).[59] In addition, considerable limitations existed, in terms of the readiness to class as non-forcible, not against the woman's will and non-rape (or not appealable rape) many cases of penetration. Thus, instances of previous, allegedly consensual sex with the defendant, or the pregnancy of the woman, were good exceptions.[60]

All appellors might be frustrated by the technical requirements of the appeal.[61] The level of detail required to be stated and repeated was demanding, as can be seen in an appeal by Felicia, widow of John Gervaise of Stamford against Richard son of Robert, for the death of her husband. Richard objected that he was a clerk and also noted that the appeal was insufficiently clear about several matters: which of two possible feasts of St Andrew and which of two possible churches of Our Lady at Stamford were meant as reference points for the scene of the crime; whether the 'ten feet from the steps' location was to the east or west of the aforesaid steps; what was the material of the murder weapon's blade; and what the precise location of the fatal wound, in inches from the jaw of the deceased. Doubts about naming and assigning parentage of the victim were also raised.[62] Appeals brought by men had similar difficulties.[63] In all appeals, it might be claimed that the action was brought for improper motives, or was 'false'.[64] Any appellant might face violence or other forms of pressure or influence which hampered

58 See, e.g., 1 *SS* p. 92 no 141 (1221); *Seipp* 1302.157rs, 1407.012. Appeal of robbery of W, brought by H and W. KB 27/518 m. 20d (IMG 305). Complications imagined relating to a revoked divorce, with the woman raped during the period between divorce and revocation: 105 *SS* pp. cxlvii, 180.

59 *Litt.*, book II, no. 190; *P and M* I, p. 39; Hyams, *KLP*, p. 150; Pulton, *De Pace*, 159b.

60 *Bracton* II, p. 416; *Mirror*, book III, c. 21; Kerr, 'Husband and Wife', p. 243; Elise Bennett Histed, 'Medieval Rape: A Conceivable Defence', *CLJ* 63 (2004), 743–69; KB 27/566 m. 21 (IMG 51).

61 Sara M. Butler, *Forensic Medicine and Death Investigation in Medieval England* (New York and Abingdon, 2015), p. 157. Rape appeal quashed for 'trivial matter', see SC 8/199/9943. Discussion of procedure on women's appeals: *Seipp* 1324.112; 1339.045rs; 1367.088ass; 1342.161rs; 1342.287ass.

62 24 *SS* 100 ff.

63 See, e.g., relating to location: KB 27/872 m.5d (IMG 459).

64 See, e.g., KB 27/177 m. 63d (IMG 5809); KB 27/177 m. 69d (IMG 5826), SC8/179/8928. Alleged false appeal by women: (robbery) KB 27/602 m. 27d (IMG 156); (H's death) KB 27/514 m. 26 (IMG 54); SC8/298/14865. Malicious procuring of indictment by men, e.g., JUST 1/1107 m. 20d (IMG 8597); woman claiming men conspired to indict her, falsely, of theft: KB 27/533 m. 35d (IMG 210). For the 'de odio et atia' procedure, see Susanne Jenks, 'The Writ and the Exception *de odio et atia*', *JLH* 23 (2002), 1–22.

them in trying to bring their cases. We hear, for example, of a woman bringing an appeal of rape allegedly assaulted to stop her doing so,[65] of another woman who was said to have been prevented from pursuing her appeal by a trumped-up suit, causing her to be imprisoned at a critical point,[66] and yet another alleging that threats were making it impossible to bring an appeal for the death of her husband.[67] Anyone bringing an appeal also faced financial and legal penalties if the case was abandoned or no conviction obtained. The importance to women of these 'gender neutral' difficulties with the appeal was, however, disproportionately large, since their alternative routes to prosecution were fewer. As well as facing all of the same difficulties and complexities of bringing an appeal which faced men, women also faced additional hurdles and problems. It might be argued that a woman's marital status disqualified her, but the same did not apply to a man.[68] Some requirements were not specifically for women's appeals, but might nevertheless have been particularly challenging for women. Thus, in particular, a raped woman must exhibit physical signs of the offence. Blood and torn clothes are suggested in some treatises as appropriate and perhaps necessary evidence that the penetration was against the woman's will, suggesting a need for quick and intimate exhibition.[69] It is true that all appellors had to act swiftly, and that those appealing for wounds as well as raped women had to exhibit themselves, but it seems plausible to suggest that the action required of a raped woman presented a particularly heavy and possibly discouraging burden, since the exhibition may well have been more intimate than that of other injuries, and the matter was regarded as more shameful than receiving a wound,[70] and since there is unlikely to be a complete discontinuity between the psychological and psychiatric response of medieval and modern women to a rape, and there is modern evidence that being subjected to rape is particularly likely to lead to conditions which would subdue the ability to take immediate, decisive action such as initiating a prosecution.[71]

65 KB 27/479 m. 29, 29d (IMG 176, 7144). See also, e.g., *Seipp* 1368.106ass, assault in Westminster Hall.

66 *Seipp* 1341.102rs.

67 SC8/345/E1330. See also SC8/334/E1192.

68 Marital status, e.g., KB 27/432 m. 60 (IMG 123); KB 27/516 m. 32 (IMG 67). Villein status: *Seipp* 1344.162rs, excommunication: *Seipp* 1329.072, 1329.171ass; KB 27/276 Rex m.9 and 9d (IMG 253 and 17).

69 *Glanvill*, XIV, 6; *Bracton* II, p. 394; *OHLE* 1, pp. 721–35. *Placita Corone*, p. 25. 60 *SS* ccii; *Britton* book 1 c. 17; *Mirror* book III, c. 21 p. 103.

70 See, e.g., Corinne Saunders, *Rape and Ravishment in the Literature of Medieval England* (Woodbridge, 2001), pp. 159–60, 171–2, 196.

71 See, e.g., Carlo Faravelli, Alice Giugni, Stefano Salvatori and Valdo Ricca, 'Psychopathology after Rape', *American Journal of Psychiatry* 161 (2004), 1483–5; Jean-Michel Darves-Bornoz, 'Rape-related Psychotraumatic Syndromes', *European Journal of Obstetrics & Gynecology and Reproductive Biology* 71 (1997), 59–65; R. Campbell and S. Raja, 'The Secondary Victimization of Rape Victims: Insights from Mental Health Professionals Who Treat Survivors of Violence', *Violence and Victims* 14

A group of fifteenth-century plea roll cases show both the importance of women's appeals for the death of their husbands at the hands of powerful interests, and also the problems in seeing them through, when opposed by those with influence, in a time of tension and weak central control. In the case of the murder of Nicholas Radford, killed in 1455, the usual criminal process did not work, due to the influence of local nobles and to the inability of his sick wife to bring an appeal.[72] The wife of William Tresham suggested that the offenders' threats were making it impossible to use the local sheriff and coroner to take action for the killing of her husband.[73] *Agnes Glover v Walter Devereux, William Herbert and others* (1457) shows an appeal brought by a widow against a group of powerful men, following an episode in which Devereux, Herbert and associates took over Hereford and its institutions for a period in 1456, forcing local judicial authorities to find Glover guilty of killing Herbert's kinsman, so that he could be hanged.[74] The irregular hanging had to be forced into the appeal formula, significantly distorting the apparent facts, showing the difficulty of using the appeal process to take action against an abuse of justice of this sort. Despite the many difficulties and obstacles, some women might show great determination in bringing appeals, against principals, accessories and those allegedly on the fringes of involvement in the deaths of their husbands. This can be seen, for example, in the efforts of an early fifteenth-century woman, Alice atte Wode, to pursue those she accused of responsibility for her husband John's 'contract killing' death at Westminster, despite the fact that they had been violent towards her and her husband in the past.[75] Alice's less robust sisters should not, however, be ignored.

(1999), 261–75; Karen G. Weiss, 'Too Ashamed to Report: Deconstructing the Shame of Sexual Victimization', *Feminist Criminology* 5 (2010), 286–310; A. Feist, J. Ashe, J. Lawrence and D. McPhee, *Investigating and Detecting Recorded Offences of Rape* (Home Office Online Report 18/07, 2007), p. 24. Anna Möller, Hans Peter Sondergaard and Lotti Helstrom, 'Tonic Immobility During Sexual Assault: A Common Reaction Predicting Post Traumatic Stress Disorder and Severe Depression', *Acta Obstetricia et Gynecologica Scandinavica* 96 (2017), 932–8.

72 G.H. Radford, 'Nicholas Radford', *Transactions of the Devonshire Association*. xxxv. 251–78; SC8/138/6864.

73 *RP* V, pp. 211–12; *TNA* C 65/101 m. 2–3.

74 KB 27/784 m. 85; KB 27/781 Rex mm. 1d and 26d and KB 27/782 Rex m. 22; *Seipp* 1457.022. See, e.g., A. Herbert, 'Herefordshire, 1413–61: Some Aspects of Society and Public Order', in *Patronage, the Crown and the Provinces in Later Medieval England*, ed. by Ralph A. Griffiths (Gloucester, 1981), pp. 103–22; Ailsa E. Herbert, 'Public Order and Private Violence in Herefordshire, 1413–61', MA Thesis, University of Wales, Swansea 1978; Gwen Seabourne, 'Judging a Hereford Hanging: Agnes Glover v. Walter Devereux, William Herbert and others, 1457', *Midland History* 45 (2020), 2–17.

75 *Seipp* 1405.080; 1405.098; KB 27/575 Rex m. 10 d (IMG 85); KB 27/577 Rex m. 2d (IMG 263); KB 27/577 Rex m. 2 (IMG 124); KB 27/578 m. 11 (IMG 25); KB 27/578 m. 57d (IMG 392); 35 *SS*, pp. 86–92, civ–cvi.

An exhaustive study of the 'success rate' of appeal cases is beyond the scope of this monograph. Information about ultimate resolution or end of these actions is very imperfect, and it is not clear how one ought to define 'success' in any case. There are examples of convictions and executions as a result of women's appeals.[76] It is, however, relevant to note that all indications are that the overall picture is one of few completed cases and convictions, a point particularly emphasised in treatments of appeals of rape.[77] This may lead to a questionable line of reasoning, from the low number of convictions to a view that this suggests that a high proportion of the allegations are likely to have been false, and, in the case of rape, that they may have been made for the purpose of achieving a disapproved marriage by means of settlement or else as the revenge of a discarded woman.[78] Seeking material compensation after rape or indeed after the slaying of a husband was, however, a course of action both practical and long-rooted, and it does not say anything about the truth of the allegation.[79] In rape cases settled by marriage, the records sometimes give a good indication that this was far from being a way of attaining a desired marriage, as we see in one early thirteenth-century Cornish case, in which a settlement by marriage between rape complainant and accused was allowed after a jury had accepted that there had been a violent attack, in that the woman complaining of rape had been seen bleeding.[80] Scholarship has made a welcome move away from seeing financial settlement as obviously less desirable to the complainant than pursuit through the courts, and away from the idea that a conviction and capital punishment was the only 'successful' outcome for the prosecutor.[81] This broader approach to the

76 See, e.g., appeals for death of H: JUST 3/167 m. 71 (IMG 154); JUST 1/189 m. 25 (IMG 60).

77 Low conviction rate in all women's appeals, and rape in particular, see, e.g., Wilkinson, *Women*, pp. 148, 151–2; Orr, 'English Women', pp. 145–9, 154, 206, 248; Kerr, 'Husband and Wife', p. 243; Settlements in rape appeals, see also *Somersetshire Pleas* no 848 p. 248, p. 256 no 887; JUST 1/1043 m. 8. For arbitration and compensation for homicide, c. 1475, see Whittick, 'Role of the Criminal Appeal', p. 64. Low conviction rate in rape indictments: Butler 'Violence and Murder', p. 339, Edward Powell, 'Jury Trial at Gaol Delivery in the Late Middle Ages: The Midland Circuit,1400–1429', in *Twelve Good Men and True: The Criminal Trial Jury in England, 1200–1800*, ed. by J.S. Cockburn and T.A. Green (Princeton, NJ, 1988), pp. 78–116, 101.

78 C.A.F. Meekings (ed.), *1235 Surrey Eyre* vol 1 (Surrey Record Society, 1979), p. 123; *Placita Corone*, p. xxviii. See Klerman, 'Women Prosecutors', p. 302; Coss, *Lady*, p. 140, C.A.F. Meekings, *Crown Pleas of Wiltshire Eyre 1249* (Wiltshire Archaeological Society, 1961), pp. 80, 88–90; J.B. Post, 'Ravishment of Women and the Statutes of Westminster', in *Legal Records and the Historian*, ed. by John Baker (London, 1978), pp. 152–3.

79 Whittick, 'Role of the Criminal Appeal', p. 65. Financial penalties for rape: M.H. Kerr, 'Angevin Reform of the Appeal of Felony', *LHR* 13 (1995), 351–91, 361; *P & M* II, p. 516 (1256). Marriage settlement after a violent rape: 1 *SS* (1201), 7. Whittick, 'Role of the Criminal Appeal', p. 63. For variation over time in judicial attitude towards settlement, see Klerman, 'Women Prosecutors', p. 274; Klerman, 'Settlement', pp. 15–18.

80 Hanawalt, 'Justice without Judgment', p. 124; 1 *SS*, no. 7, p. 3.

81 Ernst, 'Moribund Appeal of Death', p. 171; Klerman, 'Women Prosecutors', p. 312; Hurnard, *King's Pardon*, p. 204.

purposes of legal action can be bolstered by consideration of the tendency in all 'bodily harm' appeals to an emphasis on compensation rather than the physical punishment of the offender.[82] Settlement was, and remains, a frequent way of ending all manner of legal disputes.[83] In relation to rape, more recent scholarship has emphasised the financial and other risks run by women bringing appeals as a reason to doubt the falsity of their allegations. If they withdrew, or the appeal failed, serious consequences could follow, including imprisonment and financial penalty for them or those who had supported them: they were unlikely to risk frivolous suits.[84] There are other reasons which might be suggested for the failure of women's appeals, especially rape appeals, to end in conviction, including the possibility that such appeals may not be taken seriously by male authorities and juries.[85] The low 'completion rate' and 'success rate' in women's appeals are noteworthy, but there is a need for caution in the conclusions which may be drawn from them.

Other litigation initiated by or in the name of women

In addition to the appeals discussed above, women also brought a variety of less formal 'criminal' complaints bills or plaints and 'civil' actions at common law,[86] relating to rights in land, and wrongs they claimed had been done to them, seeking compensation, the return of land or another remedy. Those litigating at common law represented a relatively broad range of women, from queens downwards (though there were restrictions on the access of villein women to common law courts).[87] It was by no means the case, however, that the common law was neutral as to sex and gender, or

82 KB 27/583 Rex m. 6 (IMG 163) Settlement and pardon for one who had abducted a woman and removed her eye(s) and tongue, 1408: *CPR 1405–8*, p. 310.

83 See, e.g., in the land context, J.M. Kaye, *Medieval English Conveyances* (Cambridge, 2009), p. 18.

84 Imprisonment: *Seipp* 1321.141ss, JUST 1/721 m. 12 (IMG 353); 1325.147; 60 *SS* ccii; KB 27/720 m. 96 (IMG 196); st. of Wales 1284, c. 3, *SR* I, p. 56; *Seipp* 1348.247ass; 1366.106. Note st. Westminster II c. 12, *SR* I, p. 29.

85 *SR* I, p. 211; men of Grimsby in mercy for failure to attach a rape accused: JUST 1/479 m. 1 (IMG 1247). Dropped or failed appeals might be taken over in the king's name: see, e.g., JUST 1/1256 m. 64 (IMG 0228).

86 On plaints and bills, see Crook, *Records of the General Eyre*, p. 7; Helen M. Cam, 'Studies in the Hundred Rolls', 57; Alan Harding, 'Plaints and Bills in the History of English Law, Mainly in the Period 1250–1330', in *Legal History Studies 1972*, ed. by Dafydd Jenkins (Cardiff, 1975), 30 *SS*; 24 *SS* pp. xxi–xxx; 60 *SS*.

87 For mid-thirteenth-century land actions, see Loengard, 'What Is a Nice ... Englishwoman Doing'. In relation to appeals, Klerman, 'Women Prosecutors', pp. 314, 316, has found that most women bringing appeals were of modest circumstances. Queens, see, e.g., *Seipp* 1304.091rs; 1352.031; 1344.006rs; 1430.071;1433.072; 1479.033, KB 27/28 m. 3 (IMG 7965); KB 27/784 m. 59d (IMG 401). Prioresses, e.g., *Somersetshire Pleas* case 1521; CP 40/401 m.166d, CP 40.427 m. 84 (IMG 170); *Seipp* 1292.226rs; 1306.047rs; 1317.012ss; 1321.211ss; 1442.038; 1364.160ass; KB 27/430 m. 23 (IMG 157); Elizabeth Makowski, *English Nuns and the Law in the Middle Ages: Cloistered Nuns and Their Lawyers*

that women were accommodated as well in litigation as were men. The common law limited their ability to litigate via its rules on the disabilities of married women, and also through more indirect means, through choices about which sorts of action to entertain and facilitate.

As is well known, wives were subject to particular constraint with regard to litigation.[88] First, they could not sue their husbands at common law; thus a woman whose husband alienated her land had to await his death or their divorce to take action,[89] and a man sued for trespass against a woman might claim to be her husband, to defeat her suit. Thus, for example, it would have been regarded as a valid exception to a 1310 trespass case, in which Katerine de Ramesden alleged that Philip de Herdewyk and another man had beaten her and taken her chattels, if the Bishop of Lincoln had confirmed when asked to certify the matter that Philip was in fact Katerine's husband, as he claimed,[90] since it was a clear rule that a wife could not sue a husband.[91] This spousal immunity was occasionally used in the opposite direction; thus there is a 1338 case in which a male claiming false imprisonment was met with the objection that the defendant was his wife, and so he could not sue her.[92] There was also a rule that wives could not sue in 'civil' actions without their husband's co-operation, and that seems to have been maintained strongly.[93] Should a married woman attempt to bring a trespass action on her own, for example, she would be met by the plea that because she had a husband, she should not sue alone.[94] Fifteenth-century common lawyers seem to have had a Latin rhyme, expressing the impropriety of a married women suing alone.[95] As a consequence of this limitation, women would also face problems in litigation if they changed marital status during its course, and cases frequently revolved around whether a woman was single or married at a particular point.[96]

1293–1540 (Woodbridge, 2012), p. 29; Seipp 1455.023. For women labelled poor, see, e.g., 87 *SS*, p. lxxix.

88 See Chapter 2.

89 Sutherland, *Assize of Novel Disseisin*, p. 112.

90 CP 40/183 m. 142 d (IMG 285).

91 *Seipp* 1482.135 (which included some argument as to when this had to be raised).

92 He claimed that the 'marriage' was forced: *Seipp* 1338/009rs; CP 40/313 m. 215 d (IMG 0433).

93 Kerr, 'Husband and Wife', p. 232. Executrix, remarriage, status issues: KB 27/725 m. 13 (IMG 25); divorce in a novel disseisin action: KB 27/497 m. 28 (IMG 57); debt: JUST 1/302 m. 41d (IMG 8500); trespass, pleading as to whether a woman is sole or covert: KB 27/376 m. 57d (IMG 3280). See, e.g., JUST 1/367 m. 36d (IMG 241); Seipp 1365.111. JUST 1/1066 m. 6 (IMG 3708); JUST 1/956 m. (IMG 7898); JUST 1/367 m. 5 (IMG 12). KB 27/558 m. 22, m. 22d (IMG 46, 275); JUST 1/367 m. 33d (IMG 236); JUST 1/955 m. 13 (IMG 7593).

94 KB 27/626 m. 95d (IMG 518).

95 *Seipp* 1465.133.

96 60 *SS*, p. lxxii; 105 *SS* p. xxxiii; *Seipp* 1317.004ss. Some issues remained debatable in the sixteenth century, see, e.g., 121 *SS*, p. 350 (1549).

Women defendants were equally constrained by the disabilities in litigation which were imposed upon wives. If a case was brought which could affect the rights of a wife to an interest in land, but her husband failed to appear or participate, she was at risk of losing her interests, since in general a woman must have her husband's co-operation to defend her interest in land.[97] Wives may have been caused problems by a husband's defaults or unfitness, or his (possible but unproven) death.[98] Under Edward I, there was statutory intervention to allow the wife to act alone if her husband did not help, and common lawyers subsequently devoted particular attention to determining exactly when a wife could act alone.[99] It would be possible to see the common law in this area as 'favourable' to wives in comparison to husbands, for husbands could also lose out if they were unable to secure the participation of a wife in an action involving both of them, and that problem did not prompt comparable legal assistance. In these situations, which receive attention in several law reports, common lawyers felt obliged to follow their own construction of the marital relationship and state the maxim that a wife was 'amenable to her husband's will', despite the fact that they also showed a lack of belief in this as a current and inevitable reality, repeating that wives were 'now' less amenable to a husband's will than had formerly been the case. An interesting example of this may be seen in a Herefordshire case, *Isabella, widow of William de Myners* v. *Alice wife of Adam de Penbrugge*, recorded in the Common Pleas Roll for Michaelmas 1316. This concerned Isabella's attempt to claim dower lands currently held by Alice and her husband. Alice had failed to appear on more than one occasion and her husband, Adam, did not want this to scupper his chances of holding on to the land. He argued that Alice's default should not affect him, because Alice had left him. This received an unfavourable reception however: the response was that a wife ought to be amenable to the will of

97 Prior to legislative intervention, royal favour might be given to allow a woman to litigate alone: *CRR X*, p. 245 (1221); Orr, 'English Women', p. 40; *CRR I* pp. 153, 382 (1200–1) 62 *SS*, p. 367.

98 Issues with proof of the death of a male relation: *Seipp* 1310.032ss; 1309.054ss; 1362.005ass; 1346.011rs, disappearing and reappearing H: *Seipp* 1478.026. For a conditional resolution in such a case: *Seipp* 1285.052ss.

99 st. Westminster II c. 3. Plucknett, *Statutes*, pp. 49–50, 76, 89, 131–2, 159; 17 *SS* p. 76, 28A; p. 150 no 76A. See, e.g., 104 *SS* Case 18; (joint tenancy) *Seipp* 1292.232rs; 1292.115rs; 1292.174rs; 1292.232rs; 1306.118rs; 1310.134ss; 1310.178ss; 1311.275ss (Bereford grumbling that the law is too favourable to women and hard on men); 1312.292ss; 1315.008ss; 1323.028; 1400.007; 1410.028; 1424.057; 1336.010; 1337.074rs; 1337.125rs; 1337.150ass; 1338.274ass; 1340.142rs; 1402.060; 1406.026; 1418.029; 1421.080rog; 1425.115; 1431.072; 1447.012abr; 1480.001; 1481.087; 1341.026rs. W received on H's default, see, e.g. 98 *SS* pp. 595, 763; Walker, 'Wager of Law', p. 35. For suspicion that joint ownership could be abused, see *RP*, I, p. 66.

a husband. Adam therefore received no concession, and the court ordered that Isabella should be allowed her dower.[100]

Given the various licit and illicit means which husbands had to compel their wives' obedience and participation, however, it would be an odd perspective which saw it as a favour to allow some relief to wives, themselves without any such right to chastise or to compel, so that they could defend their interests when a husband defaulted. There is no need to suppose that all husbands and wives were likely to be unsupportive towards their spouses' interests in litigation – and, indeed, there were also fears of their co-operation to disadvantage and delay others in litigation through clever manipulation of their marital status.[101] Should there be a lack of amity, however, the fact that a wife might possibly be allowed to act alone, should her husband default, can hardly be seen as putting her in a position of 'favour' in the context of her other disadvantages.

Other aspects of litigation were not overtly set up to disadvantage women, but were modelled upon a masculine paradigm which ignored them, or did not necessarily suit them. This may appear to have been the case, for example, in relation to essoins, legitimate delays of legal process. In particular, it is notable that *Bracton* and *Fleta*'s treatments of essoins concentrate on masculine paradigms, with no discussion of pregnancy as a legitimate reason not to go to court.[102] The choice of masculine examples in these works is common enough, and does not suggest that there would be a particular problem with using pregnancy as a reason not to attend. It seems that there was some idea that there was a specific essoin relating to pregnancy, not mentioned in the treatises, as some records include reference to an essoin *de malo puerperii, de puerperio* or *de malo ventris.*[103] The lack of treatment of the matter in the treatises (in contrast, for example, to *Bracton*'s inclusion of an account of the implications of a supposedly ill man being found to have put his trousers on) does, however, mean that we are left without much information as to how it would work and at what stage of pregnancy it

100 See, e.g., *Isabella, widow of William de Myners* v. *Alice wife of Adam de Penbrugge*, CP 40/215 m. 212 (IMG 431), which is probably YB M. 10 Edw. II (52 SS) 24. Seipp 1316.055ss; 52 SS pp. 24–5. See also, e.g., 1306.196rs; 1330.823ss; 1304.057rs; 1324.180; 1355.072; 1365.129ass; 1369.055; 1371.010; 1400.007; 1424.057; 1473.019; 1311.268ss; 1337.134ass. Statement that W is amenable to H's will, but not vice versa: 1424.057, 1448.080abr. H unable to produce W: 1310.158ss. Noting that W's default can damage H: 1318.024ss; 1313.479ss. Procedure in relation to the production of W by H seen as changing or contentious: 1310.200ss; 1310.202ss; 1311.052ss; 1336.045. Limits: *Seipp* 1369.055; 1370.015; 1473.019. 1318.007ss; 1324.180; 1325.098; 1336.045; 1369.055; 1371.010, 1469.068; 1410.028; 1336.045.

101 st. Gloucester 1278, c. 10; *SR* I, p. 49.

102 *Glanvill* I, 18, 19, 28; *Bracton* IV, pp. 71, 91–5, 113, 124, 127, 143; *Fleta* book 6 c. 10; *Britton* 6.6 and 6.7.

103 67 *SS*, p. 342 no 3416, includes a woman's essoin *de malo puerperii*, and similarly 84 *SS*, no. 3144 (1208), 3720 (1208–9), 3889 (1208–9), 3913 (1208–9), for this or *de puerperio*. For a failed 1201 attempt to make an essoin *de malo ventris*, see *CRR* I, p. 383.

would be allowed.[104] Records of practice show that pregnant women might receive leave to use an attorney in cases in which personal presence was usually necessary, and scattered statements in law reports show something of the thinking of common lawyers in this area. Thus, Fortescue is shown stating that a pregnant woman could have an attorney, and that this is to avoid loss of the delivery.[105] A Year Book report of 1382 uses the example of a 'greatly' pregnant woman as a paradigm case of somebody who could not travel to court, so might have an attorney, but there is little information available as to how early in pregnancy this would be allowed.[106] Another area without information is the question of how a dispute as to the woman's condition would be resolved, whether by some version of the 'jury of matrons' procedure, seen in relation to land cases and deferral of execution, or by male inspection, as was prescribed in the case of women claiming other forms of illness.[107]

There are complaints of women being prevented from participating, even as far as the rules allowed, by force, or vexatious legal processes in retaliation for their actions or by deception. For example, plea rolls contain complaints by a mother that her daughter was removed from her home in an attempt to stop her bringing an assize,[108] by a husband that his wife was similarly stolen away in order to obstruct a land case,[109] by a widow that the man holding land she claimed in dower had trumped up a trespass suit to delay her in her action.[110] There are examples of pretences that a living woman was dead[111] and of women cheated by their lawyers.[112] Litigation could be expensive, and while law reports make a point of noting apparent generosity to or pity for 'poor women', this was far from solving the problem of funding litigation for most women, and it was recognised elsewhere that – unsurprisingly – rich women were likely to do better than the

104 *Bracton* IV, pp. 124, 128.

105 *Seipp* 1440.115.

106 *Seipp* 1382.056am. See also: JUST 1/704 m. 21d (IMG 8315) (delay granted to woman lying in childbirth); *CCR 1272–9*, p. 228 (pregnant noblewoman excused coming to recover inheritance in person); *CCR 1279–88*, 548; KB 27/260 Rex m.9; CP 40/154 m. 92d (IMG 773); 1443.060 (dower defendant 'grossly pregnant'); *CPR 1374–77*, p. 405 (attorney allowed for pregnant woman defendant in dower case). For lawyers' discussion of pregnancy and participation in litigation, see, e.g., *Seipp* 1367.018, 1430.058; 1465.158.

107 For orders that men should inspect women claiming to be too ill to attend, see: 67 *SS*, p. 113, *CRR* 1 pp. 432, 459 (prioress 1201); *CRR XV* 1233–7 p. 55 no 146; *CRR XX* (1250) no 99 p. 16, p. 44 no 262; *Seipp* 1402.045; 1430.058. *Somersetshire Pleas* no 585. For juries of matrons, see Chapter 3.

108 The mother wanted to bring the action for her: JUST 1/956 m. 18d (IMG 7909).

109 JUST 1/1080 m. 11 (IMG 1917).

110 Rose, *Maintenance*, p. 81. The widow won in a plea of conspiracy and trespass against him: KB 27/144, m. 27 (IMG 58) (1295).

111 CP 40/41 m. 3 (IMG 3645).

112 See, e.g., *Seipp* 1337.033rs; 1355.245ass; 1365.129ass; 30 *SS* no 143.

poor.[113] Women's petitions, which show what were perceived as plausible complaints about failures to do justice according to common law and gaps in the common law in relation to their grievances, covered matters as diverse as difficulties recovering land, offences against the person, enforcement of debts, trying to avoid paying up on unjust claims and recovery of land or property.[114] It was plausible for women to claim that they had been blocked from their common law rights as a result of delay, intimidation, poverty, corruption, cheating or forfeiture for another's offence.[115] Occasionally, women made requests which stretched somewhat beyond their own situation for new rules or changes in the law, or at least its practice, the better to serve women in general, as can be seen in requests for a change in the age at which girls should be able to obtain lands, and for a limit on widespread granting of charters of pardon.[116] Women might, of course, also act badly, and be the subject of complaints. Concern might be expressed about their abusive participation in litigation (maintenance), as can be seen in an ordinance of 1376 'concerning women pursuing business in ... the king's courts'. Although this is expressed in apparently general terms, however, the focus is upon the alleged misbehaviour of one particularly scandalous individual, Alice Perrers, and it should be noted that most of the maintenance statutes, from the late fourteenth century onwards, emphasise men rather than women as the problem.[117]

It is beyond the scope of a short monograph to do this justice, but it is worth raising the issue of the need for legal history to consider through a gender lens the scope of actions entertained – and not entertained – at common law. The choices being made by 'law-finders and law-makers' as to which matters should be recognised as worthy of remedy, and to whom actions should be made accessible and useful, did not represent a gender-neutral process.[118] In addition, an increase or decline in the use of actions which were specifically

113 See *Seipp* 1309.014ss, 1310.144ss, 1330.154, 1333.066, 1338.131rs, 1344.146rs; Musson and Powell, *Crime, Law and Society*, p. 255; T. Wright, *Political Songs*, ed. by Peter Coss (Cambridge, 1996), pp. 224–9. 30 *SS* No 143 p. 119.

114 Dodd, *Justice and Grace*, p. 19. Request for protection for the future: SC8/231/11510; 254/12684; 275/13736; 266/13282; 268/13356. Theft, seeking recovery of goods: SC 8/259/12902; 309/15420; 301/15011. SC 8 266/13293 (W complains of lack of conviction for a woman who poisoned her husband). SC 8/303/15149, 304/15151 (woman claiming wardship of an 'idiot' who has been abused). Rape, e.g., SC 8/295/14797, 199/9943; SC 8/76/3756 and 336/15869 (mothers trying to get action against daughters' rapists and abductors). Personal injury: SC8/39/1922; SC 8/55/2713; SC 8/23/1109. Abduction: SC 8/39/1937.

115 See, e.g., SC 8/61/3027; SC 8/ 117/5806; SC8/2/76; SC8/3/146; SC8/341/16087; SC8/120/5956.

116 See, e.g., SC 8/28/1398. SC8/39/1937.

117 *RP* II, p. 329; George Holmes, *The Good Parliament* (Oxford, 1975), pp. 6, 68–9; W. Mark Ormrod, 'The Trials of Alice Perrers', *Speculum* 83 (2008), 366–96, 394. 'Ladies' were included in a request for action relating to maintenance in 1388: Rose, *Maintenance*, p. 218; *Westminster Chronicle*, pp. 358–9; ladies giving livery mentioned as a problem in a 1429 statute: Rose *Maintenance*, p. 286; 8 Hen. VI, c. 4 (1429), *SR* II, pp. 240–1.

118 Cam, *Law Finders and Law Makers*.

for women represents a change in women's level of participation in the common law. Chief of the 'civil' actions only available to women (or women and their husbands) were the actions relating to dower.[119] This was a major area of common law activity and has received important attention in recent years.[120] In the mid-fourteenth century, dower cases by women alone or by women with a new husband were some of their most frequent actions. Nevertheless, the overall pattern was one of decline, as dower began to be supplanted by other methods of providing for widows.[121] As noted above, the decline in dower was not the only way in which widows became a less important part of the 'case-load' of common law courts, there was also a move away from intervention to uphold widows' rights in relation to chattels, this being left to other jurisdictions.[122] The decline of important woman-focused actions could be seen as forming part of a pattern of masculinisation of the scope of common law over the medieval period.

While other actions and aspects of procedure were not overtly confined to women or men, aspects of their structure and definition might be designed to a masculine model, perhaps less accommodating to women. This sort of issue is raised in the next chapter with regard to pleas of self-defence, but it might also be relevant, and is certainly a question which should be asked, in relation to the structure of 'civil' actions. One very well-known change which occurred in medieval English land law was the provision of forms of action which dealt not with questions of right, but with more limited questions associated with seisin.[123] Some, at least, of these involved consideration of physical taking of possession, possibly in the face of opposition, and had a role for physical 'self help'. Thus, to bring an action of (novel) disseisin, it was necessary to have been regarded as having been in seisin, and it was acceptable to take physical action to regain seisin, if there was an attempted ouster. *Bracton* certainly sees such action in masculine terms,

119 See also certain writs of entry designed for women: e.g., 87 *SS* pp. 99, 292–3, 296.

120 See, e.g., Brand, '"Deserving"; J.S. Loengard, '"Of the Gift of Her Husband": English Dower and Its Consequences in the Year 1200', in *Women in the Medieval World*, ed. by J. Kirshner and S. Wemple (Oxford, 1985), pp. 213–55; Joseph Biancalana, 'Widows at Common Law: the Evolution of Common Law Dower', *Irish Jurist* 23 (1988), 255–329; Sue Sheridan Walker, 'Litigation as Personal Quest: Suing for Dower in the Royal Courts, circa 1272–1350', in *Wife and Widow*, ed. by Walker (Ann Arbor, 1993), pp. 81–108; Walker, 'Wager of Law and Judgment by Default in Pleas of Dower in the Royal Courts of Late Thirteenth and Fourteenth Century England', in *The Life of the Law*, ed. by Peter Birks (London, 1993), pp. 25–42; Walker, 'Litigant Agency' in Dower Pleas in Royal Common Law Courts in Thirteenth and Early Fourteenth Century England', *JLH* 24 (2003), 1–22; Paula Dobrowolski, 'Women and Their Dower in the Long Thirteenth Century 1265–1329', in *Thirteenth Century England* VI (Woodbridge, 1997), pp. 158–9. Note changing family property practice: Coss, *Lady*, p. 86.

121 See above at 48.

122 See above at 49.

123 See, e.g., Baker, *Introduction*, pp. 250–5.

quoting a scriptural tag from the gospel of Luke about a strong, armed man.[124] Clearly women were not incapable of engaging in physically forceful actions, though examples suggest that they might need or use male help to gain the appropriate degree of control of land.[125] Gendered aspects are little explored in existing scholarship.[126] It is, however, worth at least raising the issue of whether social expectations and norms relating to women's behaviour might have left them at a particular disadvantage in actions structured around taking, demonstrating and maintaining physical possession. Did any such disadvantage diminish with the attenuation of the physical requirements for seisin in the later thirteenth century or the limitation of force in relation to taking possession of land from the time of Richard II? Giving any reliable answer to such questions would require a large-scale quantitative study of actions, over a long period of time, and it is not particularly surprising that it has not yet been attempted. Noting that there might be questions relating to gender, however, and including them within the 'overall story' of common law development, does not seem to be too much to expect. In a similar vein, it is worth considering the increased formality requirements of the common law from the late thirteenth century onwards, in areas such as the covenant and the 'forty shilling limit' in debt,[127] through a 'gender lens', inquiring whether, as seems likely, the increased formality, requiring both expense and the involvement of male professionals and value thresholds for common law suits, when combined with women's subordinate economic position and lower level of literacy, were a particular additional constraint on the utility to women of common law actions, sending them elsewhere for remedies. The standard legal historical narrative, however, has not chosen to include such considerations.[128] That narrative could also be expanded to include discussion of the gendered nature of the wrongs selected and passed over for potential remedy at common law. The nature of the offences and harms typically alleged in the expanding

124 See, e.g., Hudson *OHLE* II c. 24; Simpson, *A History of the Land Law*, p. 31; *Bracton* II, pp. 18, 21.

125 Donald W. Sutherland, *Assize of Novel Disseisin* (Oxford, 1973), pp. 106–7, 118; *Lincs RS 22* no 1425. See, e.g., Sutherland, *Assize*, p. 118. See also the story of a woman claiming land occupying it overnight, protesting her right: JUST 1/1300 m. 8d (IMG 4781). Women unable to claim their land in a court because of threats by their uncle, kept out for seven years: JUST 1/1149 m. 9 (IMG 1615).

126 Sutherland, *Assize* pp. 148, 166, 174; Statutes of forcible entry 1378–1429. 2 Ric. II st. 1 c. 6 (1378), 2 Ric. II st 2 c. 2; 5 Ric. II st 1 c. 7; 15 Ric. II c. 2; 4 Hen. IV c. 8; 8 Hen. VI c. 9. Women were sometimes portrayed leading forceful actions to enforce property rights, so that this is not entirely a matter of curbing masculine force: see, e.g., 103 *SS* p. 371 case 34.7, KB 27/217 m. 35d.

127 See, e.g., Baker, *Introduction*, pp. 340–1.

128 See, e.g., Baker, *Introduction*, c. 18, p. 343; Ibbetson, *Historical Introduction*, pp. 23–8; Baker, 'Deeds Speak Louder than Words: Covenants and the Law of Proof 1290–1321', in *Laws, Lawyers and Texts*, ed. by Susanne Jenks and others (Leiden, 2012), pp. 181–203.

trespass jurisdiction in later medieval common law are worth examining in this light.[129] The interaction between social norms and trespass jurisdiction meant that it could be less useful to women than to men. Thus, while women did bring actions for trespass to the person, and false imprisonment, and sought compensation for the injuries done them,[130] some beatings – by husbands on wives and by masters on servants – were not within the ambit of trespass actions, as long as the conduct in question was not clearly unreasonably violent according to contemporary views.[131] Approval of chastisement of a wife by a husband and chastisement of girls by those in authority over them is well evidenced.[132] Females could, likewise, legitimately be confined in the marital context, if they were villeins, or in the context of the woman's law-breaking.[133] The development from trespass to 'trespass on the case' actions, bringing a wider array of scenarios within the ambit of the common law courts, is also ripe for examination with attention to its impact upon the proportionate advantage brought to men and to women by the expansion of jurisdiction in this direction.[134] There are some tentative bases upon which a pattern of increasing masculinisation of the common law might be constructed, and there is some corroboration in studies suggesting that there was a decline in the proportion of actions brought by women in courts of common law over the course of the fourteenth and fifteenth centuries.[135] Even if this is not open to full proof, or not accepted, the possibility raised here that patterns of development were not the same for women as for men should militate against unquestioning, unified, portrayals of the linear progress of the common law.

Making statements on what the common law might have done, but did not, is fraught with danger. There are, however, intriguing insights to be gained into what women might have wanted from the common law system, but which the makers of the common law did not choose to make part of its

129 For trespass, see, e.g., Ibbetson, *Historical Introduction*, cc. 3, 4, 6.

130 See, e.g., *Seipp* 1368.106ass; 1483.004; KB 27/510 m. 35 (IMG 77). *SS* 100 p. 170, KB 27/499 m. 22d 1386H; JUST 1/158 m. 3 (IMG 8982); married woman beaten and mistreated, trespass plea (she, not H, recovers 30s). Plaint, jury find a man guilty of assault on a woman, she recovers damages: JUST 1/188 m. 14 (IMG 3248). Writ of entry for land transfer for marriage, which did not happen: CP 40/317 m. 49 (IMG 101).

131 See Sara M. Butler, *Divorce in Medieval England: From One to Two Persons in Law* (London, 2013), p. 71; *P & M* II, p. 436; JUST 2/67 m. 6.

132 Butler, *Language of Abuse*, pp. 27, 33 and c. 6; 100 *SS*, 103 *SS* p. 26. Male kin killing girls by beating, portrayed as chastisement: KB 27/626 m. 26d (IMG 591). Coroner's jury say felonious killing. Father says not guilty. A man hits a seven-year-old girl in the head, once, she dies three days later: this was said to be chastisement by a kinsman, not done with intent to kill her: JUST 1/1334 m. 27 (IMG 2593).

133 This included, from the later fourteenth century, her failure to accept employment: 100 *SS*, p. 47 case 4.3, p. 81 case 8.8, p. 100 case 10.3 KB 27/295 m. 2d; KB 27/233 m. 89; KB 27/450 m. 67 1375T.

134 See Baker, *Introduction*, pp. 350–68, 427–36.

135 See above, 79–81.

regular jurisdiction, from some of the matters raised in 'non-standardised' forms of complaint, bills and plaints, particularly in the thirteenth and early fourteenth centuries. Wrongs which they alleged, and for which they asked a remedy, included some matters which might have formed the basis for a common law action, but also went beyond this. Thus, we see allegations of assault, insult, defamation, economic loss from a cancelled marriage, loss of land or home, rape and sexual offences which did not fit into the definition of felonious rape, harassment of a pregnant and then recently delivered woman by litigation in ecclesiastical court, abduction of daughters.[136] While straightforward complaints of physical assault, for example, were entertained relatively frequently in 'regular' common law cases throughout the medieval period, from the thirteenth century onwards, sexual offences on women other than felonious rape, which were seen in plaints, did not often appear in trespass suits or, if they were part of the allegation, were not made explicit in the records which have survived. Insults did not come to be a regular part of common law jurisdiction until the sixteenth century, despite some sign that individual women wanted common law action here. To the extent that insults were covered by medieval common law, the focus of prescriptive sources was on insults to great men rather than women, though there is one, late, case at least which suggests that prominent women might be considered to be covered by the law; a complaint by Jacquetta, duchess of Bedford, that she had been slandered, heard in the Council and recorded on the Patent roll, may refer, obliquely, to the *Scandalum Magnatum* provisions.[137] When the common law did develop a more wide-ranging action for defamation, it did so in a gendered manner, accommodating more masculine concerns and leaving some of those particularly affecting women to other jurisdictions.[138] That, however, is a story which belongs to the Early Modern period.

136 Assault: *CRR XX (1250)* no 1230 p. 217; JUST 1/306 m. 4 (IMG 9057); JUST 1/1080 m. 10 (IMG 1912). H and W bring plaint for assault on W. JUST 1/628 m. 5 (IMG 478) damages go to H and W; H and W complain of defamation: JUST 1/650 m. 24d (IMG 278). Women's plaints for smashed teeth: JUST 1/23 m. 100 (IMG 1226); mayhem: JUST 1/1015 m. 12 (IMG 1228); JUST 1/934 m. 28 (IMG 5709); failed marriage: JUST 1/408 m. 99 (IMG 807); ejectment: JUST 1/486 m. 47d (IMG 2915); being put in stocks and raped (1290): JUST 1/541A m. 15d (IMG 3675); false imprisonment, e.g., JUST 1/541A m. 48d (IMG 3747); JUST 1/302 m. 77 (IMG 8354); JUST 1/573 m. 58d (IMG 843). False imprisonment of H: SS 60 no 20. Removal and mistreatment of a cow: JUST 1/628 m. 5d (IMG 499). Recovery in rape plaints: JUST 1/1016 mm. 12, (IMG 1303, 1309).

137 *P & M* II, p. 535; st. Westminster I. c. 34, *SR* I, p. 35; 2 Ric. II. st. 1, c. 5; 12 Ric. II. c. 11. See *RP* III pp. 168–70; *SR* II, p. 9, st. 1 Ric II c. 5 uses 'gentz', but mentions male positions only. Uncertainty as to whether it applies to women: Richard Crompton, *L'authoritie et iurisdiction des courts de la Maiestie de la Roygne* (London, 1637), p. 34; Thomas Starkie, *Treatise on the Law of Slander, Libel, Scandalum Magnatum and False Rumours* (London, 1813), p. 170. See *CPR 1467–77*, p. 190; *RP* VI, p. 232.

138 See, e.g., Baker, *Introduction*, c. 25; Laura Gowing, 'Gender and the Language of Insult in Early Modern London', *History Workshop Journal* 35 (1993), 1–21; David Hewitt,

Men's actions for women's injuries

We have seen above some of the limits placed on women's capacity to litigate at common law.[139] The fact that a woman could not litigate herself did not, however, mean that there was no chance wrongs done to her could be brought to the attention of the common law. Surviving collections of presentments and indictments, all made by groups of males as well as commissions and petitions identified as made by males, include accusations of the commission of many different offences against women, from homicide to fraud.[140] A wide range of women, from the wealthy to the lowly, can be seen portrayed in these actions as having been wronged. There are knights' widows, for example, but there are also those at the bottom of the social scale, as can be seen in a late fifteenth-century presentment from Southwark, stating that John Burnham, master of the Hospital of St Thomas, kept two common *meretrices*, Joan Sakkefeld and Joyce, in his room as his concubines, 'knew them carnally' whenever he wished and would not let them out to hear mass or other service for a year and more, amongst other offences. (He said he was not guilty, but made a fine 'to save trouble and expense'.)[141]

As well as bringing apparently 'altruistic' actions in relation to wrongs done to unconnected women, men might also bring actions relating to wrongs against or involving a woman connected to them. *Bracton* saw this as harm to the man through 'his people' or 'those in his power' (*potestas*), and noted that, as between spouses, there was no symmetry: while the husband could bring an action for a wrong to his wife, she could not do so if he should be wronged.[142] Plea rolls from the thirteenth century onwards contain actions in relation to *raptus*/ravishment of a wife, or loss of services of a daughter.[143] These offences are portrayed as damaging to the man who

---

'Some Cases from the Defamation Jurisdiction of the Archdeaconry of Richmond', *JLH* 19 (1998), 251–69.

139 Other limitations included those on villein women: see, e.g., in relation to false imprisonment: JUST 1/1084 m. 27 (IMG 4671); CP 40/423 m. 231d (IMG 1318), assault: JUST 1/483 m. d (IMG 2262); JUST 1/483 m. 59d (IMG 2262). Limits on 'foreign' women, see above at 29 See also *Seipp* 1483.010, KB 27/885 m.39d (IMG 290). Slain or allegedly slain women could not, of course, pursue those responsible.

140 See, e.g., SC8/97/4826; JUST 1/1032 m. 1 (IMG 2684); KB 27/351 m. 19 (IMG 1954); e.g., *CPR 1313–17*, 403 (1315); SC 8/26/1281; Dodd, *Justice and Grace*, p. 184; SC 8/27/1305; SC8/23/1108. Man hanged for killing woman: KB 27/439 m. 7 (IMG 164).

141 Knight's widow: KB 9/232/2 m. 6 (IMG 18); prioress (obtaining damages for the beating of a nun): JUST 1/457 m. 4 (IMG 4780). KB 27/921 m. 9d (IMG 552) May 1491. Prostitute (*stipendiaria*) bringing an appeal: Hanawalt, 'Justice without Judgment', p. 131; 1 *SS*, no. 16, pp. 6–8.

142 *Fleta* book II c. 1; *Bracton* II, p. 438.

143 Milsom, 'Trespass', p. 211; KB 26/121 mm 22d, 24d, 29. See also Wilkinson, *Women*, p. 150; Kerr, 'Husband and Wife', p. 228; Caroline Dunn, 'The Language of Ravishment in Medieval England', *Speculum* 86 (2011), 79–116; Seabourne, *IMW*, cc. 4, 5, 7; 100 *SS* section 8. For men's appeals for the rape/ravishment of their wives, see, e.g., KB 27/689 m. 23d (IMG 249). Father sues for ravishment of daughter: 1315.088ss, 100 SS xlv. Man

is bringing the action, but this does not mean either that they were not also seen as damaging to the woman or girl in question, or that they indicate a chattel-owner property relationship between the man and woman or girl. Such a relationship would not be consistent with the fact that when an action of trespass was brought for assault on a wife, it was not brought by the husband alone, but by the husband and wife together. Thus, for example, a fourteenth-century husband and wife might sue a surgeon for harm to the wife.[144] When percussive abortion was treated as a trespass, if the assaulted woman was married, this might be formulated as a wrong to her husband or to her and her husband.[145]

Also impinging upon the question of whether the harm was understood to be to the litigating man or also to the woman are the Plea Rolls' numerous examples of the different *raptus* offences, brought not by women, but by husbands, or by community indictment or presentment.[146] An analysis which emphasises the likelihood that some of the events behind the accusations involved wives who had consented to leaving (with 'consent' understood in a modern sense) aligns better with the idea of a focus of actions on wrong to the man than does an acceptance that a significant proportion of actions may have been based on facts which cannot now be classed as consensual. Some 'ravishment of wife and goods' cases were probably brought after courses of

---

sues for assault on his female servant, and his loss of her services: e.g., CP 40/705 m. 385 (IMG 784). Action for imprisoning P's daughter and servant, answered by the plea that the daughter went off willingly with the defendant after an agreement to marry: KB 27/450 m. 76 (1373) (IMG 1314). Damage to or sexual misconduct with, a servant treated as damage to a master or, more rarely, mistress: C 1/158/47; C 1/1/92; KB 27/450 m. 76 1373. For women suing for removal of their villeins, see, e.g., CP 40/401 m. 166d, Hil 1360. Discussion of the wrong done to H by W's adultery: *Seipp* 1486.003.

144 Milsom, 'Trespass', p. 571; KB 27/414 m. 37d (1364). Note *querela* by both spouses in relation to beating of the pregnant wife, damaging the foetus: JUST 1/804 m. 41 (IMG 2368); Pugh, *Wilts Trailbaston* no 793, assault on a wife; damages go 'to the husband in the wife's name'.

145 Presented/indicted, e.g., *Somersetshire Pleas,* No 1243; JUST 1/302 m. 85 (IMG 8370); JUST 1/1015 m. 13 (IMG 1231); JUST 1/547A m. 20d (IMG 5833); KB 9/167 m. 19 (IMG 36); JUST 3/20/4 m. 44 (IMG 105) 1411–12. Men's appeals for this: PCOG 16 p. 140; SS 1 p. 11; JUST 1/111 m. 28d (IMG 3822) 1284. Women's appeals for this: *JUST 1/ 778 m. 50 (1256);* JUST I/996 m. 40 (IMG 94) (1249); JUST 1/1006 m. 61 (IMG 9977) (1289). Butler, 'Abortion by Assault'; Pardons for assaults resulting in miscarriage: *CPR 1272–81*, 444; *CPR 1301–7*, 303. Trespass action by widow for beating causing miscarriage: KB 27/26 m. 18 (IMG 773); JUST 1/1015 m. 8. (IMG 1220). CPR 1317–21 p. 465, 470: 1319 complaint by H and W. *CPR 1422–29,* 229 (1424), Complaint by H, and by H and W separately. Assault, loss of baby, claimed damages for H and W: JUST 1/1557 m. 17 (IMG 3055).

146 Rape presentments and indictments, e.g., KB 9/361 m. 36 (IMG 73); KB 27/483 m. (IMG 131); attempts and accessories: JUST 3/167 m. 23 (IMG 198); KB 27/351 m. 22 (IMG 1960); KB 27/598 m. 10 d (IMG 561). Taking and abduction of female neifs: KB 27/626 m. 70 (IMG 155). Presentment of rape/ravishment of damsels: JUST 1/383 m.58d (IMG 1804); JUST 1/383 m. 17 (IMG 1499). Husband, guardian or father's action for ravishment,_e.g, *CRR XX* no. 38 (1250), p. 8; SC 8/23/1108; C1/69/232; C1/46/47, C1/234/71; C1/158/35; *Wilts GD and T*, pp. 369, 724.

events in which there had been no active resistance on the part of the wife, and juries do sometimes *state* that the true facts behind the complaint were an elopement,[147] but it is not possible to deduce from cases which make no such statement that the alleged abduction was fictitious, and we cannot be certain of the proportions, nor what degree of will and agreement was understood to be enough for a jury to class it as voluntary: how far beyond an absence of effective resistance did the situation have to go before it would be classed as not involuntary?[148] On the distance between medieval common law ideas of sex being 'not against the will' of a woman and modern requirements for consent in relation to sex, for example, it is difficult not to feel suspicion about the level of free choice regarded as sufficient to negate any offence, when considering a case of 1295 in which the complainant was found by a jury to have been removed from her mother's house against her will, but it was considered that the subsequent penetration was 'not against her will'.[149] Likewise too ready a deduction that, because a number of clerics were indicted and pardoned or complained that they had been falsely accused of rape or ravishment, presentments or indictments of these offences were frequently based on consensual (in contemporary or modern understanding) fornication may wrongly set in opposition the interests of women and those bringing such actions, and may thus fail to reflect the extent to which they were acting on the woman's behalf as well as that of the husband or community.[150] As noted above, it is important to ensure that historical writing is not influenced by too-quick inferences of a lack of veracity of allegations of rape in particular,[151] and it does not seem obviously implausible

147 KB 27/513 m. 16 (IMG 42) jury: D incited her (excitavit & procuravit) to elope, but did not ravish her; 100 *SS* p. 88.

148 Butler, *Divorce*, pp. 32, 49, 53; Seabourne, *IMW*, c. 7. For cases in which W was apparently driven off by H, see Seabourne, 'Copulative Complexities'. For success for the complaining husband, settlements or pardons for alleged ravishers, see KB 27/514 m. 255 (IMG 96); KB 27/498 m. 81 (IMG 178); KB 27/443 m. 53 (IMG 106); KB 27/515 m. 5d (IMG 194); KB 27/518 m. 70d (IMG 406); KB 27/516 m. 19d (IMG 200); KB 27/517 m. 5d (IMG 216). Felonious rape, ravishment, abduction, detention, presentment: KB 27/508 m. 1 (IMG 111); KB 27/594 m. 14d (IMG 590). For abduction of wife and goods cases, with a defence, see, e.g., KB 27/218 m. 7d (IMG 14) (the man an attorney claims is husband of the woman is claimed not to exist). Exception of excommunication for adultery in ravishment of wife case: KB 27/517 m. 66 (IMG 517). Alleged conspiracy between men: KB 27/515 m. 3d (IMG 190).

149 *Seipp* 1295.003rs; JUST 1/1098 m. 76 (IMG 7359).

150 Clergy attempts to seek pardon for rape, and allegations by them of false accusations: KB 27/742 m. 6 (IMG 386); KB 27/758 m. 16 (IMG 208): SC 8/97/4844; C 1/7/22; C 1/61/349; C 49/27/14 (*RP* V, pp. 152–31). Helen Lacey, *The Royal Pardon: Access to Mercy in Fourteenth Century England* (York, 2009), p. 89. Musson and Powell, *Crime, Law,* 3.12 JUST 3/203 m. 49; R.L. Storey, 'Malicious Indictments of Clergy in the Fifteenth Century', in *Medieval Ecclesiastical Studies in Honour of Dorothy M. Owen*, ed. by M.J. Franklin and C. Harper-Bill (Woodbridge, 1995), pp. 221–40.

151 The tone of some commentary on raped women has rightly been described as 'callous': Mitchell, *Portrait*, p. 120. See also Russell, 'II Trial by Battle', p. 138.

that clerics might have been more than usually inclined to misuse their relative power in order to abuse women. Frequent complaint of false allegation may suggest false allegation, but might just as well suggest high motivation to challenge accusations or convictions, and capacity to do so.[152] In the end, we cannot know, but, as suggested above, should avoid treating allegations of false accusation with any more credulity than we accord the accusations themselves.

Conclusion

Both presence and absence are important. The participation of women in the common law as litigants, although less common than men's participation, was usual, and women from relatively low to high stations in life are encountered in the plea rolls of the common law courts. The participation of women in general was often precarious, however, and was different to the participation of men. The technical and intellectual tools to limit women's ability to bring legal actions were present all along, from the statements concerning the range of appeals they could bring to the gathering of ideas of 'coverture', and should it suit those in power to use them, women's routes to participation could be blocked. It has been pointed out that it is worth considering ways in which the common law may have become more masculine over the course of the medieval period. There appears to have been a decline in the opportunities available for women to bring their cases at common law – with the increasing emphasis on indictments rather than appeals, for example, and with the decline of the hue and cry, a way for women to cause the initiation of proceedings.[153] Changes may well not have been implemented with the intention of downgrading women's level of participation: certainly there is no overt statement of a wish to do so. Likewise, decisions on the scope of common law actions and remedies, and the requirements for successful actions, do not reflect a conscious decision that actions useful to men should be accommodated by common law, and those desired by or needed by women should not. Nevertheless, an account of common law developments which neglects the possibility of different effects of doctrinal developments on men and women needs to be updated.

152 Accusations of attempted seduction, assault and imprisonment of a wife: *Seipp* 1482.115; 1482.126. Accusations of other offences, e.g., theft: JUST 3/173 m. 17 (IMG 41); KB 27/957 Rex m. 1 (IMG 111); KB 27 638 m. 19d (IMG 581). Clerical crime, other than rape, does not seem to have been doubted in the same way. See W. Rye, 'Clerical thieves temp. Edward I', *Norfolk Antiquarian Miscellany* 2 (1880), 194.

153 Bardsley, *Venemous Tongues*, pp. 38–40, 77.

6 Responsible and irresponsible women

The female defendant

Recorded in the Common Pleas roll for Michaelmas term 1421 is a trespass case in which Isabella, a 'silkwoman' of Salisbury, was accused, with her husband, John Clerk, of having beaten Agnes Howedon, her apprentice. This beating was alleged to have happened on 7th December, 1419, and to have caused Agnes damage worth £20.[1] John and Isabella, however, asserted that they had done nothing forceful, wrong or against the king's peace. Their version of events was that Agnes had secretly taken merchandise from John's shop, to one Gregory Fisher's house. On 7th December, they had found Agnes making off with goods, and had beaten her for her insolence and her wrongs. They had done this with a small willow rod, on her limbs, and in the appropriate manner for their master-apprentice relationship. Agnes, however, said that they had hit her with rather more hefty sticks or staves beyond the norm for chastisement. John and Isabella denied this, Agnes maintained it and all agreed that the matter should go to a jury.

There is much that we will never know in terms of the truth of this and many such stories told in the formulaic records of the common law – thus, it is possible that none of this happened, and supposing that something along these lines did happen, it will remain a mystery whether Isabella and John employed the customary rod or more menacing and damaging implements to beat Agnes – but there is undoubtedly more which can be done with what is left to us in terms of filling out the picture of the medieval common law's treatment of women as defendants. Even this one example raises a number of questions which have yet to be fully explored, and its juxtaposition of common law (the trespass case, and rules about the effect of marriage on responsibility and property) and local custom (apprenticeship rules, including the appropriate size of stick for chastisement, and jurisdiction relating to recovery of misappropriated goods) remind us of common law's existence within a pattern of other bodies of regulation.

Treatises such as *Glanvill* and *Bracton* gave limited space to the issue of women's legal responsibility for their misdeeds, and, indeed, their

1 CP 40/643 m. 108 (IMG 195).

descriptions often assume a male offender.[2] The classic accounts of legal history, have not expanded much on this lack of interest in women's offending.[3] Women defendants are certainly outnumbered by men in court records (with proportions varying depending on period, methods of counting and type of offence).[4] It is, however, by no means an oddity to find a woman accused of an offence or wrong, either with her husband, as here, or alone. This chapter will consider the scope of cases brought against women, and how the common law constructed and accommodated them in a system designed around the male offender. It will ask to what extent there were different ideas of male and female responsibility, what were the impacts of marriage, pregnancy and the gendered nature of routes to exculpation or the avoidance of punishment[5] and will argue for caution in adopting the idea that women were 'indulged' by the system, as some past work has claimed.

Incidence of accusations

Women defendants are present in smaller numbers than men in records of both 'civil' and 'criminal' cases. It is not, of course, possible to assert that this represents accurately the levels of offending by women (for there is always a 'dark figure' of undetected or unreported, and thus unrecorded, crime to factor in), nor even to make very clear statistical claims about changes over time, since the nature of surviving records does not allow for comparisons of like with like, but the bald finding that women are less frequently mentioned as defendants, across all series of records, is robust.[6] In 'civil' cases, this may be explained in part by the rules relating to succession to land and the effect of marriage on property holding, which those shaping the common law chose to adopt and retain. These rules made women less likely to be in control of land or personal property so as to be sued alone in respect of it, and meant that wives, unamenable to processes or outcomes involving the seizure of assets or money payments, were not worth suing without their husbands.[7] In 'criminal' matters, there were also differing levels of accusation of men and women, though the insistence on placing a male relative or husband between women and the legal system was much less strong than it was with regard to 'civil' cases. Reasons for the lower level of 'criminal' accusation of women must therefore be sought in social conditions and ideas and in their interaction with the developing common law.

2 *Glanvill* XIV, p. 1; *Bracton* II, pp. 353, 428.

3 Hyams, 'Maitland', pp. 227–30. Baker, *Introduction*, cc. 29 and 30.

4 See above p. 81–2.

5 Walker, *Crime, Gender and Social Order*, p. 75.

6 See, e.g., Clive Coleman and Jenny Moynihan, *Understanding Crime Data: Haunted by the Dark Figure* (Buckingham and Philadelphia, PA, 1996); Butler, 'Violence and Murder', p. 333, and above, 81–2.

7 See Baker, *Introduction*, pp. 285–8, 523–8.

There was one accusation of 'crime' which could not be made against women: they could not be accused of rape as a principal (though, as the example at the beginning of Chapter 5 shows, they could be seen as an accessory of some sort in these cases). Aside from this, however, women were accused of almost the same range of offences and wrongs as men, including offences of physical aggression from assault, through false imprisonment and mayhem, to homicide, including offences against men.[8] Hanawalt, noted that 'over half of the felonies women committed involved violence to persons and property'.[9] The sight of medieval women appearing as defendants in cases of violence 'which must have required masculine strength and an absence of all the qualities now considered feminine' was enough to cause horrified fascination in a Victorian barrister and legal historian, Luke Owen Pike. Having seen such records, he regarded all medieval women but those of 'very highest rank' as 'almost as brutal as their husbands ... strong in muscle but hard of heart – more fit to be the mothers of brigands than to rear gentle daughters or honest sons'.[10] The dramatic horror and confusion of this response is also seen in Pike's recreation of a husband-killing, highlighting the fact that the accused woman's name was Isolda, with all the resonances which come to that for a scholar of the medieval literary tradition, and also casting her as a 'female Othello', before ascribing her flight to a (feminine) failure of courage at the last, after she had 'shown the energy and power of a man' in committing the crime.[11] Such a view of (most) women as shockingly brutal fitted in well with his overall idea of patterns of change in this area, seen in his book's subtitle *Illustrating the Changes of the Laws in the Progress of Civilisation.* While we no longer look back at medieval records of accusations against women through the distorting lens of Victorian gender ideals, it is still important to note that neither the ideas about female weakness clearly also present in strands of medieval thinking, nor the view that women were less likely to be physically aggressive than were men, tending instead towards verbal onslaughts, nor a suggested disinclination of men to bring to official attention women's violence against them, worked to rule out the possibility that women would be accused or convicted, of violent, physically demanding offences.[12] Though they were

8 See, e.g., trespasses against a hermit and a chaplain: CP 40/421 m. 4 (IMG 9) KB 27/177 m. 50 (IMG 5618); false imprisonment of a man: KB 27/432 m. 8d (IMG 203); mayhem: KB 27/401 m. (IMG 6145); homicide: JUST 1/383 m. 36 (IMG 1539); KB 27/178 m. 62 (IMG 5995), 'infanticide': JUST 1.383 m. 8d (IMG 1799).

9 Hanawalt, 'The Female Felon', p. 254.

10 L.O. Pike, *A History of Crime in England* (London, 1873), vol 1, p. 255.

11 Op. cit., 256; the case is JUST 2/26 m. 1 (IMG 3).

12 See, e.g., Kamali, *Felony*, p. 144; Teresa Phipps, 'Misbehaving Women: Trespass and Honor in Late Medieval English Towns', *Historical Reflections* 43 (2017), 62–76, 67; Miriam Müller, 'Social Control and the Hue and Cry in Two Fourteenth-Century Villages', *JMH* 31 (2005), 29–53, 42; Karen Jones, *Gender and Petty Crime in Late Medieval England: The Local Courts in Kent, 1460–1560* (Woodbridge, 2006), pp. 92–3.

more often accused of the most serious violence along with an accomplice rather than individually (Hanawalt's study of coroners' rolls from the late thirteenth and fourteenth century showing that they were accused of killing with an accomplice in 64% of cases while males were accused of killing with an accomplice only 25% of the time, and were often procurers or abettors rather principal offenders),[13] they were not thought completely incapable of dangerous, forceful conduct. They were not regarded as too weak ever to attack males, nor too inhibited to engage in activity such as mutilation or violence against men's genitals (though the latter was a matter regarded with particular horror).[14] It was envisaged that they might be capable of misconduct regarded as treason,[15] or which could endanger the 'state' or public order.[16] Women were accused of most other 'criminal' offences: a few being accused of arson, many more accused of theft or 'offences of dishonesty'. In her study of fourteenth-century gaol delivery rolls, Hanawalt noted the relatively high level of women accused of burglary, and that 'larceny was the most common crime among female offenders'.[17] There were also vast numbers of women accused of economic or 'regulatory offences' as well as some more unusual accusations (for common law jurisdictions) such as running a brothel and witchcraft.[18] Despite an enduring myth of their immunity from common law prosecution for the killing of babies and children less than a

13 Hanawalt, 'Violent Death', p. 306.

14 Post-mortem mutilation: JUST 1/804 m. 69 (IMG 2436). Attacks on men's genitals, JUST 3/89 m. 1 (IMG 234); JUST 1/ 569A m. 9 (IMG 8133); JUST 1/1109 m. 30d (IMG 8870). *P & M* II, p. 484; *Deuteronomy* 25:11.

15 See, e.g., *CPR 1401–5*, p. 480; *CPR 1467–77*, p. 190; Bellamy, *Law of Treason*, pp. 203, 126–7, 236–7; J. Freeman, 'Sorcery at Court and Manor: Margery Jourdemayne, the Witch of Eye', *JMH* 30 (2004), 343–57, 343; Simon Walker, 'Political Saints in Later Medieval England', in *The McFarlane Legacy: Studies in Late Medieval Politics and Society*, ed. by Richard Britnell and Anthony Pollard (Stroud and New York, 1995), 77–106, 88–9; L. Diaz Pascual, 'Jaquetta of Luxembourg, Duchess of Bedford and Lady Rivers c 1416–72', *The Ricardian* 21 (2011), 67–91, 67; Kathleen Kamerick, 'Tanglost of Wales: Magic and Adultery in the Court of Chancery circa 1500', *Sixteenth Century Journal* 44 (2013), 25–45; C1/267/41; C1/229/20.

16 See., e.g.: *CCR 1323–1327*, 203; *CPR 1324–1327*, 21; *CPR 1401–5*, pp. 516–17; *CPR 1301–7*, pp. 270–1; *CPR 1327–30*, pp. 24, 213; *CPR 1327–30* pp. 221–2; *CPR 1361–4* p. 358; KB 9/72 mm. 1–5, 11 and 14; KB 27/562 Rex m. 22.] 56–7; KB 27/562 Rex m. 1(IMG 186). KB 27/482 Rex m. 39d. (IMG 447); Samuel K. Cohn jr, *Popular Protest in Late Medieval English Towns* (Cambridge, 2013), pp. 7, 185, 20; 208, 212, 24; 196, 251, 318; 304, 320; Sylvia Federico, 'The Imaginary Society: Women in 1381', *JBS* 40 (2001), 159–83; Simon Walker, 'Rumour, Sedition and Popular Protest in the Reign of Henry IV', *P & P* 166 (2000), 31–65.

Women accused of slander of a judge: *Seipp* 1356.134ass; 58 *SS* App XVIII pl. cxxxvi.

17 Arson, e.g., 83 *SS* p. 71, no 687; JUST 1/307b m. 6d. (IMG 9137): KB 27/884 m. 11 (IMG 234). Theft offences, e.g., KB 27/866 m. 9; JUST 1/409 m. 11 (IMG 35). Burglary: JUST 1/409 m. 10 (IMG 21).

Hanawalt, 'The female felon'. Counterfeiting money: JUST 3/43/2 m. 1 (IMG 135).

18 Seabourne, *Royal Regulation* cc. 3 and 4. See also, e.g., CP 40/581 m. 129 (IMG 263), CP 40/717 m. 482 (IMG 963). Brothel: KB9/363 m. 38 (IMG 85); KB 9/365 m. 12, (IMG 24):

year old, which is stressed by the *Mirror*, as Butler has shown, there are certainly cases of homicide relating to small infants.[19] In considering level and type of accusation made against women, it should be borne in mind as ever that the common law was not the only forum for accusations of offences, and gender balance might be somewhat different in other courts. For example, though there was attention to prostitution near royal residences and, to some extent, in Southwark, accusations relating to the selling of sex in itself were generally left by the common law to other authorities, reducing the proportion of women who might otherwise have appeared as defendants in common law records.[20] 'Civil' wrongs of which women were accused include trespass of various sorts, trespass on the case, abduction of heirs, disseisins, non-payment of debts, nuisances, wrongdoing relating to their holding of land or franchise rights and misbehaviour with regard to land held (e.g. waste).[21] All women might be forced to defend themselves, though different sorts of dispute or offence might be more likely to be associated with those higher or lower in the social scale. Very few members of higher social orders were accused of 'run of the mill' felonies.[22] but even queens regnant and dowager could be sued – despite the argument of Isabella of France that as a 'person of dignity and excellence', she did not need to respond to a writ of dower.[23]

In relation to those offences in which it did take an interest, the common law had quite a substantial reach, its constructions of responsibility for offences having a place for both 'principal' and 'accessory'.[24] This was important to women's liability, as women might be accused of committing a crime alone or doing so with other offenders, of participating directly but

KB 9/361 m. 39 (IMG 79). Selling five-year-old girl: KB 27/515 m. 3d (IMG 294). *P & M* II, p. 552. Witchcraft: above note 15.

19 *Mirror*, book IV c. 16; Cleveland, *Woman under the English Law*, p. 96; Sara M. Butler, 'A Case of Indifference? Child Murder in Later Medieval England', *Journal of Women's History* 19 (2004), 59–82.

20 See, e.g., *CPR 1272–81*, p. 585; *Fleta*, book 2 c. 5; *CPR 1367–70*, p. 449, *CPR 1370–74*, p. 14. KB9/366 m. 51 (IMG 102); KB 9/389 mm. 48, 49, 49d (IMG 86, 98, 99); Karras, *Common Women*, pp. 10–12, 21, 41, 150; J.B. Post, 'A Fifteenth Century Customary of the Southwark Stews', *Journal of the Society of Archivists* (1977), 418–28; Karras, *Sexuality*, p. 123; CP 40/517 m. 440 (IMG 968), *Seipp* 1456.122abr; C 16/489 m. 13d, *CPR 1454–61*, p. 610; SC8/73/3626 SC 8/27/1309.

21 See, e.g., knowingly selling putrid ale: KB 27/590 m. 36 (IMG 94); trespass: JUST 1/1055 m. (IMG 3112); KB 27/274 m. 24 (IMG 49); disseisin: *Seipp* 1342.098rs, 1342.281ass; Dower: JUST 1/804 m. 20 (IMG 2328); writ of right: JUST 1/804 m. 4d (IMG 2465); writ of entry: JUST 1/804 m. 17d (IMG 2493); Quo waranto (women are a very small minority here): JUST 1/804 m. 30 (IMG 2347); JUST 1/804 m. 36 (IMG 2360); JUST 1/804 m. 5d (IMG 2468); JUST 1/804 m. 24 (IMG 2337); nuisance: JUST 1/804 m. 7d (IMG 2473); eloigning heir: JUST 1/985 m. 14 (IMG 797).

22 Hanawalt, 'Violent Death', p. 308, notes that few members of upper orders were accused of homicide.

23 *Seipp* 1336.085.

24 Kamali, *Felony*, p. 79.

also of a variety of 'accessory' culpability, by encouraging, procuring, conspiring or consenting to an offence,[25] or they might be accused of receiving goods or offenders or assisting offenders after the offence.[26] Their alleged participation might involve physical assistance, as in the case of a man's successful plaint that a woman had held him by the hair while another man cut off his arm,[27] or they might be regarded as accessories in relation to words alone rather than any more physical intervention.[28] They might themselves be said to have been incited to commit a crime, though this was less frequent.[29] One of the more unusual cases of women being accused as accessory to homicide involved a woman, Isabella, giving a knife to her deaf husband, Eborard le Barbur, and making signs for him to kill another man, William Skynner, which he is recorded as having done.[30] The fact that the common law entertained accusations of accessories meant greater likelihood of women being accused. For example, as noted above, though they could not be accused of felonious rape, they could be accused as an accessory to rape.[31] Few such allegations show the accused women in such a prominent role as that in an indictment of a woman, one Matilda Whorewell, for helping Adam, a 'leprous man', to rape her 'beautiful' servant, Margaret, since Matilda herself was not prepared to take his money and have sex with him. Matilda was alleged to have led Adam to the room where Margaret was sleeping and locked the pair into the room, where Adam raped Margaret with particular violence, so that she died of the effects of this shortly afterwards.[32] By way of contrast, there are some rather ill-defined accusations of women's incitement to kill, which tend to indicate that accusations that offences were committed at the behest of a woman might be formed on fairly

25 See, e.g., JUST 1/804 m. 53 (IMG 2393); KB 27/623 m. 14 (IMG 209); JUST 1/303 m. 56 (IMG 8755); KB 27/294 m. 26 (IMG 404). KB 27/717 Rex m. 6d (IMG 553). Allegations of 'counselling' others to commit an offence: JUST 1/996 m. 23 (IMG 145); JUST 1/632 m. 21d (IMG 885) and JUST 1/635 m. 20 (IMG 704); KB 27/715 Rex m. 1 (IMG 156). 'Consenting' to offences, see JUST 1/1108 m. 9d (IMG 8697), JUST 1/486 m. 1 (IMG 2717). For 'procuring attack' by one man on another: JUST 1/1032 m. 1d (IMG 2695). 'Lady' ordering a man's beating, then receiving the offender: JUST 1/764 m. 1 (IMG 4928). Women's words blamed for male seditious speech, though the man was held responsible: KB 27/564 Rex m. 12 (IMG 175).

26 Receiving stolen goods: KB 27/294 m. 31 (IMG 414). Receiving offenders: JUST 1/804 m.47d (IMG 2548); KB 27/518 m. 26 d (IMG 523); JUST 1/804 m. 73d (IMG 2606). Taking food and drink to robbers (acquitted): JUST 1/1032 m. 6 (IMG 2693). Man receiving his felon wife: KB9/366 m. 14 (IMG 48).

27 KB 27/247 m. 14 (IMG 29).

28 Kamali, *Felony*, pp. 212–16, 233; *Bracton* II, p. 340; *Mirror* book I c. 9.

29 Women incited to kill: KB 27/560 m. 57d (IMG 359); KB 27/559 m. (IMG 159).

30 JUST 1/286 m. 11 (IMG 7327).

31 J. Carter, 'Rape and Medieval English Society: The Evidence of Yorkshire, Wiltshire and London, 1218–76', *Comitatus* 13 (1982), 33–63, 46; JUST 1/966 m. 32 (IMG 76). In the 'ravishment' context: *Seipp* 1369.070.

32 KB 9/167 m. 8 (IMG 17).

tenuous bases, perhaps demonstrating the influence of misogynist tropes of women's scheming malevolence,[33] such as that in the *Dialogue of the Exchequer*, which emphasised the role of women in inciting men to wrongdoing.[34]

In addition, the existence of liability for receiving felons or giving aid to outlaws, when combined with social facts, expanded the chances of women being accused of an offence. Hanawalt highlights receiving as particularly female, or of importance within accusations of female offending,[35] and it may be significant that women are used as examples of 'receivers' in registers of writs, though men are usually used in relation to other offences.[36] Given women's subordinate place to husbands and male kin, it seems likely that they would have been under some pressure to receive male kin and connections on the run who came demanding shelter. Although there was certainly an idea that non-consent could negate their culpability, however, it is not clear that the threshold for their consent was very high.[37] A woman receiving a male felon might also experience the ultimate ingratitude of his decision to turn approver and accuse her of the offence in an attempt to save his own neck.[38]

The system was clearly, and unsurprisingly, shaped with masculine norms of offending in mind. One small example of this may be seen in the fact that the formulae used in accusations of trespass included a stereotyped list of swords, bows and arrows. While women certainly used weapons to inflict injury, and there are well-known descriptions of exceptional women bearing weapons and armour, swords, shields, bows and arrows can fairly be classified as stereotypically masculine. It has been observed that there were differences between men and women in relation to training with weapons, amenability to being sworn to the assize of arms and involvement in hunting with bows or lances.[39] Using the same, weapon-centred formula for both men and women did not, however, apparently seem to medieval common lawyers

33 98 *SS*, p. 200. Words spoken by a woman said to have 'moved two men to fight': KB9/366 m. 31 (IMG 62). Female incitement as a literary trope: see, e.g., William Ian Miller, 'Choosing the Avenger: Some Aspects of the Bloodfeud in Medieval Iceland and England', *LHR* 1 (1983), 159–204, 178, 181.

34 *Dialogus de Scacc.* book II, c. 7.

35 Hanawalt, 'Female Felon', p. 131.

36 See, e.g., 87 *SS* pp. 101, 167. Note that the example of a receiver in 80 *SS* p. 338 is male.

37 Entries noting that W received felons against H's wishes, or in his absence, see, e.g., JUST 1/409 m. 20 (IMG 43), 98 *SS* p. 168.

38 Woman hanged for receiving thief and pelf: JUST 3/48 m. 29 (IMG 152). See also (brother): JUST 3/1/1 m. 12. (IMG 30).

39 Given, *Society and Homicide in Thirteenth Century England*, p. 136. See also e.g. *Bracton* II, p. 32; James Blythe, 'Women in the Military: Scholastic Arguments and Medieval Images of Female Warriors', *History of Political Thought* 22 (2001), 242–69; Steven Gunn, 'Archery Practice in Early Tudor England', *P & P* 209 (2010), 53–81, 54; M.R. Evans, 'Unfit to bear arms": The Gendering of Arms and Armour in Accounts of Women on Crusade', in *Gendering the Crusades*, ed. by Susan B. Edgington and Sarah Lambert (Cardiff, 2001), pp. 45–58. Formulae: Milsom, 'Trespass', p. 203, 'Swords, axes, bows

to be too incongruous. Weapon lists might eventually be changed to reflect the advent of firearms,[40] but there was not felt to be a need to alter the wording for those whose bearing of arms would be less likely. This might not be a matter of practical importance – for there was a great deal of fiction in the weapons lists in any case – but it is an indication of the gendered assumptions and paradigms lying behind and within common law development.

In terms of the treatment of developments in the common law's jurisdiction over the medieval period, accounts have often not mentioned the gendered nature of changes, even when they are quite stark. For example, a major 'story' of the medieval common law was the fourteenth-century expansion of trespass actions to encompass misconduct which was not really violent.[41] Conventionally, from an internal, 'doctrinal' perspective on legal history, this is portrayed in the language of 'rise', 'triumph' and, in relation to the later part of the story, the heroic military metaphor of storming a citadel.[42] This is to smooth over the many individual decisions involved in making such a change and expansion, and the potentially different impacts of changes. The actions in this expanded field were particularly likely to be related to male misconduct, regarding, as they did, wrongs done by those in positions not generally open to women, such as those of farrier, surgeon and carrier.[43] It does appear worth considering that it may chime in with the suggestion of the later medieval period having seen an increasing masculinisation of the common law in terms of development in the courts themselves, with a focus on offences of particular relevance to men, while other offences which might be focused on women's wrongdoing, women as subjects and suspects – such as scolding – were accommodated in other jurisdictions.[44] At the same time, we have noted what seems to be a trend towards greater specificity in the inclusion of women in legislative pronouncements over the course of the later medieval period, and that plaintiffs were also most likely to be male; thus we cannot reduce the complex picture of differentiation and different treatment of men and women to points on a straightforward spectrum of advantage and disadvantage in the 'position of women at common law' over the medieval period. It can, however, be pointed out, first, that ideas about women and their treatment by the common law did not stand still in these centuries, and, second, that their position, complicating though it might be, must be considered as part of any overall statement about or narrative of developments in the jurisdiction.

---

and arrows' CP 40/93 m. 14 (IMG 30); 'swords, staves etc.' KB 27/754 m. 47d (IMG 414); 'swords, staves and knives' CP 40/832 m. 322d (IMG 1539); CP 40/50 (1283) m. 17.

40 See, e.g., CP 40/882 m.308 (IMG 578).

41 Ibbetson, *Historical Introduction*, Part II.

42 See, e.g., Ibbetson, *Historical Introduction*, part II, c. 7; Baker, *Introduction*, p. 363.

43 Milsom, 'Trespass', e.g., p. 220.

44 Bardsley, *Venemous Tongues*, pp. 80, 82–9.

Escaping liability

There were various ways in which a person who had apparently committed an offence under medieval common law might avoid conviction or punishment. Trial could be avoided by claiming clergy, by fleeing to sanctuary or at least beyond the reach of the authorities, by failing to turn up for trial or escaping custody; in some cases, an out of court settlement would bring matters to an end. If the matter came to trial, following the early thirteenth-century introduction of jury trial for criminal cases, all accused persons could avoid a finding of guilt by refusing to plead and put themselves on the jury, though this would lead to harsh treatment designed to force submission.[45] Despite a finding that the accused had carried out the action alleged, conviction or punishment might not follow, again, if clergy was claimed at a later stage, or if it was found that the action had taken place with some justification or excuse, in particular, in self-defence, by accident, as lawful arrest or chastisement, whilst too mentally disordered, or too young to be held responsible or if a pardon was obtained.[46] It was not inevitable that a person regarded as having some sort of mental disturbance would avoid all punishment,[47] and nor did minority mean that an offender would be left alone by the criminal justice system. Small girls might be pardoned any offence, for example, but they were not necessarily spared trial and conviction, as can be seen in a 1284 eyre case of a six-year-old girl sent back to gaol to await a pardon after she had caused a death by dropping a stone from a cliff.[48] There was, however, an established understanding that culpability and punishment could be affected by these matters.

These escape routes showed some differences in availability and utility for men and women. Some were available to all, at least in theory, though they might accommodate men more easily than women. In other cases, it

45 See, e.g., JUST 3/48 mm. 24, 27 (IMG 56, 62).

46 Green, *Verdict*, p. 30; Kamali, *Felony*, p. 87; Hurnard, *King's Pardon*; Helen Lacey, *The Royal Pardon: Access to Mercy in Fourteenth Century England* (York, 2009), p. 69. Acquittals or pardons for offences by women not in their right mind: JUST 1/543 m. 55 (IMG 4173); KB 27/273 m. 29; JUST 1/159 m. 3d (IMG 9053); JUST 1/166 m. 28d (IMG 9739), JUST 1/374 m. 85 (IMG 2427); JUST 1/374 m. 52 (IMG 2357); JUST 1/375 mm. 52, 85 (IMG 2357, 2427); Hurnard, *King's Pardon*, pp. 161–9; JUST 1/383 m. 11d (IMG 1712). Pardon for failed execution: *CPR 1258–66*, p. 342; JUST 1/486 m. 14d (IMG 2847): *CPR 1281–92*, p. 113.

47 A 'rabid' mother, who drowned her child and fled, was subject to the usual processes to try and get her to court: JUST 1/374 m. 25d (IMG 2490). Kamali, *Felony*, pp. 55, notes that those acknowledged to be insane might still be found a felon, especially in suicide cases.

48 Hurnard, *King's Pardon*, p. 50; JUST 1/111 m 27; *CPR 1281–92*, p. 225 (pardon). Despite Coke's assertions, there was not a unified 'age of discretion' for responsibility in medieval 'criminal law': A.W.G. Kean, 'The History of the Criminal Liability of Children', *LQR* 53 (1937), 366. The youngest girl I have found executed was 13: *Seipp* 1338.182rs. There is even less clarity regarding non-felonious cases: see *Seipp* 1456.072.

was explicit that women could not use a particular method of escaping the rigours of the common law. There were also escape routes, full or partial, which were only open to particular classes of women, relating to their pregnancy or marital relationship. Although this summary suggests a rough level of equality in the availability of legal 'escape routes', and the idea of women's exclusion from some routes being balanced by their ability to use others has been embraced in some legal historical work, it seems to be the better view that the system did not 'favour' or 'indulge' them in this respect.

An example of outright exclusion of women from an 'escape route' can be seen in relation to 'benefit of clergy', under which the right of the common law to try or punish a person could be challenged. Benefit of clergy was available to men alone, since it was founded on the idea that the common law courts should not punish those in holy orders, and since women could not take holy orders.[49] This sex-based distinction became more striking once common lawyers acquiesced in the artificial extension of benefit of clergy well beyond those men who could make a plausible claim to holy orders, in the fourteenth and fifteenth centuries, since there was no move to include women in the fictionalised scope of clergy, despite later suggestions of a woman apparently claiming clergy in the reign of Edward III.[50] The results of this discrimination were particularly clear in instances in which a woman and a man were both found guilty of a criminal offence, and only the woman was executed, since he, but not she, could claim benefit of clergy.[51]

Approvers – those confessing their own guilt and accusing others of an offence, with a view to obtaining a conviction and thus not themselves being executed – were, at least from the thirteenth century, overwhelmingly male. The *Mirror* suggests a degree of doubt as to whether women could be approvers, both asserting that they could not, and also complaining as an abuse the alleged fact that they were in fact allowed to be approvers,[52]

49 A.K. McHardy, 'Church Courts and Criminous Clerks in the Later Middle Ages', in *Medieval Ecclesiastical Studies in Honour of Dorothy M. Owen*, ed. by M.J. Franklin and C. Harper-Bill (Woodbridge, 1995), pp. 165–83, 165.

50 Baker, 'The Law's Two Bodies', p. 40; L.C. Gabel, *Benefit of Clergy in England in the Late Middle Ages* (Northampton, MA, 1929), pp. 68, 87–90; Kesselring, 'Bodies of Evidence', p. 246, *Mercy*, p. 46; Baker, *OHLE VI*, p. 608; 129 *SS*, pp. 2, 47, 52, 59, 130, 155. Querying of women's exclusion: 120 *SS* p. 91. For the suggestion of a woman claiming clergy, see, e.g., Hale, *HPC* II, c. 51. Citing a case from Fitzherbert's *Graunde Abridgement* (*Coron.* H. 22 Edw. III p. 461) this states that 'anciently' professed nuns could have clergy. No such case has been traced. It may represent a misreading of KB 27/355 Rex m. 47d (IMG 8362), which is a male claim of clergy, but this is speculative. Nicholas Statham (attrib.), *Abridgement of Cases to the End of Henry VI* (Rouen, 1490), p. cxxvii, contains a note of a woman pleading clergy, but Pulton, *De Pace Regis et Regni* (1609) 207b, says no woman can have clergy, and cites the same reference to Fitzherbert.

51 See, e.g., JUST 3/167 m. 44 (IMG 96), *Seipp* 1408.017.

52 *Mirror* book V c. 17, book 1 c. 14.

but records of practice show very few women who may plausibly be so regarded.[53] Although becoming an approver did not necessarily lead to safety, nor even to a much delayed execution, this is another interesting example of apparent sex-based differentiation, contributing to the unequal position of men and women in the medieval common law.[54] It appears particularly stark in cases involving male and female offenders, when a man is able to become an approver while a woman is hanged at once.[55] It should be noted that a medieval woman's inability to act as an approver was not balanced by any immunity from being put at risk by the accusation of an approver.[56] In addition, some pardons – those for military service – were only available to males,[57] and while the theoretical basis of sanctuary did not import sex differentiation and while women did go to a church, confess and abjure, it has been shown that, in practice, women were markedly less likely to use sanctuary than were men, especially in the post-1400 period.[58]

If a case of homicide, mayhem or trespass came to court, pleading self-defence was a possible 'escape route'. A successful plea of self-defence might lead to a royal pardon or, should a jury decide on benevolent subterfuge, to an acquittal.[59] While there was no bar on women pleading self-defence, records suggest that it was not common for them to do so. The patent rolls contain hundreds of examples of entries relating to self-defence as a reason or partial reason for granting a pardon, but only a few of these relate to women said to have killed in self-defence.[60] Women were also considerably

53 For possible examples of women 'approvers', temp. Henry II, see Kerr, 'Husband and Wife', p. 222; *Wiltshire GD and T* has a rare later woman approver: no 42 and p. 12.

54 Kamali, *Felony*, p. 192; Anthony Musson, 'Turning King's Evidence: The Prosecution of Crime in Late Medieval England', *OJLS* 19 (1999), 467–79.

55 *Somersetshire Pleas* (1242–3) p. 239 no 800 (male and female thieves).

56 See, e.g., JUST 1/1339 m. 9d (IMG 3138): approver accuses his female co-thief.

57 Bellamy, *Criminal Trial*, p. 143; Powell, *Kingship, Law and Society*, pp. 232–40; Lacey, *Royal Pardon*, pp. 100–6.

58 See, e.g., JUST 1/278 m. 85d (IMG 5490). Karl Shoemaker, *Sanctuary and Crime in the Middle Ages 400–1500* (New York, 2011), p. 124; JUST 1/229 m. 14d; 1/614A m. 2; 1/230 m. 4d; 1/55 m. 21r; I/4 m. 29d; 1/614B m. 48d; 1/806 m. 17; JUST 1/4 m. 30d; JUST 1/174 m. 27d. Shannon McSheffrey, *Seeking Sanctuary: Crime, Mercy, and Politics in English Courts, 1400–1550* (Oxford, 2017), p. 19; W.C. Jordan, 'A Fresh Look at Medieval Sanctuary', in *Law and the Illicit*, ed. by Karras, Kaye, Matter, (Philadelphia, 2010), c.1, p. 20. See, e.g., JUST 1/778 m. 59 (IMG 7919); JUST 1/486 m. 14 (IMG 2747).

59 See, e.g., *Seipp* 1313.313ss; 1330.334ss, 1369.161ass; 1421.100rog. On the consequence of a finding of self-defence, see, e.g., Green, *Verdict*, c. 3.

60 Unsuccessful: *Seipp* 1321.124ss. Successful: JUST 1/804 m. 73 (IMG 2444), pardon: *CPR 1292–1301*, p. 4. SC8/278/13872; JUST 1/1277 m. 5 (IMG 2252). See, e.g., *CPR 1334–8*, pp. 109, 278; *CPR 1361–4*, p. 6; *CPR 1364–7*, p. 117; *CPR 1388–92*, p. 419. Self-defence (female v. female), accepted in a trespass case: KB 27/420 m. 58 (IMG 124). Pardon for man killing woman in self-defence: *CPR 1292–1301*, p. 4. *CPR 1258–66*, p. 615; *CPR 1266–72*, pp. 60, 112, 615; *CPR 1340–43*, p. 129. A woman attempting to arrest a man who pulled a knife on her is an example in a Year Book: *Seipp* 1302.202; SC8/278/13872.

less likely to use self-defence as a plea in 'civil' assault.[61] It is arguable that the common law's idea of self-defence was based on behaviour accepted in or expected of men, and there was difficulty fitting female behaviour into it.[62] The standard exculpatory story of acting only as a last resort, when backed into a corner or against a wall and in fear of immediate death from an opponent whose onslaught was regularly described as being conducted *viriliter*, might be considered to suit expected male v. male violence much more than male v. female violence.[63] Women would be allowed to portray themselves as having acted in self-defence, if they did fit themselves into the standard model; for example, a 1373 Buckinghamshire gaol delivery roll tells the action-packed story of a woman, Agnes atte Nasshe, dragged into a water mill by a man, John Chadde, who was intent on killing her. Agnes was said to have run away to a room high up in the mill; then John pursued her, grabbed her and drew a knife. Agnes, seeing no other way of saving her life, hit John in the chest (with her left hand, as he held her by the right hand) so that he fell to the ground, breaking his neck and dying. The jury considered that Agnes had no choice but to do this, and had not acted maliciously or with felonious intent. She was sent back to prison to await the king's grace.[64] In this unusual situation, Agnes was able to use the force of gravity to accomplish her escape from deadly peril. It seems improbable however that women would have been excused for acting in the way modern scholarship has shown to be a particularly likely response of the physically weaker person in a violent relationship, using force when not in immediate danger of death, but when a pattern of violence leaves them fearing for their lives.[65] There was no obvious community sympathy for a Northamptonshire woman who reportedly raised the hue on the husband who was beating her, then assented to the husband being killed by her brother; the siblings were both arrested.[66] It is also less clear that a killing would be seen as non-felonious if the harm feared was 'only' rape rather than death. Some sympathy seems to be shown to a woman in this situation in a Northumberland roll of 1256.

61 Women's self-defence pleas in trespass, e.g., KB 27/346 m. 46d (IMG 9895).

62 Hyams, 'Maitland', p. 232.

63 Green, *Verdict*, 36–7; Hurnard, *King's Pardon*, p. 84. Kamali, *Felony*, pp. 74–7. For trespass: *Seipp* 1455.037, 1400.041. See, e.g., *William Walravene v. John ate Hille* CP 40/413 m. 114 (IMG 226). Self-defence homicide case: H and W attack D with sticks, D kills W, jury say this was not felonious: KB 27/322 Rex m. 17d (IMG 370). For *viriliter*, see, e.g., JUST 3/1 m. 9d (IMG 55).

64 JUST 3/158 m. 21 (IMG 45).

65 For modern consideration of this issue, see, e.g., Donald Nicolson and Rohit Sanghvi, 'Battered Women and Provocation: The Implications of *R v Ahluwalia*', *Criminal Law Review* (1993), 728–38; C.P. Ewing, 'Psychological Self-Defense: A Proposed Justification for Battered Women Who Kill', *Law and Human Behavior* 14 (1990), 579–94; Vanessa Bettinson, 'Aligning Partial Defences to Murder with the Offence of Coercive or Controlling Behaviour', *Journal of Criminal Law* 83 (2019), 71–86.

66 9 *SS* p. 70 (1314).

Alice, daughter of Ivo de la Dene, stabbed Richard, son of Gamel, who was attempting to rape her. The jury described this action as having been done *se defendendo*, but, as Alice fled, how that would have been received remains a mystery.[67] In a case on the roll of the 1285 Warwickshire eyre, a jury stated that another Alice, this one the daughter of Henry Haselod, had killed her would-be-rapist, Bernard, servant of Peter de Montfort, with Bernard's own knife. There was no mention of 'in self defence' in this case, but, once again, the killer had fled.[68] A much later case, from 1437, deals with the apparent scenario of an attempted rape by Eborard Legard, a 'Frenchman', on Joan Chamberleyn, which ended by Joan hitting Eborard over the head (more than once) with a candlestick. This was treated as self-defence, but it is somewhat ambiguous on the issue of whether killing a would-be rapist could be regarded as understandable enough to go unpunished, since there was also a suggestion that there was a potentially deadly knife attack on Joan by Eborard (after she had fought off his rape attempt, he decided to kill her). Whether this was a 'makeweight' to ensure that this qualified as self-defence (thus showing doubts about whether deadly force could be used when the alternative was 'only' rape and not death) or whether it was what was actually thought to have occurred cannot now be known.[69]

Men did claim self-defence in trespass cases or mayhem cases, saying that they struck when being attacked by a woman,[70] though it was fairly unusual for them to initiate action based on a claim that a woman had beaten them.[71] There are few cases in which a male is said to have killed a female in self-defence, though clearly this was not inconceivable. In the rolls of the eyre of Hereford 1292, for example, there is a record of a case in which Geoffrey, son of Reginald, was reported to have killed Matilda Syward. She was said to have caught him in bed with her daughter (age not specified) and held on to him as she raised the alarm. Others came, one man, Simon the servant, hitting him with an iron fork, meaning to kill him. Geoffrey stabbed Matilda, then fled. Matilda died. The jury stated that Geoffrey could not have escaped from Matilda without wounding her, and the iron-fork-wielding Simon would have killed him had he not escaped;

67 *P & M* II, p. 477; *Northumb. AR*, p. 85.

68 JUST 1/956 m. 41 (IMG 7847).

69 JUST 3/220/2 m. 57 (IMG 80); JUST 3/210 m. 29d (IMG 0141); Maddern, *Violence and Social Order*, p. 98.

70 See, e.g., *Seipp* 1330.541ss; KB 27/578 m. 57 (IMG 127); CP 40/643 m. 452 (IMG 888); CP 40/643 m. (IMG 979); KB 27/472 m. 48 (IMG 98); KB 27/670 m. 102 (IMG 263). KB 27/431 m. 38d (IMG 304); KB 27/566 m. 3d (IMG 285); KB 27/577 m. 7 (IMG 15). KB 27/583 m. 46 (IMG 97); KB 27/595 m. 21d (IMG 280); KB 27/719 m. 46d (IMG 374); KB 27/721 m. 45 (IMG 95); KB 718 m. 96 (IMG 204); KB 27/782 m. 12 (IMG 26); KB 27/867 m. 24d (IMG 275); CP40/711 m. (IMG 838). H says he was defending W from a woman: KB 27/623 m. 4d (IMG 229). Unsuccessful: KB 27/626 m. 71 (IMG 157); KB 27/818 m. 40 (IMG 89); KB 27/857 m. 26 (IMG 59). Mayhem: KB 27/491 m. 59 (IMG 125).

71 Woman sued for breaking a man's close and beating him: KB 27/350 m. 120 (IMG 3702).

Geoffrey received a pardon, on grounds of a sort of self-defence, here conceived as encompassing killing X to escape the probable lethal attack of Y.[72] The jury was to the fore in the development of self-defence: a picture of juries taking action to enforce 'community' views about homicide, sometimes against the apparent, strict rules of the 'official' criminal law, has been championed by Thomas A. Green. Exclusively male, the members of the jury were likely to cast self-defence in the mould of their sympathies and their own experiences and expectations of confrontation.[73] This was not straightforwardly 'anti-women' – since women's forceful action in defence of family members might also be seen in a favourable light, as in the case of a woman who helped her father when he was under attack, hitting his assailant with an axe. She was reported for this by a jury at the eyre of Yorkshire 1257, but pardoned as her father's defender.[74] Some women also included defence of a husband or an infant in their explanations of apparently violent or wrongful conduct.[75] Woman might intervene physically in protection of other women from male attack or in a fight between men, though this might lead to serious injury to them rather than the man in question.[76] Nevertheless, women who committed violent acts may well have been running a greater risk than were their male equivalents, and would be running a very great risk if they used violence against the man with the greatest opportunity to threaten or use violence against them – a husband – as will be discussed further below.

As with self-defence, the concept of accident or misadventure was an 'escape route' with a gendered dimension.[77] The common law in practice accepted that accidental injury or killing was not worthy of punishment as a felony. Sometimes, women's killings fell into this category,[78] but it would be fair to say that the possibility of a misadventure finding for harm which came to pass as a result of play or martial practice was particularly useful for men. *Bracton* and *Fleta*'s examples of 'death through play' or accidental homicide are notably masculine, both in linguistic expression and, it

72 JUST 1/302 m. 69, m. 69d (IMG 8330, 8556); JUST 1/303 m. 59 (IMG 8761); *CCR 1288–96*, p. 184.

73 Thomas A. Green, 'Societal Concepts of Criminal Liability for Homicide in Medieval England', *Speculum* 47 (1972), 669–95.

74 JUST 1/1109 m. 30d (IMG 8869), *CPR 1247–58*, p. 150. For the perceived duty of men to protect women, see Elisabeth van Houts, 'Family, Marriage, Kinship', in *A Social History of England 900–1200*, ed. by Julia Crick and Elisabeth van Houts (Cambridge, 2011), c. II.5, p. 134; and, e.g., JUST 1/804 m. 71d (IMG 2595); JUST 2/67 m. 30 (IMG 136); JUST 1/302 m. 59 (IMG 8308); KB 27/578 m. 68d (IMG 414); *Seipp* 1469.079; 1469.082.

75 Green, 'Societal', p. 681; C. 9260/792 no. 15. (1361), 103 *SS*, pp. 261–2; trespass, removal by woman of a hawk attacking an infant, Case 21.6, CP 40/441 m. 147 (IMG 296) 1371.

76 See, e.g., JUST 1/739 m. 55d (IMG 1739); JUST 1/739 m. 92d (IMG 1810). JUST 1/118 m. 53d (IMG 4922); JUST 1/739 m. 55d (IMG 1739); JUST 1/739 m. 92d (IMG 1810); *PCCG* 31.

77 For accident, see Kamali, *Felony*, p. 235; *Bracton* II, pp. 341, 384.

78 Hurnard, *King's Pardon*, p. 176; JUST 1/615 m. 8d; *CPR 1272–81*, pp. 311, 457; *CPR 1292–1301*, pp. 29, 66.

might be thought, in factual scenario (hunting with spears, playing with a ball, throwing stones, archery).[79] Given male domination of positions with law-enforcement roles, defences of lawful arrest were also more relevant to men than to women.[80] Likewise, although the case at the beginning of this chapter involves a woman defendant claiming to have been engaged in reasonable chastisement of an employee, given the greater number of situations in which men were allowed or expected to chastise, as husbands, fathers and employers, this was a plea more regularly available to men than to women.[81]

Anger or provocation was not a 'defence' or 'excuse' as far as the common law was concerned, but some cases bring in the idea and suggest a degree of jury sympathy. In particular, homicides by men whose wives were caught in a compromising position with another man were not officially excused in medieval common law whatever much later commentators might have asserted,[82] but this may be an instance in which the common law diverged from popular sentiment (or at least the sentiment of male jurors). There are, in relatively early cases, signs of a body of opinion considering wounding or castration of the lover a not inappropriate response,[83] and medieval juries might show sympathy for the husband who killed his wife's lover, portraying it as self-defence.[84] For example, what might appear to be

79 *Bracton* II, pp. 341, 384; *Fleta* book 1 c. 31, Bk 1 c. 22. Archery: Green, *Verdict*, p. 88. On the masculine nature of ball games see, e.g., F.P. Magoun, Jr., 'Football in Medieval England and in Middle-English Literature', *American Historical Review* 35 (1929), 33–45. JUST 1/996 m. 39d (IMG 176) (Jury: the wound inflicted with D's knife did not cause death). See also JUST 1/307 m. 9 (IMG 9121); KB 27/471 m. 26 (IMG 185). JUST 1/676 m. 2 (IMG 4752): woman 'ran onto a sword held by her son and killed herself'.
Men wrestling, leading to death, pardon: KB 27/641 m. (IMG 214). Male defendants in archery deaths, e.g., JUST 1/804 m. (IMG 2450), *CPR 1292–1301*, p. 5 (misadventure). See also JUST 1/135 m. 11 (IMG 6967), *CPR 1292–1301*, p. 2; Hurnard, *King's Pardon*, p. 279; JUST 1/1060 m. 13d. Girls said to have killed another child in play by mistake: *London Eyre 1244* Lond RS 1970, no. 133. See also the 1284 Cornish eyre of deadly play with stones, above at 129. For a less forgiving line on male 'sports', see the report of Fyneux CJ's speech in *Seipp* 1496.029.

80 See, e.g., *Seipp* 1505.051.

81 100 *SS* Case 2.13; CP 40/449 m. 262; *CRR XVI 1237–42*, p. 24 no 101 (woman chastises daughter to death). For male 'chastisement' cases, see KB 27/626 m. 26d (IMG 591); JUST 1/1334 m. 27 (IMG 2593) and the reference to chastisement of an adulterous wife in JUST 3/1 m. 9d. (IMG 0055). For a jury accepting the story that a woman had fled in fear of her violent husband, see JUST 1/804 m. 65d (IMG 2590).

82 Krista Kesselring, 'No Greater Provocation? Adultery and the Mitigation of Murder in English Law', *LHR* 34 (2016), 199–225; *P & M* II, p. 484; *Seipp* 1486.003, CP 40/893, m. 244 (IMG 448). See also, for the unacceptability of killing a wife's lover, JUST 1/996 m. 30d (IMG 157). (1306–7).

83 1257, 1288 and 1305–6 instances of castration in such circumstances, though these were seen as offences by the common law: JUST 1/1109 m. 27 (IMG 8791); JUST 1/210 m. 43d (IMG 5127) (1288); JUST 1/791 m. 1 (IMG 1482).

84 Kesselring, 'No Greater Provocation?', p. 204; Green, *Verdict*, pp. 42–3; JUST 3/1 m. 9d (IMG 0055). See also JUST 1/118 m. 55 (IMG 4771): men kill a clerk in a room with a man's wife: pardons on condition of fighting in Scotland. Petition of a man alleged to

a rather suspicious story of pursuit and unavoidable homicide in self-defence was given by a jury late in the reign of Edward I, noted in a 1307 gaol delivery record. John Mustarde had, apparently, come upon his wife sitting with another man, Thomas Osmond, in the house of a third party. Thomas, according to the jury, then pursued and attacked John, following him into John's home, and only when there was no escape did John happen to hit Thomas with a handy pole-axe. The alleged fact of John seeing his wife sitting with Thomas seems legally irrelevant, but it appears to have played some role in the jury's mind. John was expected to be pardoned, as this was found to be self-defence.[85] To what extent do we see gendered difference here? We might expect considerably less sympathy with a woman who behaved in a similar way, given differing ideas about the anger and physical aggression of men and women and differing expectations of chastity in husbands and wives.[86] A married woman's sexual jealousy was seen as a believable motive for procuring the homicide of 'the other woman'.[87] As long as she directed her reprisals against the 'other woman' rather than against her husband, while the fact that she had been wronged clearly did not amount to an exculpation, it may be that there was some sympathy for a woman committing an offence in this context. This is suggested by the questions about the culprit's age and mental competence which seem to have been put to the jury in a case of 1306 in which an abused wife, Joan, wife of Edmund Sneed, was found to have ripped out the eyes of Christiane, daughter of Thomas de la Twychene, who had, according to the jury, been involved in adultery with Joan's husband.[88] The posing of these questions gives the impression of an active attempt to find a reason not to condemn Joan. Outside the marital context, it is not impossible that some sympathy lay behind determinations that a woman's action did not cause a death, as in a case in which a woman was said to have been provoked by a man's defamatory words and hit him with a tool, but his death was found to have been caused by a fever and not the blow.[89] Sympathy did not, however, stretch to the situation in which a woman took violent action against her own husband, however adulterous or provoking he might have been, as we will see below.

Duress as an 'escape route' also had gendered aspects, though its status as a 'general defence' was as yet only at the 'under construction' stage in the medieval common law. Treatises considered duress, force and fear in

have killed his supposed 'dishonourer': SC8/103/5109 (he alleges that this is false, as a matter of causation, though care is also taken to portray the deceased unfavourably).

85 JUST 1/966 m. 10 (IMG 8921).

86 See, e.g., Elizabeth Papp Kamali, 'The Devil's Daughter of Hell Fire: Anger's Role in Medieval English Felony Cases', *LHR* 35 (2017), 155–200, 168, 175–6, 190.

87 JUST 1/409 m. 7 (IMG 16).

88 JUST 1/1032 m. 4d (IMG 2700). Edmund and Joan were reported to have supported Christiane thereafter.

89 JUST 1/956 m. 41 (IMG 7847).

relation to invalidation of a gift or transfer of land and definitions of the sort of fear which would count in such cases are expressed in masculine terms. *Bracton* for example, borrowing terminology from Romanist sources, defines the relevant fear as 'an agitation of the mind caused by danger, present or future', which is 'immediate' fear of death or physical torture, and which is the sort of fear which 'may occur in a resolute man' (*in virum constantem*) rather than a 'weak or timid' one (*cuiuslibet vani vel meticulosi hominis*).[90] The use of *vir* makes it hard to see this as gender-neutral, whatever one might conclude about the inclusivity of *homo*.[91] Defences of duress are evident in records relating to debt, in which it is clear that being kept imprisoned until one seals an obligation, if established, is a valid exception to the debt action. This was used by both men and women.[92] Ideas of duress are less obviously effective as defences outside the context of debt. A woman's explanation that she was present at a killing by others and concealed them, in part at least because of their threats to kill her, did not save her from death, for example.[93] The increased likelihood of pressure being brought to bear by husbands on wives to transfer their lands was mainly dealt with – to the extent it was dealt with – through the formal mechanisms associated with the fine process and the possibility of challenging transfers after the husband's death with a *cui in vita* action.[94] An explicit idea of coercion and compulsion as a defence is, however, encountered in pronouncements and cases on what would later be called 'the doctrine of marital coercion' in relation to 'criminal' offences. Commentators have often portrayed the treatment of married women as generous, in that they were shielded from adverse consequences of their offending behaviour by this doctrine. An eighteenth-century legal scholar, for example, put it in these terms:

> [T]he laws have always been very merciful in regard to femes covert, for they are not amenable to punishment for a bare theft, committed under the coercion of or in the company of their husbands, neither shall they be deemed accessory for receiving their husbands, who have been guilty of a felony, though it is said that men become accessories by receiving their guilty wives…[95]

90 *Bracton* II, p. 65; *Fleta* book 3, c. 7. See also *Bracton* II, p. 296, on the action *quod metus causa*. On the resolute, not timid, man as a Romanist borrowing: 8 *SS*, p. 180, 184.

91 See Chapter 1.

92 Woman's defence of imprisonment and force: CP 40/427 m. 85 (IMG 172).

93 1 *SS* (1202) p. 28, no 77. On uncertainties surrounding duress, see Milsom, 'Trespass'; p. 581, note 32, John Hudson 'Emotions in the Early Common Law (c. 1166–1215)', *JLH* 38 (2017), 130–54; Kamali, *Felony*, p. 235; 100 SS, xli (duress pleas based on st. 6 Ric. II st 2 c 5; *SR* II, 31).

94 See above p. 40.

95 Richard Wooddeson, *A Systematical View of the Laws of England* (Oxford, 1792), pp. 1, 261, Lecture XVI, p. 447.

A twentieth-century commentator on the medieval common law stated simply that:

> [A] woman who committed a felony jointly with her husband could not be held guilty of it since she was under his dominion.[96]

Both statements, particularly the latter, give an exaggerated view of the 'shielding' effect of marriage for women in terms of culpability. Such accounts also tend to ignore the fact that the reason the common law had begun to develop ideas to exculpate wives was that they might be inculpated, or disadvantaged, because of their marriage. They are insufficiently attuned to the fact that these ideas developed not as general doctrines, but in relation to specific types of offence, and that, in fact, part of their early development concerned the exculpation of men as well as the exculpation of women. There was neither an automatic immunity for married women and married women alone, with regard to all felonies, nor a formed and straightforward legal 'doctrine of marital coercion' during the medieval period.[97] The common law did hold husbands responsible in 'civil' cases and some non-capital criminal cases, in the sense that they were obliged to pay compensation for their wives' misdeeds.[98] This was rather different of course, being a practical necessity given the choice which had been made to bar wives from rights in chattels. It need not be seen as requiring an idea that the wife was actually always dominated by the husband to such an extent that she could not be responsible or culpable.

Thirteenth-century treatises had something to say about both the possibility of the wife being exculpated by virtue of the fact or presumption that she was dominated by her husband, and also the situation of the husband of an offending wife, who might perhaps be deemed responsible for his wife's actions. There was particular concern with theft, which showed a continuation of the interest in theft and receiving stolen goods evident in older legal codes.[99] Treatise accounts combine statements that punishment should only be imposed upon those actually offending, with a recognition of the theoretical and/or practical power of husbands over wives (and consequent difficulties in holding wives responsible for actions or situation which may not have been their own choice). There are illustrations of situations in which culpability can be presumed (particularly when stolen goods are found under a wife's lock and key), probably descending from older treatments of this matter.[100] Slightly different interpretations are given as

96 *Wilts GDT*, p. 24.

97 *Bl. Comm.* IV pp. 27–8; Gerry Rubin, 'Pre-Dating Vicky Pryce: The Peel Case (1922) and the Origins of the Marital Coercion Statutory Defence', *Legal Studies* 34 (2014), 631–59.

98 See, e.g., *Crown Pleas of the Eyre of Devon* 1238, ed. by Henry Summerson, no 524.

99 Older law: *P & M* I, p. 33, Hudson *OHLE* II, p. 168.

100 *Fleta* book 1 c. 36; *Bracton* II, p. 428.

to why a woman might be held not culpable in relation to such offences. *Bracton*, considering theft, gives an explanation based on the common law construction of the relationship between spouses and chattels – the wife is not to be held liable for theft by her husband, 'because it is not she who has it [i.e. the stolen thing] within her *potestas* but her husband'.[101] An explanation might, instead, be based on the husband's legal power or (factual or presumed) domination over his wife.[102] Concern was not all with the wife however: *Bracton* also considered whether a husband was liable for his wife's thefts. The answer was 'not inevitably': the idea of his responsibility for her or control over her did not stretch this far. There was, however, work for him to do if he wanted to be held innocent, in that he needed to demonstrate that he had not consented to her misdeeds.[103] In relation to wives and culpability for crimes committed by or with their husbands, on the whole, they were not simply regarded as irresponsible and unamenable to law if they were thought to have been involved in an offence with their husbands. *Bracton* states that 'the wife must … not be discharged in every case'.[104] The idea of the dominated wife was clearly not the only available construction of the marital relationship: *Bracton* also contemplated a homicide scenario in which a husband held the victim whilst the wife took the active role in the killing, and suggested at least limited capacity for the wife's independent action when it placed upon her the tricky duty 'neither [to] accuse her husband nor assent to his felony, but … to hinder him so far as she is able'.[105]

In records of cases, we see women being held not responsible for felonies because of a lack of knowledge of a key fact, such as that goods received were stolen,[106] or on the grounds of coercion (whether actual or presumed) in cases of theft, harbouring thieves, robbery, even homicide.[107] As with the *Bracton* account, there was no irrebuttable presumption of coercion, and occasional records indicate careful inquiry into its presence or absence.[108]

101 *Bracton* II, p. 428.

102 *Bracton* IV, p. 287; *Fleta* book VI c. 50; refers to the case of Roger de Fanborne and his wife Agnes. Roger was hanged, Agnes released as she was 'under her husband's rod; Rubin, 'Pre-Dating Vicky Pryce', p. 637.

103 *Bracton* II, p. 428; *Fleta* book 1, c. 36. See Kamali, *Felony*, pp. 61–2. Note earlier ideas of responsibility spreading to kin rather than spouse: *LHP*, p. 223.

104 *Bracton* II, p. 428.

105 *ibid.*; *Fleta* book 1 c. 36. Compare Thomas of Chobham's, *Manual for Confessors*, c. 1215: Sharon Farmer, 'Persuasive Voices: Clerical Images of Medieval Wives', *Speculum* 61 (1986), 517–43.

106 JUST 1/135 m. 28 (IMG 7010); David Crook, 'The Seditious Murder of Thomas of Sibthorpe and the Great Statute of Treasons 1351–2', *Historical Research* 88 (2015), 402–16.

107 Wilkinson, *Women*, p. 164; M.T. Clanchy, 'Highway Robbery and Trial by Battle in the Hampshire Eyre of 1249', in *Medieval Legal Records*, ed. by Hunnisett and Post, (London, 1978), p. 56; Kamali, *Felony*, p. 2; *Crown Pleas of the Wiltshire Eyre*, ed. and tr. C.A.F. Meekings (Devizes, 1969), pp. 180, 238; JUST1/996 m. 26d (IMG 151) (1249). JUST 1/996 m. 37 (IMG 86); Hanawalt Westman, 'The peasant family', p. 13; JUST 3/125 m. 9d.

108 JUST 3/125 m. 9d (IMG 62).

A confession of participation or evidence of wives' own independent criminal activity might override any presumption of coercion by a husband.[109] Women might also be seen as the dominant partner in relation to theft, with the husband a mere accessory or receiver.[110] In relation to certain types of offence – those outside the home – there is a good case for suggesting that there was, over the course of the thirteenth century, a move from assuming the liability of wives present at their husbands' offences to a more 'firmly exculpatory' view (at least in relation to theft), and there are certainly examples of what appears to be a presumption that wives acted under their husbands' compulsion.[111] In the reign of Edward III, there does seem to have been an expectation that if women were taken for crimes committed with their husbands, it should be asked whether this had occurred through the husband forcing the wife's action, something which suggests that this was an acceptable explanation, but not that it was presumed to be the case in every instance of misconduct by a married woman.[112] By the latter part of the fourteenth century, there are signs of language of 'coverture' crossing over into the 'criminal' context, and perhaps moving towards a more ready presumption of a will overborne. Thus, in a 1363 case concerning an indictment alleging that a husband and wife received felons, it was pleaded that the wife had been, at the critical time and was still, 'covered by her husband Richard' and 'wholly under his *potestas*, so that she could not contradict him', and that, since the indictment did not mention either that she committed an offence or consented to it or that she received the felons without his knowledge, it was insufficient.[113]

That such claims of necessary coercion through marriage were not always a safe route for women can be seen in a case of 1366 in which Alice, 'servant of Walter Baret', was appealed alongside Walter in relation to thefts of various objects from a church. Walter claimed clergy successfully. Alice said that since she was his wife rather than his servant as the appeal stated, she would not answer for things done in her husband's presence. A jury found that both Walter and Alice were guilty of the offence that Alice was indeed Walter's wife, but that she had committed the offence of her own malice without her husband's coercion. Alice was remitted to gaol to await the gaol delivery. At the delivery, it was ordered that she should be hanged because she had committed the offence, and this had not been through coercion of

109 *Northumb. AR*, 332; 98 *SS*, p. 168. H not liable for W's larceny when he was not present and had no knowledge of it. Kiralfy *Source Book* p. 37; 24 *SS*, p. 81; 98 *SS* p. 791; *Seipp* 1322.018. Kerr, 'Husband and Wife', pp. 236, 280.

110 SC 8/254/12666.

111 Henry Summerson, 'Maitland and the Criminal Law in the Age of Bracton', in *The History of English Law*, ed. by Hudson (Oxford, 1996), pp. 115–43, 116; JUST 1/564 m.3 IMG 7317), theft; Kerr, 'Husband and Wife', pp. 236–7.

112 Kerr, 'Husband and Wife', p. 237; 97 *SS*, 179.

113 KB 27/412 m. 34d (IMG 582).

her husband.[114] This case certainly shows the existence of a belief in a robust presumption of coercion, but clearly it could be rebutted, and juries were prepared to look past it. In addition, it should be noted that Alice's claim of presumed coercion or the absence of a requirement to answer related to the specific situation of offences committed in the husband's presence: it was not a formula suggesting a blanket immunity for married women. In the late fourteenth century, Alice and other women who were said to have committed offences with their husbands were certainly still being accused, convicted and hanged.[115] Another wife, found to have been coerced, seems to have run the risk of execution in a case of 1353. She had confessed to a theft of bread, but said that this was done at the command of her husband (or, more precisely, by the man who was her husband at the time of the offence). She was not executed, but the report suggests that this was a matter of judicial favour rather than a matter of routine. She had not helped her cause by confessing to the theft, referring to command rather than coercion, nor perhaps by taking too big a step away from the 'crime committed in husband's presence' cases.[116] In the sixteenth century, the 1353 case may have been interpreted as illustrative of a conception of marital coercion which had become more generous to the wife, as a reading of 1551 seems to elide command and coercion, by adding the idea that a wife owes obedience to her husband.[117] The default position in the medieval common law would appear to have been some expectation of influence by husband over wife. 'Marital coercion' as an exculpatory doctrine in felony cases was certainly not, however, equivalent to the situation of irrebuttably presumed wifely irresponsibility seen in some aspects of 'civil' law, in which we find such statements as that of a mid-fifteenth-century Chancellor that everything done by a married woman was to be regarded as having been done *per drede de son baron*,[118] and it is quite possible that the strength of presumption of lack of culpability varied with the type of offence.

Later legal tradition would emphasise the idea of favour and generosity in this context. There is, however, a danger of exaggeration of the idea that it excused women who were not in fact coerced. A balanced assessment requires an admission that we cannot know that there was not in fact significant coercion within marriages. We should also bear in mind the possibility of marriage having the opposite effect on women's legal liability – that of what might be called 'marital contagion'. The facts of married life put spouses in a position in which they might be accused of wrongdoing by virtue of proximity to the commission of an offence, or through cohabitation,

114 JUST 3/156 m. 5 (IMG 0015).

115 JUST 3/179 m. 5 (IMG 10). H and W, with others, convicted as accessories to homicide, on appeal by the wife of the deceased.

116 *Seipp* 1353.165ass.

117 132 *SS*, p. 192.

118 *Seipp* 1467.038.

by virtue of proximity to the proceeds of crime. Against any 'advantage' or 'indulgence' to women must be weighed the 'collateral damage' to wives (and families) of their husbands' offences and convictions, including forfeiture, expropriation, economic loss and loss of freedom,[119] as well as the risk that they themselves would fall under suspicion of guilt because of proximity to him and his offences, in circumstances ranging from those wives present at their husbands' offences (whether or not actively participating), through those who 'received' their felon husbands or their stolen goods to the Yorkshire wife noted in the eyre of 1257 who had wanted to pull her husband out of a pond in which he had drowned himself, perhaps in order to try and escape the economic consequences of his 'self-felony'.[120] Perhaps, above all, the material on 'petty treason', to be discussed below, throws significant doubt on the idea that married women were, overall, shown 'mercy' by the common law.

Another 'escape route' sometimes portrayed as generous to women relates to pregnancy. Evidence that executions of those felons confirmed to be pregnant should be deferred until after the birth predates the period of this book, and the possibility of such deferral was maintained through and beyond the medieval period.[121] It was justified on the grounds of a need to prevent the killing of the foetus.[122] Convicted women used claims of pregnancy in an attempt to defer execution, and were sometimes successful in doing so.[123] Consideration of the area has been complicated and distorted by later developments and theories, leading to the linked ideas that pregnant felons were generally given a complete reprieve as opposed to a deferral of execution,

119 See K.J. Kesselring, 'Felony Forfeiture in England, c. 1170–1870', *JLH* 30 (2009), 201–26; Seabourne, *IMW*, cc. 1 and 3; C.D. Ross, 'Forfeiture for Treason in the Reign of Richard II', *EHR* 71 (1956), 560–75; J.R. Lander, 'Attainder and Forfeiture, 1453 To 1509', *Historical Journal* 4 (1961), 119–51; Anne Crawford, 'Victims of Attainder: The Howard and De Vere Women in the Late Fifteenth Century', *Reading Medieval Studies* 15 (1989), 58. Orders to eject wives and children of attainted jurors from their lands: *Seipp* 1368.087, 1504.010. Suffering of the family of an official who not done his duty: 98 *SS*, p. 11; *Wilts GD and T*, no 119.

120 Yorkshire eyre 1257. JUST 1/1109 m. 30d (IMG 8870). For a theft case, see, e.g., W dragged into H's theft: apparently arrested but not indicted m. 11 (IMG 28). For capital punishment for a woman noted to have been present with her husband at a (multiple) homicide, see *CRR VIII*, 273 (1220).

121 *Bracton* II, p. 429; *Fleta* book 1 c. 36; *Mirror* book IV, c. 16; J.C. Oldham, 'On Pleading the Belly', *Criminal Justice History* 6 (1985), 1–64, 2; Harris Stoertz, 'Pregnancy and Childbirth', p. 271.

122 JUST 3/210 m. 16 (IMG 35). Note, however, that there were limits to this: see below, p. XXX

123 Deferrals, e.g., JUST 1/374 m. 32d (IMG 2504); RCR vol I p. 204 (deferred burning for homicides – 1198); Kerr, 'Husband and Wife', p. 237; *Wilts GD and T*, pp. 34, 81; JUST 1/1108 m. 22 (IMG 8723); JUST 3/220/2 m. 77 (IMG 106); JUST 3/1/4 m. 42d (IMG 207). JUST 3/48 m. 2d (IMG 99); JUST 3/48 m. 28d (IMG 145), m. 40d (IMG 176); JUST 3/113 m. 6 d (IMG 27); JUST 3/189 m. 5 (IMG 13); JUST 3/217/3 m. 39 (IMG 55); JUST 1/1334 m. 1d (IMG 2673); JUST 1/966 m. 7 (IMG 8917).

and that this was part of a doctrine of 'benefit of the belly', regularly involving false claims and declarations of pregnancy, comparable to the (increasingly fictionalised) male-only doctrine of benefit of clergy.[124] Recent work has shown the idea of fictionalised generosity to medieval women to have been a comforting myth. In the medieval period (and into the early modern period), women's pregnancy was less of a shield than had been suggested.[125] Butler's study of the later medieval period has shown that pregnant women could not count on being pardoned, and there was not routine collusive false declaration of pregnancy: the 'matrons', tasked with determining the truth of claims of pregnancy, did find some not pregnant.[126] It is also the case that some obviously pregnant women were hanged and that not all pregnancies 'counted' for the purpose of deferral.[127] The increasingly evident requirement that the foetus be found to have 'quickened' meant that those pregnancies which had not reached this relatively advanced stage would not result in deferral. Even an advanced pregnancy might, on some views, not serve as a basis for deferral; if the woman had used a previous pregnancy to defer execution, there was a view that she could not do so again even if there was a new pregnancy. Mid-fourteenth-century Year Book reports note the hanging of women, despite their claims of pregnancy, because they had benefited from previous deferrals. Some disquiet is recorded, along with the suggestion that this is a change from the past, but objections do not appear to have prevailed.[128] The idea that the 'once only' rule for pregnancy deferrals was not of long duration seems to be supported by a Warwickshire case from the end of Edward I's reign. Alice, sister of Hugh ad Fontem, had been convicted of homicide. At least some thought it appropriate to send her back to prison, deferring her execution on the grounds of a new pregnancy, despite the fact that she had already had such a deferral, and had had the baby on which that first deferral was based, before becoming pregnant once more.[129] The idea that one could only use the pregnancy deferral on one occasion seems to have become orthodox by the mid-fifteenth century.

124 J.M. Beattie, cited in Oldham, 'On Pleading', p. 19, and Butler, 'Pleading', pp. 133–4. Walker, *Crime, Gender and Social Order*, p. 197; J.S. Cockburn, *Calendar of Assize Records, Home Circuit Indictments Eliz I and James I* (London, 1985), p. 122, suggests fiction.

125 Kesselring *Mercy*, App II, p. 78; Walker, *Crime, Gender*, p. 197; Butler, 'Pleading', pp. 133, 140.

126 Butler, 'Pleading', pp. 133–4, 136, 142. 'Not pregnant': e.g., JUST 3/220/2 m. 182 (IMG 243); JUST 3/173 m. 26 (IMG 61); JUST 3/188 m. 17d (IMG 411): *Seipp* 1348.279ass (1348): JUST 3/195 m. 72d (IMG 415). For claims with excessive gestation periods, see Butler, 'More than Mothers', p. 28.

127 Henry Summerson, 'Attitudes to Capital Punishment in England 1200–1350', in *Thirteenth Century England VIII*, ed. by M. Prestwich, R. Britnell and R. Frame (Woodbridge, 2001), pp. 123–34, 131: 1258 case, hanging of a heavily pregnant convict: JUST 1/1187 m. 11. (IMG 27).

128 *Seipp* 1338.259ass, 1349.019ass; 1351.055; 132 *SS*, p. 235.

129 JUST 1/966 m. 7 (IMG 8917).

Baker's Selden Society volume on readings on Magna Carta includes a reading which he dates 1455–60, which states this as incontrovertible, though its explanation leaves something to be desired – such a woman should be executed when pregnant a second time 'inasmuch as she lost all manner of answers when she took the first answer, so that she cannot be saved by any fresh cause'. It works as an explanation only if considered to relate to the woman alone, and ignoring statements which highlight the need not to kill innocent foetuses.[130]

Some women who obtained a deferral also obtained a pardon, but this was not inevitable, and some were hanged in due course.[131] The suggestion that women received 'indulgent' treatment in this respect cannot be sustained.[132] The rejection of the idea of 'benefit of the belly' as a generous 'easy way out' for women convicted of felony suggests wider problems with constructions of past courts and administrations as generous or lenient to women, and of women as fraudulent in claims relating to reproduction. None of this is to suggest that women were executed in greater numbers than men, nor even that a smaller proportion of accusations against men than accusations against women resulted in execution; the point is to highlight that the common law's range of 'escape routes' was gendered, and that those routes available to women were not as 'indulgent' to them as has been suggested in what has become the orthodox common law narrative. Why might previous scholars have thought there was consistently favourable treatment of pregnant women? Partly, it is a case of 'reading back' the ideas and practices of the more recent past – in which it would not be unjust to see the treatment of pregnant convicts as more generous – into the more distant past, perhaps also retrospectively systematising and treating practices as if they conformed to a clear, accepted and articulated doctrine, when that does not seem to have been the case in the medieval period. Partly, it may have been a device to enable women's encounter with the common law to be neatly encapsulated and then ignored, to move back to the more interesting business of men.

Disposal and punishment

In completed 'civil' cases, where the defendant was not acquitted, we see orders relating to land or money. The marital status of a female defendant had a bearing on the detail of the destination of both. In 'criminal'

130 132 *SS*, pp. lxix, 235.

131 Pardons: see, e.g., Butler, 'More than Mothers', p. 14 '1228, 1248, 1253: *CCR 1227–31*, 53; *CPR 1247–58*, 20; *CCR 1251–53*, 501', *CPR 1313–17*, 20, *CPR 1350–54*, 10, 366; *CPR 1354–8*, 99, 515; *CPR 1364–7*, 103, *CPR 1370–74*, 122; *CPR 1374–7*, 269, *CPR 1381–5*, 243; *CPR 1391–96*, 8, 28, 317; *CPR 1396–9*, 516; *CPR 1405–8*, 299; *CPR 1408–13*, 267; *CPR 1436–41*, 356. Not: Butler, 'Pleading', p. 143; JUST 3/36/1 m. 17. Escape, sanctuary, abjuration: 24 *SS*, p. 96.

132 See, e.g., *Wilts GD and T*, p. 24 'indulgencies'.

cases, we see financial penalties and corporal penalties, up to and including capital punishment, for women as well as men. On the whole, punishment for those convicted of felony was not differentiated by sex in the common law,[133] though *Britton* worried about the need to make adjustments in some mayhem cases, depending on whether the assailant was a man or a woman – for what the author advocated as the usual rule of 'member for member' punishment could not apply if a woman attacked a man's genitals. In this case, she was to lose a hand instead, a justification for this penalty being found in the fact that this was the 'member wherewith she committed the offence'.[134] Generally, however, death by hanging and forfeiture of such property as was held by the convict were available to deal with both men and women. Some lesser offences had different punishments for men and women, however,[135] and in the case of some of the most serious offences, death sentences were differentiated based on marital status and/or sex.[136] The most spectacular cases, to be dealt with below – those ending in burning of the female convict – were not common, but they deserve detailed consideration, as they are useful windows on both the medieval common law's treatment of women and the ways in which that treatment has been portrayed in subsequent work.

Women, marriage, treason, heresy and fire

> The severity of the punishments meted out to women by the criminal law were, however, throughout the period excessive.[137]

> It was a common sight to see the body of a woman burning because she had murdered her husband, though it must be said that the hangman generally managed to strangle the prisoner before the flames touched her body.[138]

133 No differentiation by sex: *Glanvill* 1. 2; *Bracton* II, pp. 298–9. Burning for plotters against their lord's safety: *D.* 48.19.28.11; *P. & M.*, ii, p. 504 n.; cf. *CCR 1227–31*, p. 53: woman convicted of husband's death ordered to be burnt. *Bracton* II, p. 318, punishment for 'lese-majesty' is drawing, breaking and hanging, while for theft or homicide it is 'simple hanging'; II, 349 punishment of a clerk for apostasy: degrading then burning; *P & M*, I, p. 437, n. 4. For sex as a matter to take into account in sentencing, in some canon law sources: Schrage, 'Women Do Not Sit as Judges', pp. 377–89.

134 *Britton* book 1, c. 26 no. 1.

135 See, e.g., *SR* I, pp. 199–200.

136 For sex differentiated execution in other jurisdictions, see, e.g., 18 *SS*, p. 75; 21 *SS* p. xxxiv; Henry Summerson, 'Trials by Ordeal in a Kentish Court in the Early Thirteenth Century', *JLH*, 41 (2020), 332–42, 340; Mia Korpiola, 'Rethinking Incest and Heinous Sexual Crime: Changing Boundaries of Secular and Ecclesiastical Jurisdiction in Late Medieval Sweden', in *Boundaries*, ed. by Musson (London, 2005), c. 8, p. 111; J. Borsje, 'Rules and Legislation on Love Charms in Early Medieval Ireland', *Peritia* 21 (2010), 172–90, 178.

137 Cleveland, *Woman under the English Law*, p. 158.

138 Cleveland, *Woman under the English Law*, p. 118.

Death by burning was not restricted to female felons. From an early period, burning was suggested as an appropriate punishment for arsonists, probably because of a combination of the seriousness of the offence and an idea of 'fit' or analogy to the offence, 'so that they may be punished in the manner as they have offended'. Both men and women were burnt for arson.[139] The association of arsonists and death by burning was not complete either in theory or practice, however, with examples of arsonists being imprisoned or hanged rather than burnt, and disagreement amongst late-thirteenth century commentators as to the correct penalty.[140] The idea seems to have become attenuated in the later thirteenth century, with examples of post-mortem or partial burning.[141] Thirteenth-century treatises recommended burning as a punishment in some other areas: sodomy, apostasy, sorcery and being a 'renegade and miscreant'.[142] Evidence of use of such a punishment is hard to find for medieval England, however.[143] In theory, death by fire was also the prescribed response for all recalcitrant heretics once royal justice took a role in this area. The idea of burning as the appropriate penalty for confirmed heretics was an old one, widespread and persistent in Europe, and not unknown in England in the thirteenth century.[144] Early fifteenth-century legislation, expressed without sex differentiation, prescribed burning in a high or prominent place and forfeiture of property for heresy.[145] In practice, while

139 Summerson, 'Burning Issues', pp. 101, 105, 107, 110, 111; *LHP* pp. 108–9; *Glanvill*, 1, 3; *Britton* book 1 c. 10. *PCCG* no 216 p. 52; Women burnt: 1 *SS* no.191, *Eyre of London 1244* no. 146 (1240–1).

140 Summerson 'Burning Issues', pp. 110, 111; JUST 1/761 m. 33d. 111; *Mirror*, book IV c. 15 (punishment formerly burning, now hanging); *Britton* book 1 c. 10 (burning for arsonists).

141 Summerson, 'Burning Issues', p. 111, examples from Norwich in 1272 (burning after death of arsonists, including a woman): W. Rye, 'The Riot Between the Monks and Citizens of Norwich in 1272', *Norfolk Antiquarian Miscellany* 2 (1880), 27, 45, an account of the 1283 execution of Dafydd ap Gruffudd stating that organs were to be burnt because he had burnt houses and villages, and a hanging, then burning of an arsonist in Carlisle in 1292: JUST 1/137 m. 30. See also the prescription of death by fire for some arson in the customs of Waterford, c. 1300 18 *SS*, p. 177.

142 P & M II, p. 546: *Fleta* Book 1 c. 35; *Britton*, book 1 c. 10.

143 Possible post-mortem burning of a witch on the orders of the clergy, 1279: *P & M* II, 552: *Northumb. AR*, p. 343. For a 1324 example of burning associated with sorcery in Ireland, see A. Neary, 'The Origins and Character of the Kilkenny Witchcraft Case of 1324', *Proceedings of the Royal Irish Academy* 83C (1983), 333–50.

144 *Britton* book I c. 11, note z; *Heresy and Authority in Medieval Europe*, ed. by E. Peters, (Philadelphia, 1980), pp. 71, 74, 80. A.E. Larsen. 'Are all Lollards Lollards', in *Lollards and Their Influence in Late Medieval England*, ed. by Fiona Somerset and others (Woodbridge, 2003), p. 61; Maitland, *The Deacon and the Jewess in Roman Canon Law in the Church of England* (London, 1898), pp. 158–9. *Mirror* book IV, c. 14, burning for heresy. This chapter does not differentiate punishment for men and women.

145 *De Haeretico Comburendo* (1401); 2 Hen. IV, c. 15, *SR* II, pp. 125–8; 2 Hen. V, st. 1, c. 7; *SR* II, pp. 181–4; A.K. McHardy, 'De Heretico Comburendo 1401', in *Lollardy and the Gentry in the Later Middle Ages*, ed. by Margaret Aston and Colin Richmond (New York, 1997), pp. 112–26. F.D. Logan, *Excommunication and the Secular Arm in Medieval England: A*

women were amenable to burning as recalcitrant heretics, those sentenced to the flames before the sixteenth century were predominantly male.[146] This difference is best explained by women's perceived and real lesser prominence within Lollardy (despite some well-known exceptions), mirroring their generally less prominent role in religious life and public life.[147]

In both arson and heresy, the prescription of fire was linked to the nature of the offence only. In other cases, it was aspects of the offender's identity (sex or marital status) which were determinative of amenability to burning. These aspects might be relevant to punishment only, or to both guilt and punishment. There are signs of a particular association between women and the punishment of burning. Some early records show women burnt as a punishment apparently for ordinary homicide,[148] though punishment for this and most other felonies was generally hanging. *Britton* recommended the burning of women for treason.[149] The most consistent evidence of theory and practice of burning of women related to those found guilty of offences which would come to be categorised as species of treason: first, the killing of a superior and, in particular, a husband and, second, counterfeiting coinage, always taken very seriously, as an affront to the king.[150] The link between these offences and burning of women predated the explicit designation of the offences as treason: women, but not men, were burned for counterfeiting coinage before the 1352 Act (men being drawn and hanged),[151] and wives who killed husbands were burned before this same legislation called such killings a species of treason.[152] The reason for the burning of women is never articulated. The later idea that it was in some way connected to an idea of

Study in Legal Procedure from the Thirteenth to the Sixteenth Century (Toronto, 1968), pp. 191–4; P.R. Cavill, 'Heresy, Law and the State: Forfeiture in Late Medieval and Early Modern England', *EHR* 129 (2014), 270–95, 271. *P & M* II, p. 546, notes 1160s corporal punishment (not burning) of heretics.

146 Heresy, case against males, e.g., JUST 3/206 m. 7d (IMG 1258).

147 See Shannon McSheffrey, *Gender and Heresy: Women and Men in Lollard Communities, 1420–1530* (Philadelphia, 1995), pp. 109–23, 151–65; Claire Cross, 'Great Reasoners in Scripture: The Activities of Women Lollards 1380–1530', in *Medieval Women*, ed. by D. Baker (Oxford, 1978), pp. 359–80.

148 Hurnard, *King's Pardon*, p. 169: JUST 1/818 m. 47 (IMG 4479). For pre-conquest association of women and punishment by fire, see Hudson *OHLE* II, p. 186.

149 *Britton* book 1 c. 9 no. 3.

150 On treason, see in particular Bellamy, *Law of Treason*; *Glanvill* book I, 2, XIV. 1: *Bracton* II, p. 334; *Fleta* book 1, c. 21; *Placita Corone*, xxxvi–xxxvii, 21–2.

151 *Fleta* book 1 c. 22. See Bellamy, *Law of Treason*, p. 2, and, e.g., female counterfeiter burned, men drawn and hanged: JUST 3/1/1 m. 6d (IMG 52) 1310; (1347) KB 27/349 Rex m. 2 (IMG 2970); Woman counterfeiter to be burnt, 1375: JUST 3/158 m. 4d (IMG 64); man drawn and hanged for consent to killing of his lord: JUST 3/36 m. 2 (1296). Women burned for counterfeiting: JUST 3/41/1 m. 17 (IMG 0040).

152 Men or women could be condemned for the 'petty treason' of killing a master/mistress: *Seipp* 1440.120; KB 27/714 m. 164 (IMG 334).

decency in their treatment is unconvincing.[153] Burning was a particularly spectacular way to die, and one which had clear resonances with the tortures of hell.[154] The choice of this method of execution not for all crimes by women but only for what were apparently regarded as particularly serious female crimes is likely to indicate that it was regarded as a worse death than hanging, though it is difficult to make a comparison of the suffering involved in the two types of death.[155] We have no evidence from this period for the minor comfort of the idea that those sentenced to burn died not from the fire and smoke but from 'mercy-strangling'.

> A foolish doctrine, whereby allegiance was presumed to exist between husband and wife, was used as an argument for burning the wife to death in the event of her killing her husband.[156]

It is not surprising that in a hierarchical society, special opprobrium would be cast on killing of 'higher up' individuals: pre-fourteenth-century sources suggest the killing of feudal lords as particularly heinous, and also stressed the additional culpability in killing a father or mother,[157] while the legislation of 1352 singled out the king and key members of the royal family, masters and husbands. The association in the Statute of Treasons of husband-killing with other homicides going against hierarchical structures (master-servant, abbot-monk) and, slightly more loosely, with the set of offences of thought and deed against the king and selected members of the royal family lying at the core of the definition of treason is interesting. That concern with husband-killings should be emphasised in the mid-fourteenth century leads to the possibility that it was part of the concerned programme of reform in the wake of the Black Death and its frightening dislocation and disturbance of expectations.[158] It may also be considered to have formed part of the heightened attention of legislators to women, which was noted in Chapter 1, to have developed after the Black Death. In this statute, there was attention not only to women as offenders against their husbands, but also as potentially wronged parties, with the inclusion of offences against royal women being designated as treasons. The inclusion of husband-killings

153 Ruth Campbell, 'Sentence of Death by Burning for Women', *JLH* 5(1984), 44–59, 54; Bl. *Comm.* IV, 93.

154 See, e.g., A.E. Bernstein, *Hell and Its Rrivals: Death and Retribution amongst Christians, Jews and Muslims in the Early Middle Ages* (Ithaca, NY and London, 2017); *Mark* 9:47–8; *Matthew* 25:31–46; *Revelation* 14:11.

155 Rarity of death by fire as a method of suicide, probably for practical reasons: Alice and Gwen Seabourne, 'Suicide or Accident? Self Killing in Medieval England', *British Journal of Psychiatry* (2001), 43–7.

156 Cleveland, *Woman under the English Law*, p. 158.

157 *Bracton* II, p. 334. *Fleta* book 1 c. 16.

158 Bellamy, *Law of Treason*, p. 123. Crook, 'Seditious Murder of Thomas of Sibthorpe', argues that particular (male) cases influenced the Statute.

amongst treasons is probably best seen as, in part, a new formalisation of the conceptual positioning of what was already seen as a serious affront to accepted social order, and was already subject to a different penalty from that for 'ordinary' homicide. It was not, however, initially assimilated to treason in the language which was used in accusations. Thus, Matilda Kene, who was in 1292 accused of killing her husband, was said to have done so *nequiter et in felonia* rather than using a specialised term suggesting sedition or treason, such as *proditorie.*[159] Treason as a separate and coherent concept was itself 'under construction' in this period. The 1352 legislation was probably the first step in the assimilation of husband-killing with the solidifying concept of treason, with the 'petty treason' label, by which it was known to later generations of lawyers, coming into greater use for this conduct in the fifteenth century.[160]

Cases of wives killing husbands had appeared on rolls from the late twelfth century onwards, and there are indications of burnings for this offence from at least the early thirteenth century.[161] Differentiation between a wife's punishment for killing her husband (burning) and that of another woman convicted of the same offence (hanging) can be seen in a case from

159 JUST 3/87 m. 8 (IMG 105). She preferred to face the statutory penalty for refusal to plead rather than a trial.

160 For the later sense, see Bellamy, *Law of Treason*, p. 229; *RP* IV, 260b (1423) – 'Petty treason' term used 1423, SC 8/307/15328, 1497 statute *SR* II, p. 639.

161 Kerr, 'Husband and Wife', p. 240; *CRR V*, p. 64, 1207: accused wife passed ordeal of iron; 59 *SS* p. 338 pl. 743 (fled): Coss, *Lady*, 134: Nicholas Vincent, 'Simon of Atherfield d. 1211, a martyr to his wife', *Analecta Bollandiana* 113 (1995) p. 349–61. Burning, 1212, 62 *SS*, 322, *CRR VI*, 306. Other examples of burning of wives, e.g., JUST 1/538 m.13 (IMG 3188); JUST 3/35B m. 53d (IMG 0217); JUST 1/705 m. 6d (IMG 8411); JUST 1/573 m. 78 (IMG 563); JUST 3/92 m. (IMG 403), JUST 1/374 m. 42 (IMG 2331); JUST 3/74/2 m. 5 (IMG 0023); 1315 JUST 3/111 m. 9 (IMG 22); JUST 1/1108 m. 17 (IMG 8657); KB 27/243 Rex m. 7 and 7d (IMG 261 and 250); JUST 3/1/3 m. 7d (IMG 0153); JUST 3/18/5 m. 29 (IMG 329); JUST 3/28/1 m. 5 (IMG 0013); 1357 JUST 3/139 m. 4d (IMG 82) two cases; JUST 3/166 m. 7 (IMG 16); 1380 KB 27/476 Rex m. 19 (IMG 0521); JUST 3/173 m. 26 (IMG 61); KB 27/508 m. 4 and m.6d (IMG 116, 252);JUST 3/177 m. 49 (IMG 107); JUST 3/180 m. 30 (IMG 67); JUST 3/177 m. 27 (IMG 0058); JUST 3/180 m. 30 (IMG 67); JUST 3/168 m. 9 (IMG 10); KB 27/561 Rex m. 2d (IMG 402); JUST 3/195 m. 72d (IMG 0415); KB 27/638 m. 20d (IMG 0583); JUST 3/197 m. 8 (IMG 21); JUST 3/202 m. 4 (IMG 827). There were also, of course, instances in which a woman abjured, e.g., JUST 1/778 m. 55 (IMG 7912); fled, e.g., JUST 1/303 m. 53 (IMG 8749); JUST 1/383 m. 57d (IMG 1800)); escaped from gaol, e.g., 2 *SS*, 154; died in gaol, e.g., JUST 1/166 m. 19 (IMG 9590); refused to plead, e.g., JUST 3/87 m. 8 (IMG 105); was acquitted: JUST 1/883 m. 4d (IMG 516); KB 27/883 m. 69d (IMG 416); including when a supposedly slain husband turned up in court: 1306 (JUST 3/105 m. 9 (IMG 18)); had a sentence deferred for pregnancy, e.g., JUST 3/113 m. 6d (IMG 27); JUST 3/189 m. 5 (IMG 13)) or was pardoned (see, e.g., Mitchell, *Portraits*, c. 6). Murderous Maud? The case against Maud Mortimer of Richard's castle; *CPR 1301–7*, pp. 69, 378, pardon 'for a felony she is said to have committed'; JUST 1/1334 m. 43d (IMG 2753); SC8/278/13872, *KB 27/608 m.7 (IMG 89);* KB 9/366 m. 32 (IMG 0064); KB 29/114 m. 12d (IMG 0080); KB 29/115 m. 11 (IMG 32); KB 27/893 m. 8d R (IMG 602). See also, for procedure at the local level, *London Eyre 1276* no. 209.

the eyre of Kent of 1293–4.[162] Burnings of husband-slayers were not common; only very occasionally does a gaol delivery roll have more than one such burning.[163] This penalty was not always employed; for reasons which are not apparent, convicted husband-slayers were sometimes hanged rather than burnt.[164] Nevertheless, the idea that burning of husband-killers was very rare, or specifically associated with mid-fourteenth-century legislation and later fourteenth-century conditions, can be overdone.[165] Records, reports and recommendations of the burning of convicted husband-killers can be found throughout the late medieval period.[166] There seems no doubt that burning was the accepted punishment from the early fourteenth century onwards. Had it not been the case that burning was a realistic possibility, the accusation that Hugh Despenser the younger had, in 1322, threatened to have Alice de Lacy burned as the cause of her husband's death (*qele estoit cause de la morte son Baron*) and that she had complied with him because she feared for her life (*pur doutee de sa morte*) would not have made sense.[167] It did make sense because the threat of burning for the killing of a husband was real and could be made even against women from the highest social positions.[168] There are sufficient records to show that burning was not just a remote, theoretical possibility, but something to fear and expect. Common lawyers and those involved in the administration of justice accepted that this was the correct response to this offence, and acted upon this view in husband-slaying cases.

Two instances of burning have received particular attention from modern commentators. Juliana Murdak was burnt for being 'of counsel and precept' with those who killed her husband in 1316.[169] Nobody else was executed for this crime: one probable offender claimed benefit of clergy, another turned approver.[170] The 1387–8 case of Elizabeth Walton, according to the

162 JUST 1/374 m. 63 d (IMG 2563).
163 JUST 3/139 m. 4d (IMG 82).
164 JUST 3/199 m. 5 (1423) (IMG 568); JUST 1/383 m. 58 (IMG 1584).
165 Kerr, 'Husband and Wife', p. 240, and Strohm, *Hochon's Arrow*, p. 39, suggest few burnings before the mid-fourteenth century.
166 See above note 161.
167 Natalie Fryde, *The Tyranny and Fall of Edward II 1321–1326* (Cambridge, 1979), p. 113; Miscellaneous Books, duchy of Lancaster, D.L. 42/11, f. 66v.
168 Aside from Alice de Lacy, those accused included women labelled *domina*, wives of a *dominus* and a gentleman: JUST 1/306 m. 8 (IMG 9068); JUST 1/306 m. 8d (IMG 9088); *CPR 1301–7*, pp. 334, 378, 402, 410, 427, 440; JUST 1/1334 m. 43d (IMG 2753), KB 27/889 m. 22d (IMG 201), JUST 3/28/1 m. 5 (IMG 13).
169 97 *SS*, pp. 216–17.
170 97 *SS*, pp. 216–17; *Plea Rolls for Staffordshire*, ed. by G. Wrottesley, pp. 30–4; William Salt Society x, 38; xiv, 18; KB 27/241 m. 12d (IMG 237): KB 27/242 Rex mm. 4, 31, (IMG 322, 378) and 31d (IMG 368); KB 27/243 Rex m. 7 and 7d (IMG 261 and 250). See also *CCR 1323–7*, 413; *CCR 1318–23*, 299, 471; *CIPM* II, 657; V, 555. For property ramifications of the case and the interest of law reporters: *Seipp* 1330.430ss and 1330.704ss; 97 and 98 *SS* pp. 216–17, 588–9; *CPR 1340–43*, p. 98 and *CPR 1348–50*, p. 340. Coss suggests an

Westminster chronicle, saw a wife inciting a priest to kill her husband. The priest received 'condign punishment' and the woman was burnt.[171] These two cases are clearly interesting and important. They show the triple disadvantage for women of a system conceiving responsibility for homicide in relatively wide terms, and treating with particular opprobrium homicides going against hierarchical norms, but shutting women out from 'escape routes' available to men. Neither woman was alleged to have struck the fatal blow, and yet only they were executed, and they were executed by burning.

Although I would emphasise the long-term view of burning as a penalty for women who killed their husbands, it could also be argued that there may have been a particular royal and municipal interest in husband-killings in the later fourteenth century. This is suggested by criticisms of apparently unauthorised exercises of jurisdiction in this area in Yorkshire in 1378[172] and a case from Dartmouth in 1390. These showed both eagerness by local authorities to burn female petty traitors and an idea that this was something over which the 'centre' should have some control. The latter case, for example, emerges from the 1390 patent roll pardon for the mayor of Dartmouth, for having had Denys, wife of William Beaumont, burnt, after she had been convicted for killing William by poison, without obtaining royal permission for the burning.[173] The presence of a particular interest in burning husband-slayers at this time might conceivably be linked to roughly contemporary concern with women's troubling behaviour, disrupting patterns of family authority, which also saw changes in legislative provisions on the effect of women's sexual or marital misconduct on their rights to land.[174] Scrutiny of the boundaries of authority and the attention of chroniclers should not, however, be confused with changes to the normal operation and accepted understanding of the common law. Burning had been the orthodox penalty for husband-slayers for a considerable time, and continued to be so regarded thereafter: burning was, for example, confirmed as the

illicit relationship between Juliana and a constable: Peter Coss: 'An Age of Deference', in *A Social History of England 1200–1500*, ed. by Rosemary Horrox and W. Mark Ormrod (Cambridge, 2006), pp. 31–72, 48; *Lady*, pp. 131–8.

171 *Westminster Chronicle*, p. 322; KB 27/508 m. 4 and m. 6d (IMG 116, 252). See, e.g., Hanawalt, *Wealth of Wives* c. 6 note 78; Paul Strohm, 'Treason in the Household', in *Hochon's Arrow: the Social Imagination of Fourteenth Century Texts*, ed. by Strohm (Princeton, NJ, 1992), pp. 121–44.

172 This involved W's alleged participation in the killing of H, but the focus was on a clerical participant, and the (lack of) authority of those who had condemned the killers. KB 27/468 Rex m. 19 (IMG 131); 88 *SS*, pp. 5–7.

173 *CPR 1388–92*, p. 253. A royal order also was given in the Walton case, KB 27/508 m. 4d (IMG 252).

174 Phifer, 'Property, Power', p. 212; Hawkes, 'Preliminary Notes on Consent in the 1382 Rape and Ravishment Laws of Richard II', *Legal History* 11 (2007), 117–32.

penalty for wives who killed husbands in the late fifteenth century too, in the discussions of lawyers reported in a Year Book note of 1483.[175]

Some records give further insights into ideas around this, particularly sex- and gender-charged offence. Accusations include descriptive information which might have been taken as intensifying the offence – or explaining how a woman could have managed it – such as that the husband was in his bed or that the killing was done at night.[176] Allegations of husband-slaying include poisonings, use of weapons and killings in the context of a fight.[177] Some records note concealment of the corpse by throwing it in a well or river, putting it in an oven or in the case of one Kentish wife in 1334, convicted and burnt for killing her husband, chopping it up, feeding part to the dogs and burying the rest.[178] There is no sign of a disinclination amongst male community representatives to put women at risk of burning, as can be seen in the inclusion of a clarificatory statement at the end of an indictment of 1446, in which it is made clear that Joan, now wife of John Margetson, one of her co-accused, was married to William atte Talys when he was slain.[179] There was to be no question of this being dealt with as a 'mere' homicide, and no risk of a failure on the grounds of incorrect description of Joan's status.

Husband-slaying accusations include women acting alone and acting with others, and, in particular, 'consenting' or similar whilst others (generally males) perform the actual killing. There are records of accusations of wives working with a sister, brother, son, a servant, a lover (several of them clerics), a lover who is also a servant or another individual.[180] Some early cases suggest a ready suspicion of wives. A record of 1207, for example, shows a woman accused of procuring her husband's killing, apparently

175 *Seipp* 1483.037; for property ramifications of petty treason, see *Seipp* 1449.070abr. For the burning of a young employee for killing her mistress: *Seipp* 1338.182rs; 1338.278ass; Bellamy, *Law of Treason*, pp. 87, 227. A Nottinghamshire servant convicted of murdering her mistress was hanged, not burned (1413, JUST 3/56/8 m. 2 (IMG 6), m. 15 (IMG 27); JUST 3/195 m. 64d (IMG 397). W kills H: Seipp 1322.018; 1338.182rs. Reports relating to the Murdak case: 1330.430ss and 1330.704ss (property). Bellamy, *Law of Treason*, p. 227; A. Fitzherbert, *La Graunde Abridgement* (London, 1516), I, f. 259.

176 JUST 1/538 m. 13 (IMG 3188).

177 JUST 1/135 m. 14 (IMG 6975); JUST 1/306 m. 8 (IMG 9068); JUST 1/306 m. 8d (IMG 9088); KB 27/883 m.69d (IMG 416); *CPR 1388–92*, p. 253; JUST 3/167 m. 39 (IMG 86). 1422 decapitation with a sword: JUST 3/197a m. 9 (IMG 21) (axe); JUST 1/374 m. (IMG 2331); (knife) JUST 1/573 m. 61 (IMG 527); slit throat: JUST 1/739 m. 90 (IMG 1613); axe SS 88 p. 118: KB 27/561 m. 2d, 1401 (IMG 402); JUST 1/573 m. 61 (IMG 527).

178 JUST 3/92 m. 3 (IMG 403); KB 9/366 m. 32 (IMG 0064); KB 27/893 m. 8dR (IMG 602). W strangling H, then disposing of the body in an oven: Pike, *History of Crime* I, p. 256, JUST 2/26 m. 1 (IMG 3). JUST 3/28/1 m. 5 (IMG 13).

179 KB 9/253 m. 14 (IMG 28) 1446. See, however, KB 27/285 m. 14 (IMG 461).

180 JUST 1/135 m. 14 (IMG 6975); JUST 3/92 m. 3 (IMG 403); JUST 1/486 m. 11d (IMG 2842), JUST 1/538 m. 15d (IMG 3248); KB 27/883 m. 69d (IMG 416); *Seipp* 1483.037. *Others* JUST 1/303 m. 53 (IMG 8749); 88 *SS*, p. 14; KB 27/889 m. 22d (IMG 201); KB 27/690 Rex m. 3 (IMG 218); Maddern, *Violence*, pp. 46, 104, KB 27/690 Rex m. 3; SC8 215/ 10727; JUST 3/202 m. 4; KB 9/366 m. 32 (IMG 0064), KB 27/893 m. 8d (IMG 602).

on the basis of local awareness of quarrelling between the spouses over her alleged multiple adulteries, and removal of chattels from the matrimonial home, but notes her vindication by ordeal of hot iron.[181] Another wife was accused in a jury's perhaps far-fetched narrative of secret signs and signals to let her alleged lover in to her house to kill her husband; she was, however, not tried.[182] One wonders how it could plausibly be thought to be known by those drawing up an indictment in Wiltshire in 1305 that 'Joan' who was the wife of Richard de Langeleton had procured unknown men to slay Richard her husband at Coveleston.[183] In the later fifteenth century, Fortescue noted a case which seems to support the idea that women might be presumed with relative alacrity to be involved in 'domestic' murders of their husbands.[184] As an illustration of the disadvantages which could come with speedy legal processes, 'the Chancellor' tells 'the Prince' of a case he had seen at a Salisbury gaol-delivery session. A woman had been indicted for the death of her husband. She was convicted and burned 'within the year', but at a later session, the slain man's servant confessed that he had committed the murder alone and that the burnt woman had in fact been completely innocent.[185] Accusations might also be made some time after the alleged killing, leaving women at risk of disastrous consequences long after the loss of a husband, as can be seen in a case from the London eyre roll of 1276, recording an appeal in 1269–70 against a woman accused of killing her husband by the administration of a 'poison drink' in 1263–4.[186]

The accusation or punishment of a woman as 'accessory' (with a hint that she is in fact the evil mastermind and driving force) is not unusual.[187] We cannot, of course, know the truth of the episodes behind the accusations. It may be true that women would be likely to seek assistance of those with greater strength or opportunity to kill their husbands, but the common portrayal of the woman scheming behind the scenes may reflect gender-based assumptions of the male triers and indicters that they were involved, but not able to take a principal active role.[188] It is interesting to note that accounts might vary in terms of where blame and impetus were placed: thus, the

181 1 *SS* p. 55. See also, e.g., Orr, 'English Women', p. 234, *PCCG* nos 254, 379 (in the latter, a woman seems to have been suspected because she was not in bed with her husband when he was attacked. Her story was that she had been in another room in bed with a sick child).

182 *PCCG* 1221, no 254.

183 *Wilts GD and T*, p. 108 no 586 (acquitted).

184 John Fortescue, Francis Gregor, et al., *De Laudibus Legum Angliae; A Treatise in Commendation of the Laws of England* (Cincinnati, OH, 1874) C 53 212.

185 This case, if it is a real one, has not been identified.

186 *London Eyre 1276*, no. 209.

187 See, e.g., 1 *SS* p. 55, no. 101 (1207). Marion, wife of Hugh Dobin, was suspected of procuring Hugh's death. Some reason for this suspicion is given, in her alleged adultery and removal of chattels from the marital home. She passed the ordeal of iron.

188 Hanawalt, 'Female Felon', p. 124, Crime, 117'. Strohm, *Hochon's Arrow*, 135.

same killing might be assigned to a wife and servant in one account, without differentiation and, in another account, to the servant as principal with the wife consenting.[189] The murder of husbands by wives said to have been involved with another man has had a fascination for contemporary authors and modern scholars. Finding an illicit sexual aspect to a killing might be a useful strategy for contemporaries wishing to stress a causal link between immorality and insubordination on the one hand, and more violent disorder on the other.[190] In later commentary, speculation as to the presence of an illicit affair as the background to homicide, or its concealment, has proved difficult for some to resist, even when contemporaries left no record of such a suggestion, something which might be thought to tell its own story of ideas about women. In the case of a woman acquitted of a death in 1375, speculation involves a number of questionable steps. The case concerned the death of William Cantilupe, and the accusation and acquittal of his wife, Maud, and others. One account gives as the only 'plausible explanation' worthy of mention the theory that Maud was the driving force behind the killing, a view arrived at by a questionable path starting from the fact that Maud later married the local sheriff, instrumental in her acquittal, moving to the idea that he must have wanted to marry her at the time of the killing, then to the idea that they were lovers at that time, to her guilt, to her having been the driving force behind the murder.[191] Even more recent authors may fall into this sort of mood, for example, on the basis of the terse and tendentious records of the common law, opining that Juliana Murdak is likely to have been a 'sexually bewitching woman'.[192]

The apparent threat of Hugh Despenser the younger to have Alice de Lacy burned (as a husband-murderer) as 'the chief cause of her husband's execution'[193] (her husband having been despatched for rising against the king) suggests an expansive idea of what might conceivably count as 'killing' of a husband. It is not clear that there was a suggestion that Alice had in any sense caused her husband's actions, and this is best seen as a false

189 JUST 3/8/6 m. 11 (IMG 92); JUST 3/8/6 m. 35 (IMG 128).

190 Strohm, *Hochon's Arrow*, 135–7, notes the Westminster chronicle alteration of the story to focus on an illicit sexual relationship. See also M. Hamel, 'The Wife of Bath and a Contemporary Murder', *Chaucer Review*, 14 (1979), 132–9.

191 *Records of Some Sessions of the Peace in Lincolnshire: 1360–1375*, ed. by Rosamund Sillem, Publications of the Lincoln Record Society, XXX (1936), pp. lxv–lxxv. On this case, see also F. Pedersen, 'Motives for Murder: The Role of Sir Ralph Paynel in the Murder of William Cantilupe (1375)', in *Continuity, Change and Pragmatism in the Law: Essays in Memory of Professor Angelo Forte*, ed. by A. Simpson, L.M. Wilson, S. Styles, and E. West (Aberdeen, 2016a), pp. 68–93 and 'Murder, Mayhem and a Very Small Penis', *American Historical Association*, AHA (2016), 1–32.

192 Coss, *Lady*, p. 138.

193 See further above, note 167. See also the alleged false accusation of husband-killing against a woman and a male servant (husband being alive): C1/45/128 dated 1433–43 or 1467–72.

accusation, though it is one with instructive aspects in relation to understanding of the scope of the offence. Other cases show that presence at the scene of one's husband's death might be enough to raise the possibility of being held in some way culpable.[194] The limits of the conspiracy/accessory concept, or perhaps of the idea of causation of death, appear to have been reached with an allegation in the 1340s that two men and a woman had conspired to cause the death of the woman's husband, to acquire his goods, by causing him to be imprisoned and hanged; nothing was to be done in this case, according to the endorsement of the petition of the mayor and aldermen of London.[195] On the authority of a story told by a medieval justice, Spigurnel, in a Year Book report of the reign of Edward II, Hale tells us that a wife's attempt to kill her husband also attracted the penalty of burning, though the case to which Spigurnel referred in 1322 is yet to be identified, and the story he told does not necessarily suggest a 'pure' attempt, i.e. one in which the husband certainly recovered afterwards. All that is clear from the story is that the husband was said to have survived long enough to drag himself before justices of gaol delivery who were already sitting, and denounce the wife and her lover as responsible for the attack on him. What was understood to have become of him afterwards is not clear, and Fitzherbert and Staunford's earlier retellings do not make it clear that this was a pure, and completely unsuccessful, attempt rather than one which caused a lingering, and not an immediate, death.[196] There is room for further research on medieval ideas about attempts in general, and this issue may not have been treated in the same way for all offences.[197] It is not implausible that the expansive definition of treason, encompassing planning or desiring an outcome, as opposed to acting to ensure its achievement, might lead to the treatment of an attempted killing by wife of husband as 'petty treason', but this is not yet clear.[198]

Conclusion

The medieval common law did not have an explicit doctrine of the nature and limits of responsibility, much less an explicit theory of when and how

194 A man's wife and son, present at his killing, arrested, but acquitted: JUST 1/1108 m. 19d (IMG 8715).

195 SC8 59/2929.

196 Hale, *HPC* 1, 378; *Seipp* 1322.018; Fitzherbert, *Graunde Abridgement* (London, 1577), Corone 383; Staunford, *Les Plees del Coron (1557)* I, p. 10; F.B. Sayre, 'Criminal Attempts', *Harvard Law Review* 41 (1928), 821–59, 824–5; Bellamy, *Law of Treason*, App. II, p. 227. On attempts and intention, see *Fleta* book 1 c. 23, *Bracton* II, p. 342; KB 9/245 m. 68 (IMG 127).

197 Baker, *Introduction*, p. 524; A. Kiralfy, 'Taking the Will for the Deed: the Mediaeval Criminal Attempt', *JLH* 13 (1992), 95–100, 97.

198 *Bracton* II, p. 334; *Fleta* book I, c. 21; Bellamy, *Law of Treason*, especially c. 5; *Seipp* 1440.121.

this might differ for men and women or sub-groups of women. Nevertheless, there are themes which can be discerned and uncertainties or changes which should be noted.

There are some striking asymmetries between the common law's treatment of men and women with regard to doctrines and ideas of culpability, as, for example, in relation to benefit of clergy and 'petty treason'. There are also some subtler ones, such as the apparently gendered nature of self-defence and accident, in which the common law worked through male paradigms which did not necessarily accommodate women as constructed by medieval social and legal thought. Another example is found in the formulae for pardons for almost all purposes rather than one specified offence, which emerged in the later fourteenth century, made explicit exclusions for homicide and 'the rape of women', this formula being used for pardons even when the recipient was herself a woman. Arguably this was not entirely irrelevant, given the alternative definitions of raptus and the existence of accessory liability, but it is best seen as indicative of the lack of specific accommodation for women in the legal system.[199] Marital status made a considerable difference to women accused of 'civil' wrongs such as trespass or non-payment of a debt. Its impact upon 'criminal' responsibility is clear with regard to inculpation – as the cases on husband-slaying demonstrate – but less certain with regard to exculpation.

This chapter has stressed the need to re-examine the comforting ideas of favour and balance seen in some previous work on women's responsibility, in terms of the extent to which the common law developed ways to limit their liability. While their civil liability might be obscured by the mediating presence of a husband, and the logic of his role in relation to property and whatever may have been the case in previous ages, both single and married women in the later medieval period were assumed to be responsible for their own 'criminal' actions, liable to criminal penalty in principle and in practice. The law was not restrained by stereotypes of female passivity or weakness from blaming women for forceful actions, and nor should we be too keen to find favour to women in the system, exaggerating the extent to which they might escape criminal liability or punishment, in order to regard this as balancing their position. When a man might take advantage of a fictionalised process of claiming clergy while a woman, charged with the same offence, might be burned, it is hard to think of women as having been the objects of favour. Nor are we likely to comfort ourselves with the thought that, while medieval women may have been harshly treated, they were rather brutish, and so may not be regarded as appealing objects of pity:

> [T]he women of these times were in many cases wanting in pity, decency, and all the better attributes of the sex … devoid of patience, gentleness,

199 See, e.g., KB 27/47 m. 20 (IMG 173); KB 27/893 m. 6 (IMG 269). Lacey, *Royal Pardon*, p. 89.

and sympathy. ... Crimes of violence, such as the strangling with her own hands of a lover or husband, were by no means unknown; and if the criminal law punished women with severity, many of those who suffered had by their behaviour almost forfeited the right to be regarded as belonging to what is termed the gentler sex.[200]

200 Cleveland, *Woman under the English Law*, p. 158 And see Pike, above p. 123.

Conclusion

The future of women's legal past

An eighteenth-century treatise on law relating to women spotted what appeared to be an oddity in this area, noting that 'Our old laws and customs relating to women are many of them very merry, though the makers of them might possibly be grave men'.[1] Those focusing on classical or doctrinal legal history have often dealt with the treatment of women in the history of the common law, if not with merriment, at least with a lack of willingness to take it seriously as a worthy subject for examination. It would be a slight exaggeration to say that it has been a case of 'Maitland says nothing, and so, as usual, no one else does either!',[2] since there have been important studies of aspects of this history in recent years, particularly by those based in history departments rather than law schools. Nevertheless, there remains a need to bring consideration of women in from the margins of all types of legal historical study, doctrinal and social, 'internal' and 'external'. Not to do so would be out of line with the blossoming of modern study on women and gender, in both history and law. It can no longer be acceptable to present as a study of the history of the common law which excludes the application to half of the population of that law, or which treats half of the population as an uninteresting appendix, of relevance only in relation to real property. Such an approach risks leaving understanding of medieval law in general and that relating to women in particular cut off and mired in the analysis of legal historians of earlier eras. This book has tried to make a start with the considerable task of bringing the common law part of the 'old laws and customs relating to women' into the mainstream of legal history, noting some of the pitfalls to be avoided in doing so, and suggesting some possible constructions of the material which is available.

One of the points which has emerged is that in undertaking studies of women and the common law, legal historians should be prepared to embrace complexity and nuance rather than seeing attention given to women (or other groups other than the standard free, non-'foreign' male) as a distraction

1 Anon., *A Treatise of Femes Coverts or the Lady's Law* (London, 1732), p. vii.
2 Hyams, 'Maitland and the Rest of Us', p. 229.

likely to produce regrettable derogation from neat narratives, such as those of the 'rises' of centralisation and professionalisation of the common law, and the development, proliferation and manipulation of forms of action. Chronology of the common law's involvement in the lives of, and interest in, women is not necessarily the same as its attention to and accommodation of men and their interests.[3] In addition, given the dissonances and inconsistencies seen in much learned medieval discourse relating to women, it would be odd to expect a developing body of law to stand entirely apart and to give clear, comprehensive answers on the legal position of women. It is clear that the medieval common law approach to women displayed considerable intellectual tension. A series of contradictions seem to lie at the heart of the common law in this area, with women placed between poles of unity and division; responsibility and irresponsibility; capacity and incapacity; visibility and invisibility; audibility and inaudibility. While it was a commonplace of medieval misogyny that women were unable to maintain consistent views and behaviour, in studying this material, it is tempting to feel that the charge of inconsistency would be better levelled at those involved in trying to accommodate women in the man-shaped structures of the common law. Rather than following this feeling, and falling into the trap of condescension towards the lawyers and people of long-distant ages, however, it would be more constructive to see an overall picture of fluidity in much treatment of women and in women's relationship with the common law.

Our investigations should avoid an over-emphasis of an analysis based on hard and fast rules and exceptions. It is vital, as much in this book testifies, to understand that the medieval common law was not always a clear and straightforward body of strict rules against which 'practice' can be measured and exceptions identified. The relationship between law and practice in this period in particular was more complex and more intimate than that. While some rules relating to women in the medieval common law were quite settled by the later twelfth century, elsewhere, 'the law' might be indistinct, contested or in flux, and might not have reached a clearly defined shape before the end of the medieval period. Furthermore, on occasions when it is reasonable to discuss rules and exceptions, it is important not to look only at 'upward' exceptions – i.e. those instances of women somehow rising above apparently prescribed limitations – but also at those who did not manage this,[4] and perhaps found themselves unable even to take advantage of those mechanisms and procedures which were prescribed as part of the common law. Both an ability to act and limitations on that ability were present in the lives of medieval women, and are to be found embedded in the medieval common law.

3 The idea of differential chronology has long been mooted in 'mainstream' history: Joan Kelly, 'Did Women Have a Renaissance?', in *Women, History and Theory: The Essays of Joan Kelly* (Chicago, IL, 1984), c. 2.

4 Bardsley, *Women's Roles*, pp. 2, 129, 140; Mitchell, *Portraits*, p. 127.

Just as medieval litigants frequently settled cases informally rather than pursuing them to reach a definitive conclusion, and just as medieval courts did not always come to a decision, we, looking backwards over the centuries, should not expect to be able to see all of the surviving sources and come up with one neat and definitive account of women and the medieval common law. There is scope for further refinement and revision, however, with ever closer investigation into the mass of records of the common law – the scope of which being far more than can be encompassed by one monograph or one academic lifetime – and I hope that some of the points made here will encourage or even annoy other legal scholars sufficiently to prompt them to turn to the common law records in search of women, their experiences and the intellectual environment which they encountered when faced with legal difficulties in this formative period for the common law. C.S. Kenny expressed a hope that 'some hand, more skilful and less busy than [his] own, [would] complete the story [of married women and the law] which [he] left half-told';[5] but it is probably more sensible to adopt the view of a pioneering woman legal historian that completion is neither possible nor particularly desirable, and to embrace the idea that 'The story does not end there. No story can end, in history.'[6]

5 Kenny, *History*, p. viii.
6 Cam, *Law Finders*, p. 21.

Select bibliography

Manuscripts: The National Archives (Kew)

C1 Chancery: Early Pleadings and Proceedings
CP 40 Plea rolls of the Common Bench/Court of Common Pleas
JUST 1 Justices in Eyre, of Assize, of Oyer and Terminer, and of the Peace, etc: Rolls and Files
JUST 2 Coroners' Rolls and Files
JUST 3 Gaol Delivery Rolls and Files
KB 9 Indictment files, Court of King's Bench
KB 26 and 27 Plea Rolls, King's Bench
SC8 Ancient Petitions

Printed primary sources

Bracton on the Laws and Customs of England, ed. by George Woodbine and Samuel Thorne (4 vols, Cambridge, MA: Harvard University Press, 1968–77).
Bracton's Note Book: A Collection of Cases Decided in the King's Courts during the Reign of Henry III, ed. by Frederic W. Maitland (3 vols, London: C.J. Clay, 1887).
Britton, ed. by F. Nichols (2 vols, Oxford: Clarendon Press, 1865).
Calendar of Close Rolls (London: HMSO, 1892–1963).
Calendar of Patent Rolls (London: HMSO, 1891–).
C.E.H. Chadwyck-Healey (ed.), Somersetshire Pleas, *Civil and Criminal from the Rolls of the Itinerant Justices, c. 1200–56* (London: Harrison and Sons, 1897).
Chew, Helena and Martin Weinbaum (eds.), *The London Eyre of 1244* (London: London Record Society, 1970).
Coke, Edward, *Institutes of the Laws of England* (4 vols, London, 1628–44).
Corpus luris Canonici, ed. by A. Friedberg (Leipzig: Tauchnitz, 1879).
The Course of the Exchequer and Constitutio Domus Regis, ed. by Charles Johnson, F.E.L. Carter, D.E. Greenway (Oxford: Clarendon Press, 1983).
Curia Regis Rolls Preserved in the Public Record Office (London: HMSO, 1922–).
Fitzherbert, Anthony, *Graunde Abridgement* (London: Tottell, 1577).
Fleta vols 2–4, ed. by H.G. Richardson and G.O. Sayles (3 vols, London: Selden Society, 1955–84).
Fortescue, John, *De Natura Legis Naturae*, tr. by Chichester Foitescue in *Works*, ed. by T. Fortescue (London: Privately Printed 1869).
Fortescue, John, *De Laudibus Legum Angliae*, ed. by F. Gregor and A. Amos (Cincinnati, OH: Robert Clarke and Co, 1874).

Glanvill, The Treatise on the Laws and Customs of the Realm of England Commonly Called, ed. by G.D.G. Hall (London: Nelson, 1965).
Hale, Matthew, *Historia Placitorum Coronae* (London: Nutt and Gosling, 1736).
Hershey, Andrew, 'An Introduction to and Edition of the Hugh Bigod Eyre Rolls, June 1258–February 1259: P.R.O. JUST 1/1187 & JUST 1/873', Ph.D. thesis, King's College London, 1991.
Jenkins, Dafydd, *Hywel Dda, The Law* (Llandysul: Gomer Press, 2000).
Knighton's Chronicle 1337–1396, ed. and tr. by G.H. Martin (Oxford: Clarendon Press, 1995).
Leges Henrici Primi, ed. by Leslie J. Downer (Oxford: Clarendon Press, 1972).
Littleton, Thomas, *Tenures*, ed. by Eugene Wambaugh (Washington, DC: John Byrne and Co., 1903).
The Mirror of Justices, ed. by W. Whittaker, *Selden Society* vol. 7 (Oxford: Professional Books, 1893).
The Old Tenures c. 1515 and The Old Natura Brevium c, 1518, ed. by Morris S. Arnold (Chicago, IL: Professional Books, 1980).
Page, W. (ed.), *Three Early Assize Rolls for the county of Northumberland, saec XIII* (Durham: St Andrews & Co, 1891).
Palmer, Robert and Elspeth Palmer, *The Anglo–American Legal Tradition*, http://aalt.law.uh.edu.
Paris, Matthew, *Chronica Majora*, ed. by H. Luard (7 vols, London: Longman, 1872–83).
The Parliament Rolls of Medieval England, ed. by Chris Given-Wilson, Paul Brand, Seymour Phillips, Mark Ormrod, Geoffrey Martin, Anne Curry and Rosemary Horrox (16 vols, Woodbridge: Boydell Press, 2005).
Placita Corone or La Corone Pledee Devant Justices, ed. by John Kay (London: Selden Society, 1986).
Placitorum Abbreviatio (London: Record Commissioners, 1811).
Pugh, Ralph B. (ed.), *Wiltshire Gaol Delivery and Trailbaston Trials 1275–1306* (Devizes: Wiltshire Record Society, 1978).
Putnam, Bertha Haven (ed.), *Proceedings before Justices of the Peace in the Fourteenth and Fifteenth Centuries, Edward III to Richard III* (London: Spottiswoode, Ballantyne, 1938).
Rotuli Litterarum Clausarum, ed. by T. Duffus Hardy (London: Record Commissioners, 1833–44).
Rotuli Litterarum Patentium, ed. by T. Duffus Hardy (London: Record Commissioners, 1835).
Seipp, David (ed.), *An Index and Paraphrase of Printed Year Book Reports 1268–1535* http://www.bu.edu/law/*Seipp*/.
Sillem, Rosamund (ed.), *Records of Some Sessions of the Peace in Lincolnshire: 1360–1375*, Publications of the Lincoln Record Society, XXX (Lincoln: Lincoln Record Society Hereford, 1936).
Statutes of the Realm, ed. by A. Luders, T.E. Tomlins, J. France, W.E. Taunton and J. Raithby (London: Record Commission, 1810–27).
Staunford, Sir William, *Les Plees del Coron, 1571*, ed. by Peter Glazebrook (London: Professional Press, 1971).
Stenton, Doris (ed.), *The Earliest Lincolnshire Assize Rolls AD 1202–1209* (Lincoln: Lincoln Record Society, 1924).

Summerson, Henry, *Crown Pleas of the Devon Eyre 1238* (Exeter: Devon and Cornwall Record Society, 1985).

The Westminster Chronicle 1381–1394, ed. by L.C. Hector and Barbara Harvey (Oxford: Oxford University Press, 1982).

Woodbine, George E., *Four Thirteenth Century Law Tracts* (New Haven, CT: Yale University Press, 1910).

Selden society volumes

Vol. 1, for 1887, *Select Pleas of the Crown vol. 1 1200–1225*, ed. by F.W. Maitland.

Vol. 8, for 1894, *Select Passages from Bracton and Azo*, ed. by F.W. Maitland.

Vol. 9, for 1895, *Select Cases from the Coroners' Rolls, 1265–1413*, ed. by Charles Gross.

Vol. 10, for 1896, *Select Cases in Chancery, 1364–1471*, ed. by W. Paley Baildon.

Vol. 15, for 1901, *Select Pleas, Starrs etc. of the Jewish Exchequer 1220–1284*, ed. by J.M. Rigg.

Vol. 17, for 1903, *Year Books of 1 and 2 Edward II (1307–1308 and 1308–1309)*, ed. by F.W. Maitland.

Vol. 18, for 1904, *Borough Customs Vol. I*, ed. by Mary Bateson.

Vol. 19, for 1904, *Year Books of 2 and 3 Edward II (1308–1309 and 1309–1310)*, ed. by F.W. Maitland.

Vol. 20, for 1905, *Year Books of 3 Edward II (1309–1310)*, ed. by F.W. Maitland.

Vol. 21, for 1906, *Borough Customs vol. II*, ed. by Mary Bateson.

Vol. 22, for 1907, *Year Books of 3 and 4 Edward II (1310)*, ed. by F.W. Maitland and G.J. Turner.

Vol. 24, for 1909, *The Eyre of Kent of 6 and 7 Edward II (1313–1314), Vol. I*, ed. by F.W. Maitland, L.W. Vernon Harcourt and W.C. Bolland.

Vol. 30, for 1914, *Select Bills in Eyre 1292–1333*, ed. by W.C. Bolland.

Vol. 31, for 1915, *Year Books of 5 Edward II (1311–1312)*, ed. by W.C. Bolland.

Vol. 33, for 1916, *Year Books of 5 Edward II (1312)*, ed. by W.C. Bolland.

Vol. 34, for 1917, *Year Books of 6 Edward II (1312–1313)*, ed. by Paul Vinogradoff and Ludwik Ehrlich.

Vol. 37, for 1920. *Year Books of 8 Edward II (AD 1314)*, ed. by W.C. Bolland.

Vol. 50, for 1933, *Year Books of 1 Henry VI (A.D. 1422)*, ed. by C.H. Williams.

Vol. 51, additional for 1933, *Select Cases in the Exchequer Chamber*, ed. by M. Hemmant.

Vol. 58, for 1939, *Select Cases in the Court of King's Bench under Edward I* vol. III, ed. by G.O. Sayles.

Vol. 59, for 1940, *Rolls of the Justices in Eyre for Gloucestershire, Warwickshire and Shropshire 1221, 1222*, ed. by Doris M. Stenton.

Vol. 60, for 1941, *Select Cases of Procedure without Writ under Henry III*, ed. by H.G. Richardson and G.O. Sayles.

Vol. 62, for 1943, C.T. Flower, *Introduction to the Curia Regis Rolls 1199–1230.*

Vol. 80, for 1963, *Novae Narrationes*, ed. by Elsie Shanks and S.F.C. Milsom.

Vol. 84, for 1967, *Pleas before the King or his Justices* 1198–1212. Vol. IV, ed. by Doris Mary Stenton.

Vol. 85, for 1968, *The Eyre of London 14 Edward II (1321)*, vol. I, ed. by Helen M. Cam.

Vol. 87, for 1970, *Early Registers of Writs*, ed. by Elsa de Haas and G.D.G. Hall.

Vol. 96, for 1980, *The Shropshire Eyre Roll of 1256*, ed. by Alan Harding.
Vol. 97, for 1981, *The Eyre of Northamptonshire 1329–30 Vol. 1.*, ed. by Donald W. Sutherland.
Vol. 98, for 1982, *The Eyre of Northamptonshire 1329–30 Vol. 2.*, ed. by Donald W. Sutherland.
Vol. 100, for 1984, *Select Cases of Trespass in the King's Courts, 1307–1399, Vol. I*, ed. by Morris S. Arnold.
Vol. 102, for 1986, *The Notebook of Sir John Port*, ed. by J.H. Baker.
Vol. 103, for 1987, *Select Cases of Trespass in the King's Courts, 1307–1399, Vol. II*, ed. by Morris S. Arnold.
Vol. 105, for 1989, *Readings and Moots at the Inns of Court in the Fifteenth Century*, Vol. II, ed. by Samuel E. Thorne and J.H. Baker.
Vol. 106, for 1990, *English Lawsuits from William I to Richard I, vol. I. William I to Stephen*, ed. by R.C. Van Caenegem.
Vol. 109, for 1993. *Reports from the Lost Notebooks of Sir James Dyer Vol. I*, ed. by J.H. Baker.
Vol. 111, for 1995. *Earliest English Law Reports*, vol. I, ed. by Paul Brand.
Vol. 112, for 1996, *Earliest English Law Reports*, vol. II, ed. by Paul Brand.
Vol. 114 for 1997 Select Cases in Manorial Courts 1250–1550: Property and Family Law, ed. by L.R. Poos and Lloyd Bonfield.
Vol. 115, for 1998, *Reports of Cases by John Caryll vol I. 1485–1499*, ed. by J.H. Baker.
Vol. 116, for 1999, *Reports of Cases by John Caryll Vol. II. 1500–1522*, ed. by J.H. Baker.
Vol. 121, for 2004, *Reports of Cases in the Time of Henry VIII, Vol. II*, ed. by J.H. Baker.
Vol. 122, for 2005, *Earliest English Law Reports*, vol. III, ed. by Paul Brand.
Vol. 129 for 2012, *The Rights and Liberties of the English Church: Readings from the Pre-Reformation Inns of Court*, ed. by Margaret McGlynn.
Vol. 132 for 2015 *Selected Readings and Commentaries on Magna Carta 1400–1604*, ed. by J.H. Baker (London, 2015).

Secondary sources

Archer, Rowena E., 'Rich Old Ladies: The Problem of Late Medieval Dowagers', in *Property and Politics: Essays in Later Medieval English History*, ed. by T. Pollard (Gloucester: A. Sutton, 1984), 15–31.
Arnold, Morris S., et al. (eds.), *On the Laws and Customs of England: Essays in Honour of Samuel E. Thorne* (Chapel Hill: University of North Carolina Press, 1981).
Auchmuty, Rosemary, 'Legal History', in *Great Debates in Gender and Law*, ed. by Rosemary Auchmuty (London: Red Globe Press, 2018), 173–84.
Baker, J.H., *The Law's Two Bodies* (Oxford: Oxford University Press, 2001).
Baker, J.H., *The Oxford History of the Laws of England vol. VI 1483–1558* (Oxford: Oxford University Press, 2003).
Baker, J.H., *The Men of Court 1440–1550* (London: Selden Society, 2012).
Baker, J.H., *The Reinvention of Magna Carta* (Cambridge: Cambridge University Press, 2017).
Baker, J.H., *Introduction to English Legal History*, 5th edn (Oxford: Oxford University Press, 2019).

Bardsley, Sandy, *Women's Roles in the Middle Ages* (Westport, CT and London: Greenwood Press, 2007).

Beattie, Cordelia, 'Your Oratrice: Women's Petitions to the Late Medieval Court of Chancery', in *Women, Agency and the Law, 1300–1700*, ed. by Bronach Kane and Fiona Williamson (London: Pickering & Chatto Publishers, 2013), 17–30.

Beattie, Cordelia, 'Married Women's Wills: Probate, Property, and Piety in Later Medieval England', *LHR* 37 (2019), 29–60.

Bellamy. John G., *The Law of Treason in England in the Later Middle Ages* (New York: Cambridge University Press, 1970).

Bellamy, John G., *The Criminal Trial in Later Medieval England: Felony before the Courts from Edward I to the Sixteenth Century* (Toronto: University of Toronto Press, 1998).

Bennett, Judith M., 'Medieval Women, Modern Women: Across the Great Divide', in *Culture and History, 1350–1600*, ed. by David Aers (New York: Harvester Wheatsheaf, 1992), 147–75.

Blamires, Alcuin, Karen Pratt and C.W. Marx (ed. and tr.), *Women Defamed and Women Defended: An Anthology of Medieval Texts* (Oxford: Clarendon Press, 1992).

Brand, Paul, *The Making of the Common Law* (London: Hambledon Press, 1992).

Brand, Paul, *The Origins of the English Legal Profession* (Oxford: Wiley-Blackwell, 1992).

Brand, Paul, 'Deserving and Undeserving Wives: Earning and Forfeiting Dower in Medieval England', *JLH* 22 (2001), 1–20.

Brand, Paul, *Kings, Barons and Justices: the Making and Enforcement of Legislation in Thirteenth Century England* (Cambridge, Cambridge University Press, 2003).

Brand, Paul, 'Judges and Juries in Civil Litigation in Later Medieval England: The Millon Thesis Reconsidered', *JLH* 37 (2016), 1–40.

Brand, Paul, and Joshua Getzler (eds.), *Judges and Judging in the History of the Common Law and Civil Law from Antiquity to Modern Times* (Cambridge: Cambridge University Press, 2012), 44–55.

Brundage, James, 'Juridical Space: Female Witnesses in Canon Law', *Dumbarton Oaks Papers* 52 (1998), 147–56.

Butler, Sara M., 'A Case of Indifference? Child Murder in Later Medieval England', *Journal of Women's History* 19 (2004), 59–82.

Butler, Sara M., 'Abortion by Assault: Violence against Pregnant Women in Thirteenth-and Fourteenth-Century England', *Journal of Women's History* 17 (2005), 9–31.

Butler, Sara M., *The Language of Abuse: Marital Violence in Later Medieval England* (Leiden and Boston, MA: Brill, 2007).

Butler, Sara M., 'Discourse on the Nature of Coverture in the Later Medieval Courtroom', in *Married Women and the Law: Coverture in England and the Common Law World*, ed. by Tim Stretton and K.J. Kesselring (Montreal: McGill-Queen's University Press, 2013), 24–44, c. 2.

Butler, Sara M., 'Pleading the Belly: a Sparing Plea? Pregnant Convicts and the Courts in Medieval England', in *Crossing Borders: Boundaries and the Margins in Medieval and Early Modern Britain: Essays in Honour of Cynthia J. Neville*, ed. by Sara M. Butler and Krista J. Kesselring (Leiden: Brill, 2018), 131–52.

Butler, Sara M., 'More than Mothers: Juries of Matrons and Pleas of the Belly in Medieval England', *LHR* 37 (2019), 1–44.

Butler, Sara M., 'Violence and Murder in Medieval Europe', in *Cambridge World History of Violence, Volume 2: AD 500–AD 1500*, ed. by Matthew Gordon, Richard Kaeuper, Harriet Zurndorfer (Cambridge: Cambridge University Press, 2020), c. 16.

Butler, Sara M. and Krista J. Kesselring (eds.), *Crossing Borders: Boundaries and Margins in Medieval and Early Modern Britain: Essays in Honour of Cynthia J. Neville* (Leiden and Boston, MA: Brill, 2018).

Cadden, Joan, *Meanings of Sex Difference in the Middle Ages* (Cambridge: Cambridge University Press, 1993).

Cam, Helen M., *Law Finders and Law Makers in Medieval England* (London: Merlin Press, 1962).

Campbell, Ruth, 'Sentence of Death by Burning for Women', *JLH* 5 (1984), 44–59.

Cannon, Christopher, 'The Rights of Medieval English Women: Crime and the Issue of Representation', in *Medieval Crime and Social Control*, ed. by Barbara A. Hanawalt and David Wallace (Minneapolis: University of Minnesota Press, 1999), 156–85.

Carter, J. 'Rape and Medieval English Society: the Evidence of Yorkshire, Wiltshire and London, 1218–76', *Comitatus* 13 (1982), 33–63.

Cleveland, Arthur Rackham, *Woman under the English Law: From the Landing of the Saxons to the Present Time* (London: Hurst and Blackett Ltd, 1896).

Cohn, Samuel K., *Popular Protest in Late Medieval English Towns* (Cambridge: Cambridge University Press, 2013).

Conaghan, Joanne, *Law and Gender* (Oxford: Oxford University Press, 2013).

Coss, Peter, *The Lady in Medieval England 1000–1500* (Stroud: Sutton, 1998).

DeVun Leah, 'Erecting Sex: Hermaphrodites and the Medieval Science of Surgery', *Osiris*, 30, *Scientific Masculinities* (2015), 17–37.

Dodd, Gwilym, *Justice and Grace: Private Petitioning and the English Parliament in the Late Middle Ages* (Oxford: Oxford University Press, 2007).

Dubber, Markus D. and Christopher Tomlins (eds.), *The Oxford Handbook of Legal History* (Oxford: Oxford University Press, 2018).

Dunn, Caroline, 'Damsels in Distress or Partners in Crime? The Abduction of Women in Medieval England', Ph.D. Fordham University (2007), https://research.library.fordham.edu/dissertations/AAI3286418/.

Dunn, Caroline, 'The Language of Ravishment in Medieval England', *Speculum* 86 (2011), 79–116.

Dunn, Caroline, *Stolen Women in Medieval England: Rape, Abduction and Adultery 1100–1500* (Cambridge: Cambridge University Press, 2012).

Erler, Mary, and Maryanne Kowaleski (eds.), *Women and Power in the Middle Ages* (Athens: University of Georgia Press, 1988).

Erler, Mary, and Maryanne Kowaleski, *Gendering the Master Narrative: Women and Power in the Middle Ages* (New York: Cornell University Press, 2003).

Ernst, Daniel R., 'The Moribund Appeal of Death: Compensating Survivors and Controlling Jurors in Early Modern England', *AJLH* 28 (1984), 164–88.

Everard, J., 'Public Authority and Private Rights: Women in the English Royal Courts of Justice 1196–1250', in *Sexuality and Gender in History*, ed. by Penelope Hetherington and Philippa Maddern (Centre for Western Australia History at the University of Western Australia, 1993), 123–44.

Goldberg, Peter Jeremy Piers, *Women, Work and Life Cycle in a Medieval Economy* (Oxford: Oxford University Press, 1992).

Goldberg, Peter Jeremy Piers (ed.), *Women in England c 1275–1525* (Manchester: Manchester University Press, 1995).

Goodrich, Peter, 'Gynaetopia: Feminine Genealogies of Common Law', *Journal of Law and Society* 20 (1993), 276–308.

Green, Monica H., 'Bodies, Gender, Health, Disease: Recent Work on Medieval Women's Medicine', *Studies in Medieval and Renaissance History* 3rd series 2 (2005), 1–46.

Green, Monica H., *Making Women's Medicine Masculine: The Rise of Male Authority in Pre-Modern Gynaecology* (Oxford: Oxford University Press, 2008).

Green, Thomas, *Verdict according to Conscience: Perspectives on the English Criminal Jury 1200–1800* (Chicago, IL: University of Chicago Press, 1985).

Hanawalt, Barbara A., 'The Female Felon in Fourteenth Century England', *Viator* v (1974), 253–68.

Hanawalt, Barbara A., 'Violent Death in Fourteenth and Early Fifteenth Century England', *Comparative Studies in Society and History* 18 (1976), 297–320.

Hanawalt, Barbara A., 'Whose Story Was This? Rape Narratives in Medieval English Courts', in *Of Good and Ill Repute: Gender and Social Control in Medieval England*, ed. by Barbara A. Hanawalt (Oxford: Oxford University Press, 1998), 124–41.

Hanawalt, Barbara A., *The Wealth of Wives: Women, Law and Economy in Late Medieval London* (Oxford: Oxford University Press, 2007).

Harris-Stoertz, Fiona, 'Pregnancy and Childbirth in Twelfth-and Thirteenth-Century French and English Law', *Journal of the History of Sexuality* 21 (2012), 263–81.

Harris-Stoertz, Fiona, Midwives in the Middle Ages: Birth Attendants 600–1300', in *Medicine and the Law in the Middle Ages*, ed. by Walter J. Turner and S.M. Butler (Leiden: Brill, 2014), 58–87.

Hawkes, Emma, '"She Was Ravished against Her Will, What So Ever She Say": Female Consent in Rape and Ravishment in Late-Medieval England', *Limina* 1 (1995), 47–54.

Hawkes, Emma, 'She Will Protect and Defend her Right…' Women's Knowledge of Common Law and Equity in Late Medieval England', in *Medieval Women and the Law*, ed. by Noël James Menuge (Woodbridge: Boydell, 2000),148–51.

Hawkes, Emma, 'Judging Female Judges: Sir John Fortescue's Vision of Women as Judges in *De Natura Legis Naturae*', *Limina* 8 (2002), 93–112.

Holt, J.C., 'Presidential Address: Feudal Society and the Family in Early Medieval England: IV. The Heiress and the Alien' *TRHS* 35 (1985), 1–28.

van Houts, Elisabeth, 'Gender and Authority of Oral Witnesses in Europe (800–1300)', *TRHS* 9 (1999), 201–20.

van Houts, Elisabeth (ed.), *Medieval Memories: Men, Women and the Past, 700–1300* (London and New York: Routledge, 2013).

Hudson, John (ed.), *The History of English Law, Centenary Essays on 'Pollock and Maitland'* (Oxford: Oxford University Press, 1996).

Hudson, John, *Oxford History of the Laws of England vol. II, 871–1216* (Oxford: Oxford University Press, 2012).

Hyams, Paul R., 'Maitland and the Rest of Us', in *The History of English Law*, ed. by John Hudson (Oxford: Oxford University Press for the British Academy, 1996), 213–41.

Ibbetson, David, *A Historical Introduction to the Law of Obligations*' (Oxford: Oxford University Press, 1999).

Ibbetson, David, 'What Is Legal History a History Of?', in *Law and History* (Current Legal Issues 6), ed. by Andrew Lewis and Michael Lobban (Oxford: Oxford University Press, 2004), 33–40.

Jansen, Douglas C., 'Women and Public Authority in the Thirteenth Century', in *Queens, Regents and Potentates, Women of Power I*, ed. by Theresa M. Vann (Woodbridge: Boydell and Brewer, 1993), 91–105.

Jenks, Susanne, '*Occidit… inter brachia sua*: Change in a Woman's Appeal of Murder of her Husband', *JLH* (2000), 119–22.

Jenks, Susanne, 'The Writ and Exception *de odio et atia*', *JLH* 23 (2002), 1–22.

Johns, Susan M., *Noblewomen, Aristocracy and Power in the Twelfth Century Anglo-Norman Realm* (Manchester: Manchester University Press, 2003).

Kamali, Elizabeth Papp, 'The Devil's Daughter of Hell Fire: Anger's Role in Medieval English Felony Cases', *LHR* 35 (2017), 155–200.

Kamali, Elizabeth Papp, *Felony and the Guilty Mind in Medieval England* (Cambridge: Cambridge University Press, 2019).

Kamali, Elizabeth Papp and Thomas A. Green, 'A Crossroads in Criminal Procedure: the Assumptions Underlying England's Adoption of Trial by Jury', in *Law and Society in Later Medieval England and Ireland: Essays in Honour of Paul Brand*, ed. by Travis R. Baker (London and New York: Routledge, 2018), 51–82.

Kane, Bronach, *Popular Memory and Gender in Medieval England: Men, Women and Testimony in the Church Courts, c.1200–1500* (Woodbridge: Boydell Press, 2019).

Kane, Bronach and Fiona Williamson, *Women, Agency and the Law 1300–1700* (London: Pickering & Chatto, 2013).

Kantor, Georgy, Tom Lambert, and Hannah Skoda, *Legalism: Property and Ownership* (Oxford: Oxford University Press, 2017).

Karras, Ruth Mazo, *Common Women: Prostitution and Sexuality in Medieval England* (New York and Oxford: Oxford University Press, 1996).

Karras, Ruth Mazo, *Sexuality in Medieval Europe: Doing unto Others*, 2nd edn (London and New York: Routledge, 2005).

Kenny, Courtney S., *The History of the Law of England as to the Effects of Marriage on Property and on the Wife's Legal Capacity* (London: Reeves and Turner, 1879).

Kerby-Fulton, Kathryn, Katie Anne-Marie Bugyis and John Van Engen (eds.), *Women Intellectuals and Leaders in the Middle Ages* (Woodbridge: Boydell and Brewer, 2020).

Kerr, Margaret H., 'Husband and Wife in Criminal Procedure in Medieval England', in *Women, Marriage and Family in Medieval Christendom: Essays in Memory of Michael M Sheehan CSB*, ed. by Constance M. Rousseau and Joel T. Rosenthal (Kalamazoo, MI: Medieval Institute Publications, Western Michigan University, 1998), 211–251

Kesselring, Krista J., *Mercy and Authority in the Tudor State* (Cambridge: Cambridge University Press, 2003).

Kesselring, Krista J., 'Felony Forfeiture in England, c.1170–1870', *JLH* 30 (2009), 201–26.

Kesselring, Krista J., 'Bodies of Evidence: Sex and Murder (or Gender and Homicide) in Early Modern England, c. 1500–1680', *Gender and History* 27 (2015), 245–62.

Kesselring, Krista J., 'No Greater Provocation? Adultery and the Mitigation of Murder in English Law', *LHR* 34 (2016), 199–225.

King, Helen, *The One Sex Body on Trial: The Classical and Early Modern Evidence* (Farnham: Ashgate, 2013).

Klapisch-Zuber, Christiane and others (eds.), *A History of Women in the West II: Silences of the Middle Ages* (Cambridge, MA: Harvard University Press, 1992).

Klerman, Daniel, 'Settlement and the Decline of Private Prosecution in Thirteenth-Century England', *LHR* 19 (2001), 1–65.

Klerman, Daniel, 'Women Prosecutors in Thirteenth Century England', *Harvard Journal of Law and the Humanities* 14 (2002), 271–313.

Lacey, Helen, *The Royal Pardon: Access to Mercy in Fourteenth Century England* (Woodbridge: York Medieval Press, 2009).

Laqueur, Thomas, *Making Sex: Body and Gender from the Greeks to Freud* (Cambridge, MA: Harvard University Press, 1990).

Leeming, Mark, 'Lawyers' Uses of History, from *Entick v Carrington* to *Smethurst v Commissioner of Police*', Francis Forbes Lecture, Supreme Court of New South Wales (2020). http://www.forbessociety.org.au/wordpress/wp-content/uploads/2016/02/Forbes-Lecture-2020_-Justice-Leeming.pdf.

Loengard, Janet S., 'Rationabilis Dos: Magna Carta and the Widow's "Fair Share" in the Earlier Thirteenth Century', in *Wife and Widow in Medieval England*, ed. by Sue Sheridan Walker (Ann Arbor: University of Michigan Press, 1993), 59–80.

Loengard, Janet S., 'Which May Be Said to Be Her Own': Widows and Goods in Late Medieval England', in *Medieval Domesticity: Home, Housing and Household in Medieval England*, ed. by M. Kowaleski and P.J.P. Goldberg (Cambridge: Cambridge University Press, 2008), 162–76.

Loengard, Janet S., 'What Is a Nice (Thirteenth-Century) Englishwoman Doing in the King's Courts?', in *The Ties That Bind: Essays in Medieval British History in Honor of Barbara Hanawalt*, ed. by Linda E. Mitchell, Katherine L. French and Douglas L. Biggs (London: Routledge, 2010), 55–70.

Maddern, Philippa, *Violence and Social Order East Anglia 1422–1442* (Oxford: Clarendon Press, 1992).

Maddern, Philippa, 'Widows and Their Lands and Texts in Fifteenth Century Norfolk', *Parergon* 19 (2002), 123–50.

Masschaele, James, *Jury, State, and Society in Medieval England* (New York: Palgrave Macmillan, 2008).

Maurer, Helen, *Margaret of Anjou: Queenship and Power in Late Medieval England* (Woodbridge: Boydell Press, 2003).

McIntosh, Marjorie, *Controlling Misbehavior in England 1370–1600* (Cambridge: Cambridge University Press, 1998).

McSweeney, Thomas J., *Priests of the Law: Roman Law and the Making of the Common Law's First Legal Professionals* (Oxford: Oxford University Press, 2019).

McVitty, E. Amanda, 'Engendering Erudition: Masculinity and Legal Authority at England's Medieval Inns of Court', *Gender and History* 32 (2020), 447–64.

Menuge, Noel J., *Medieval Women: Texts and Contexts in Late Medieval Britain* (Leiden: Brepols, 2000).

Milsom, S.F.C., 'Trespass from Henry III to Edward III', *LQR* (1958), 195–224; 407–36; 561–90.

Mitchell, Linda E., *Portraits of Medieval Women: Family, Marriage and Politics in England 1225–1350* (New York: Palgrave Macmillan, 2003).

Mulholland, Maureen and Brian Pullan (eds.), *Judicial Tribunals in England and Europe, 1200–1700* (Manchester: Manchester University Press, 2003).

Musson, Anthony and W. Mark Ormrod, *The Evolution of English Justice: Law, Politics and Society in the Fourteenth Century* (London: Palgrave, 1999).

Musson, Anthony and Edward Powell, *Crime, Law and Society in the Later Middle Ages* (Manchester: Manchester University Press, 2009).

Orr, Patricia R., 'English Women at Law: Actions in the King's Courts of Justice, 1194–1222', Ph.D. thesis, Rice University (1989) https://scholarship.rice.edu/handle/1911/16275.

Orr, Patricia R., '*Non potest appellum facere*: Criminal Charges Women Could Not, but Did, Bring in Thirteenth Century English Royal Courts of Justice', in *The Final Argument: The Imprint of Violence on Society in Medieval and Early Modern Europe*, ed. by D.J. Kagay and L.J.A. Villalon (Woodbridge: Boydell Press, 1998), 141–62.

Palmer, Robert C., *English Law in the Age of the Black Death 1348–81* (Chapel Hill: University of North Carolina Press, 1993).

Phifer, Michael, 'Property, Power and Patriarchy: The Decline of Women's Property Right in England after the Black Death', PhD dissertation (University of Houston, 2014) https://uh-ir.tdl.org/bitstream/handle/10657/725/PHIFER-DISSERTATION-2014.pdf?sequence=1&isAllowed=y.

Pike, Luke Owen, *A History of Crime in England: Illustrating the Changes of the Laws in the Progress of Civilisation* (London: Smith, Elder and Co., 1873).

Plucknett, Theodore Frank Thomas, *Statutes and Their Interpretation in the First Half of the Fourteenth Century* (Cambridge: Cambridge University Press, 1922).

Plucknett, Theodore Frank Thomas, *Legislation of Edward I* (Oxford: Clarendon, 1949).

Pollock, Frederick and Frederic William Maitland, *The History of English Law before the Time of Edward I*, 2 vols (Cambridge: Cambridge University Press, 1895).

Powell, Edward, 'Arbitration and the Law in England in the Late Middle Ages', *TRHS* 33 (1983), 49–67.

Powell, Edward, *Kingship, Law and Society: Criminal Justice in the Reign of Henry V* (Oxford: Oxford University Press, 1989).

Power, Eileen, 'The Position of Women', in *The Legacy of the Middle Ages*, ed. by Charles George Crump and Ernest Fraser Jacob (Oxford: Oxford University Press, 1926), 401.

Rackley, Erika and Rosemary Auchmuty, *Women's Legal Landmarks: Celebrating the History of Women and Law in the UK and Ireland* (Oxford: Hart, 2018).

Rigby, Stephen H., *English Society in the Later Middle Ages: Class, Status and Gender* (London: Palgrave, 1995).

Rose, Jonathan, 'Studying the Past: The Nature and Development of Legal History as an Academic Discipline', *JLH* 31 (2010), 101–28.

Rose, Jonathan, *Maintenance in Medieval England* (Cambridge: Cambridge University Press, 2017).

Russel, M.J., 'Trial by Battle and the Appeals of Felony', *JLH* 1 (1980), 135–64.

Sandberg, Russell, 'The Time for Legal History: Some Reflections on Maitland and Milson Fifty Years on', *Law & Justice* 180 (2018), 21–37, 25.

Schrage, Eltjo, 'Women Do Not Sit as Judges, or Do They – The Office of Judge in Vincentius Bellovacensis' Speculum', *Fundamina* 16 (2010), 377–89.

Scutt, Jocelynne A., *Women and Magna Carta: A Treaty for Rights or Wrongs?* (London: Palgrave Macmillan, 2016).

Seabourne, Gwen, *Royal Regulation of Loans and Sales in Medieval England: Monkish Superstition and Civil Tyranny* (Woodbridge: Boydell Press, 2003).

Seabourne, Gwen, *Imprisoning Medieval Women: The Non-Judicial Confinement and Abduction of Women in England, c.1170–1509* (Farnham: Ashgate, 2011).

Seabourne, Gwen, 'Copulative Complexities: The Exception of Adultery in Medieval Dower Actions', in *Law and Legal Process: Substantive Law and Procedure in English Legal History*, ed. by Matthew Dyson and David Ibbetson (Cambridge: Cambridge University Press, 2013), 34–55.

Seabourne, Gwen, 'It Is Necessary That the Issue Be Heard to Cry or Squall within the Four [Walls]': Qualifying for Tenancy by the Curtesy of England in the Reign of Edward I', *JLH* 40 (2019), 44–68.

Seipp, David J., 'The Concept of Property in the Early Common Law', *LHR* 12 (1994), 29–91.

Seipp, David J., 'Jurors, Evidences and the Tempest of 1499', in *The Dearest Birth Right of the People of England: The Jury in the History of the Common Law*, ed. by John W. Cairns and Grant McLeod (Oxford: Hart, 2002), c. 5.

Seipp, David J., 'The Law's Many Bodies and the Manuscript Tradition in English Legal History', *JLH* 25 (2004), 74–83.

Seipp, David, 'Formalism and Realism in Fifteenth-Century English Law: Bodies Corporate and Bodies Natural', in *Judges and Judging in the History of the Common Law and Civil Law from Antiquity to Modern Times*, ed. by Paul Brand and Joshua Getzler (Cambridge: Cambridge University Press, 2012), 44–55.

Sheehan, Michael M., *Marriage, Family and Law in Medieval Europe: Collected Studies*, ed. by James K. Farge (Toronto: University of Toronto Press, 1997).

Skinner, Patricia, *Studying Gender in Medieval Europe: Historical Approaches* (London: Palgrave Macmillan, 2018).

Smith, R.M., 'Women's Property Rights under Customary Law: Some Developments in the Thirteenth and Fourteenth Centuries', *TRHS* 36 (1986), 165–94.

Spring, Eileen, 'The Heiress-at-Law: English Real Property Law from a New Point of View', *LHR* 8 (1990), 273–96.

Stevens, M.F., 'London Women, the Courts and the 'Golden Age': A Quantitative Analysis of Female Litigants in the Fourteenth and Fifteenth Centuries', *London Journal* 37 (2012), 67–88.

Storey, R.L., 'Malicious Indictments of Clergy in the Fifteenth Century', in *Medieval Ecclesiastical Studies in Honour of Dorothy M. Owen*, ed. by M.J. Franklin and Christopher Harper-Bill (Woodbridge: Boydell Press, 1995), 221–40.

Stretton, Tim, 'Coverture and Unity of Person in Blackstone's *Commentaries*', in *Blackstone and His Commentaries, Biography, Law, History*, ed. by Wilfrid Prest (Oxford: Hart, 2009), 111–28.

Stretton, Tim, 'Women, Legal Records, and the Problem of the Lawyer's Hand', *JBS* 58 (2019), 684–700.

Stretton, Tim and Krista J. Kesselring (eds.), *Married Women and the Law: Coverture in England and the Common Law World* (Montreal: McGill University Press, 2013).

Stringer, Rebecca, *Knowing Victim: Feminism, Agency and Victim Politics in Neoliberal Times* (London and New York: Routledge, 2014).

Strohm, Paul, *Hochon's Arrow: The Social Imagination of Fourteenth-Century Texts* (Princeton, NJ: Princeton University Press, 1992).

Summerson, Henry, 'Maitland and the Criminal Law in the Age of Bracton', in Hudson, *The History of English Law: Centenary Essays on 'Pollock and Maitland'*, ed. by John Hudson (Oxford: Oxford University Press for the British Academy, 1996), 115–43.

Sutherland, Donald W., *Assize of Novel Disseisin* (Oxford: Clarendon Press, 1973).
Walker, Garthine, *Crime, Gender and Social Order in Early Modern England* (Cambridge: Cambridge University Press, 2003).
Walker, Sue Sheridan, 'Litigation as Personal Quest: Suing for Dower in the Royal Courts, circa 1272–1350', in *Wife and Widow in Medieval England*, ed. by Sue Sheridan Walker (Ann Arbor: University of Michigan Press, 1993), 81–108.
Walker, Sue Sheridan, 'Wager of Law and Judgment by Default in Pleas of Dower in the Royal Courts of Late Thirteenth and Fourteenth Century England', in *The Life of the Law*, ed. by Peter Birks (London: Hambledon Press, 1993), 25–42.
Walker, Sue Sheridan, *Wife and Widow in Medieval England* (Ann Arbor: University of Michigan Press, 1993).
Walker, Sue Sheridan, '"Litigant Agency" in Dower Pleas in Royal Common Law Courts in Thirteenth and Early Fourteenth Century England', *JLH* 24 (2003), 1–22.
Whittick, Christopher, 'The Role of the Criminal Appeal in the Fifteenth Century', in *Law and Social Change in British History*, ed. by John Alexander Guy and Hugh G. Beale (London: Royal Historical Society, 1984), 55–72.
Wilkinson, Louise J., 'Women as Sheriff', in *English Governance in the Thirteenth Century*, ed. by Adrian Jobson (Woodbridge: Boydell Press, 2004), 111–24.
Wilkinson, Louise J., *Women in Thirteenth-Century Lincolnshire* (London: Royal Historical Society and Boydell Press, 2007).

Index

Note: Page numbers followed by "n" denote footnotes.

For Product Safety Concerns and Information please contact our EU
representative GPSR@taylorandfrancis.com
Taylor & Francis Verlag GmbH, Kaufingerstraße 24, 80331 München, Germany

www.ingramcontent.com/pod-product-compliance
Ingram Content Group UK Ltd.
Pitfield, Milton Keynes, MK11 3LW, UK
UKHW020003200926
475702UK00015B/2451

* 9 7 8 0 3 6 7 7 4 5 2 2 6 *